ISABELLA
STEWART
GARDNER

and Fenway Court

By MORRIS CARTER

Illustrated and with a Foreword by G. Peabody Gardner

Published by the Trustees

ISABELLA STEWART GARDNER MUSEUM

BOSTON

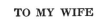

TO MY WIFE

FOREWORD

A S A YOUTH and young man I was fortunate in having
seen a good deal of my Great-aunt Isabella Stewart
Gardner (Mrs. Jack) because of her visits with my family each
summer and her frequent appearances at informal family meals.
My Great-uncle Jack I saw only occasionally as I was at board-
ing school most of the time and he died when I was only ten
years old; even so I realized how much my Father admired and
loved him.

Aunt Belle had a strong feeling of loyalty for Uncle Jack's
family and took a keen interest in their doings. When I was at
Harvard she followed my career in athletics enthusiastically,
going so far at times as to sit on a snowbank to watch me play
hockey in the Stadium (no artificial ice in those days). It was
probably shortsighted of me not to have taken more advantage
of my opportunities to know this remarkable woman. When I
was in college I sometimes did my studying while seated in the
flowery and fragrant courtyard at Fenway Court and got to
know some of her brilliant young devotees such as Henry
Sleeper, Arthur Pope and A. Piatt Andrew, especially the
latter, for he was an instructor at Harvard and known familiarly
as "Doc." I never really knew them intimately as I was consider-
ably younger and did not participate in any of the wonderful
parties they gave for her.

After my marriage Aunt Belle used to come and dine with us
occasionally and was particularly fond of my wife, who had come

FOREWORD

to Boston from another city just as she had. My last memory
of her was when she arrived in a taxi at our house in Brookline,
which had formerly been hers, at eight o'clock on a lovely morning in April, the 14th to be exact, which was her birthday. She
had been notified that our son John Lowell Gardner was born
earlier that morning and wanted to see him and, if possible, hold
him in her arms. This she did for the nurse brought him down,
well swaddled, and placed him in her lap. She then returned to
Fenway Court which because of her ill health she had not left
for several months and was never to leave again. I hope and
believe that she felt this happy coincidence of birthdays was
ordained and that it was, in a sense at least, a slight compensation for the loss of her adored little son.

My earliest remembrances of Morris Carter are rather tenuous;
as time went on they became less so but still remained somewhat
vague for a number of years. However I could not help being
aware of his existence in spite of his modest self-effacement. He
was devoted to Aunt Belle and never departed far from her
beck and call. I suspect, though, that everything was not always
"Sunshine and Roses" as is indicated by this quotation from his
book: "Yet she had just regard for faithful service, even if she
did not choose the usual methods of showing appreciation, and
those who remained long in her employ developed an affection
for her and a devotion to her which it was often difficult for them
to explain even to themselves."

This book of Morris Carter's is without doubt the best, most
accurate and understanding of any of the books or articles that
have been written about Mrs. Jack. All too many have been

FOREWORD

trivial, misleading and often malicious. This does not apply to Louise Hall Tharp's excellent book "Mrs. Jack" nor to Aline B. Saarinen's sketch of her in "The Proud Possessors" nor of course to George L. Stout's book "Treasures from the Isabella Stewart Gardner Museum."

There is no question about Mrs. Jack's dependence on Carter's help and her firm confidence in his ability and loyalty. This is clearly demonstrated by her having the good sense to provide that he would become the Director of the Museum on her death and her extraordinary perspicacity in providing that he should remain the Director for so long as he wished. In other words she did not want anyone else who might be the President or a Trustee to give the impression that they were in the driver's seat and might seek to impose their own ideas rather than adhering strictly to hers, thereby giving the impression that Morris Carter was subservient to them.

An exceptionally mild-mannered man, he looked as if he might easily be intimidated, but such was not the case, especially with the ironclad mandate he had to back him up. It is my impression that there was an attempt by one individual to reduce him to a more subordinate position. This is not surprising, for the individual concerned, fine man though he was, had been known on occasion to brush aside any opposition to his wishes in a rather cavalier fashion. In a confrontation with Carter he soon learned that Mr. Milquetoast was Mr. Granite. Thereafter all went well without ill feeling.

He was eminently well fitted for his job and thoroughly versed in what Mrs. Jack's wishes for the future were. He was

FOREWORD

scrupulously loyal to them, did everything that he felt she would have wanted done and nothing that he felt might displease her. When his search for a successor was so brilliantly successful he no doubt believed that his inspiration had come direct from Mrs. Jack and I am inclined to agree!!

G. PEABODY GARDNER

JANUARY 20, 1971

PREFACE

DURING her later years Mrs. Gardner was frequently urged, by the friends who knew best how exceptionally interesting her life had been and how delightfully she could narrate her experiences, to write her memoirs. The request was always greeted with that wonderful rippling, musical laugh which suggested the enjoyment of something hugely amusing, incredibly absurd. But when the request was made by a member of the Gardner family who was very dear to her, she was good enough to take the matter seriously, and after a moment's hesitation said deliberately: 'I — can't — do — it.' At the age of eighty, she felt unequal to the labor of sifting, formulating, and dictating her recollections; life itself was still a delight, but recording it would be drudgery. She had never made a practice of keeping a journal, although she did write a detailed account of her longer journeys. Everywhere she bought photographs, and the albums in which she mounted them, with brief notes of dates and of special events, furnish a chronological outline of her travels. The chronicle of her life in Boston has been pieced together from letters written by her and by her friends, from anecdotes she herself told, and from a considerable variety of other sources.

The title of this book might well have been 'The Life of Isabella Stewart Gardner, as told by the Town of Boston.' Many of her friends will recognize their contributions to the story; I thank them all for their aid in creating this account of

PREFACE

the 'fascinating Mrs. Jack'; my especial thanks are due to Mrs. Gardner's cousin, Mr. Theodore F. Hicks, the confidential secretary and afterward partner of her father, who has furnished information in regard to Mrs. Gardner and her family which should forever refute many of the legends current during her lifetime.

To Mrs. George H. Monks, a niece of Mrs. Gardner, and to Mr. Harold Jefferson Coolidge, her nephew, the President of the Trustees of the Isabella Stewart Gardner Museum, I am particularly indebted for their kindness in reading my manuscript; their suggestions and corrections have saved me from many mistakes.

MORRIS CARTER

BOSTON, 1925

CONTENTS

ILLUSTRATIONS

ILLUSTRATIONS

The title-page device is taken from the corporate seal of
the Isabella Stewart Gardner Museum, Incorporated,
designed by Mrs. Gardner.

ISABELLA STEWART GARDNER
AND FENWAY COURT

ISABELLA STEWART GARDNER
AND FENWAY COURT

. .
.

CHAPTER I

ALPHA

IN Boston, where pride of race flourishes, although many
families begin their history with the year 1620 and some
even later, Mrs. Gardner's simple statement that she was
descended from Robert Bruce and that she and Mary Queen
of Scots were leaves on the same family tree, was received with
amused incredulity. It was too fantastic. Indeed, it was too
strange for fiction, but not for truth.

Mrs. Gardner belonged to the Invernahyle branch of the
Appin Stewarts. Her genealogy is given in 'The Stewarts of
Appin, by General H. J. Stewart, F.S.A. Scot., and Lieutenant-
Colonel Duncan Stewart, Late 92d Highlanders,' where her
name appears on page 170 (eighth line from the bottom, to be
exact). There are documented records of the family as far back
as the middle of the twelfth century, and various genealogists
assert that the Stewarts were descended from King Fergus I, a
contemporary of Alexander the Great. Mrs. Gardner quite
naturally had a cult for Mary Stuart and for the martyred
Charles I. She possessed a few precious Stuart relics:[1] fragments of silk and lace, said to be parts of dresses once worn by
Mary Stuart; a Book of Hours printed by Symon Vostre in 1514

[1] Now in the collection at Fenway Court.

[3]

and given to the Queen by her husband, François II; it has their autographs, and those of her mother-in-law, Catherine de Médicis, and of her uncle, Cardinal de Lorraine. On Christmas Eve, when mass was celebrated in Mrs. Gardner's private chapel at Fenway Court, it sometimes seemed as if her costume had been influenced by her favorite portrait of Mary Stuart. In the picturesque fanaticism of the Order of the White Rose, she took an æsthetic interest. The first and only issue of 'The Royal Standard,' published in September, 1900, when 'Ralph von Cram' was Prior of the Order in North America, is more entertaining than 'The Lark' and similar little magazines intended to amuse. All such humorous publications gave Mrs. Gardner pleasure. The death of Charles of England, king and martyr, was occasionally — not regularly — commemorated at Fenway Court by a little supper for a few enthusiasts, and an intimate, romantic service in the chapel. Endowed with those gifts of fascination and charm for which the crowned Stuarts were famous, Mrs. Gardner happily was not shadowed by their ill-fortune.

Her grandfather, James Stewart, a son of Thomas Stewart and Mary Brough (whose portrait hangs at Fenway Court), emigrated from Scotland, married Isabella Tod, of Suffield, Connecticut, and lived out his life as a prosperous gentleman farmer at Jamaica, Long Island. Through her grandmother, Isabella Tod, Mrs. Gardner was descended from the Kents, Dwights, and Dudleys of Connecticut, and from two of the early governors — Governor Thomas Welles and Governor Robert Treat.

In 1826, David Tod, the father of Isabella Tod Stewart,

ALPHA

made a journey from his daughter's home to Utica, Buffalo, Pittsburgh, Philadelphia, and New York, visiting the scattered members of his enterprising family. In the following letter to his daughter, he gives an account of the journey:

BEDFORD [PA.] Sept. 5th, 1826

DEAR ISABELLA

Your letter to your Brother of the 29th last month came to hand yesterday, by which I conclude you are all well, as you say nothing to the contrary. You will recolect I left you the 12 July, I reached Utica, 240 miles, in three days — left the packet Boat, went 50 miles to Turin, where Brother Augustus Kent[1] & Sister Albro lives, found them all well, staied one night, returned to Utica, proceeded on the Canal to Bufalo which I reached in 4 days — now from you 520 miles, then in the steam Boat Henry Clay on lake Erie, to Painsville, where Mr Ford lives 100 miles — from this & three other places on the lake (viz) Erie, Fair Port, & Cleveland, stages to Pitsburgh run three times a week. I got to Warren 70 miles in two days from the lake — M^r McCurdy, Wife & Child gaind home two days before my arrival, —

.   .   .   .

I staid at Warren three days — David Tod, Georges second son who is in a lawyers Office here, conveyed me in a Dearbourn as one horse waggons are call'd here, to his fathers in Youngstown, where I found your Brother Wife & two Children, all well and living on the best & well they may, a good Chiken may be had for a six-pence, butter 5 cts Beef 2 to 1 ct the lb — wheat 36 cts, Eggs 3 cts Doz, everything in like proportion. Stage hire from N. York to Pitsburgh, from 3 to 4 cents but from the latter place to Phil^a 6 cts. George was luckily at home, & busy with hay & harvesting. Corn, Meadows, and pasturing, hereabouts has suffered with the drougth, yet George net from 12 Acers as many tuns of verry good hay, the ground has been mowed constantly for 23 years, without any manure whatever, — I staid at Youngstown four weeks, the last night at Ingersols, his wife is little, red haired, handsome, neat & active. — reached Pitsburgh in two days, staid there three, and reached here in two. John[2] was on his circuit, did not get home till five days — all verry well. — Alas how oblivious is the grave, and how emphatically call'd the place of forgetfulness, the Mistres of this family has not been dead six months, estimable for every valuable quallity, usefull in every possible situation, — one would think amongst her acquaintances there were few to appreciate her worth, few to imitate her

---

[1] His wife's brother.   [2] Another son.

[5]

virtues, and none sensible how soon they may be called to follow her. Your Brother as usual is constantly in the whirl of business, what little time he has for reflection I believe his mind is fully impres'd with a just sense of the erepairable loss of Mrss. Tod. — The Children are verry promising, and well taken care of by Mrss. Fisher, who is a verry affectionate & judicious manager, — you mention my staying here the winter, not recolecting that 4 shirts, as many cravats, and stockings, are the only articles not on my back, I believe shall spend the winter in Connecticut, but whereever I shall be let it not in the least obstruct your scheme of spending the winter in N. York, you have long enough been a slave to others, may well be allowed three or four months time, under your own controal. — I have not yet seen Johns farm, the people here speak of it in the highest terms, 9 or 10 hundred Acers, can cut 3 or 400 Tons good hay, Aples for 3 or 4 hund: Bal^s living water in spring & running brooks, — good for wheat, — & free from stones — I shall stay here perhaps till sometime in Oct^r — tell Charles to write me, if he has anything to say — or David — remember me to all the three

I am

Dear Daughter your Affectionate father

DAVID TOD

miles	
Alb	160
Buff	360
Erie	100
Warren	80
Pitsburgh	70
Bedford	100
Phila	200
N.Y	100
	1170

P. S. It is not yet determined how little Belle is to get to you. You will be pleas'd with her or I am mistaken.

November 7, 1827, David Tod died, and Isabella Tod Stewart received the following letter from her brother George, which gives further details of her family history:

BRIER HILL [YOUNGSTOWN, OHIO] Feby 7th 1828

MY DEAR SISTER

I have for a long while — indeed, too long a while, omitted to write you: — I feel ashamed for this seeming — though it may be adjudged, an actual neglect. I will urge no apology however but will assure you — that there is no want of affection for my dear Sister, to which, any of the above *matters*, can be ascribed. —

The death of our father was promptly and kindly announced to us by our much esteemed nephew, James Stewart — your Son. — The news came to us, unexpectedly; for we had not heard, that he was under the influence of any disease in any sense alarming; — yet, from his advanced age, a much

ALPHA

longer continuance, here, could not have been much calculated on, reasonably. — His age, with me, is doubtful; — but from my best recollection, from, the sayings of our grandmother Kent — Uncle Augustus, and others, in Suffield, the place of *our* nativity, he was born in 1746 — and I think in October — on this supposition he had seen 81 years at least. Both the times that he visited Ohio — he was asked by me how old he was — *that* he could not, with certainty tell; but on his own estimate, he was about three years younger. It was, I thought, not a little strange, that a man of his mind and intelligence, should not have had some confident opinion on the subject. He said, when I was in New York, either in 1814 or 1816, that the credentials of his birth, which he obtained in Scotland, was lossed at sea — but thought he was but 15 when he first landed in America, at Boston. I will write on this subject to our Uncle Augustus Kent, now living, if living at all, in the black river Country, in the state of New York. Can you, my dear Sister, give me any information on the subject? — If so, be pleased to do it.

My Son, the Doctor, shew me a letter from James, a day or two since, informing him that you had regained your health. This information I received with great joy — for I had felt very anxious about you, since receiving the letter of your son, informing of the death of his Grand-father.

We look for you to make us a visit next Summer — we look for that pleasure with much certainty: the visit of no person on earth could give us more pleasure. — We have had intimations, that you thought of a Western *trip*, last Season — your Sister Sally [1] was sure that you would be forthcoming: — but do not disappoint *her* again — you may rest assured of a real welcome for your dear self, — and whomsoever it may be your pleasure to bring with you. — My wife I left with Mrs McCurdy, this day week — she has not yet returned — I should look for her tomorrow were not the roads indescribably bad — if she does not return by tomorrow evening, I will make them a visit the next day. Our daughter Mary was with us a week during the only *cold* weather we have had this season (winter). Your Sister, since the death of old Miss Kitty, will not put herself on a saddle, unless for a mile or two; and the waggoning is so bad that Mr McCurdy dares not to venture.

Mary — Julia Ann — Grace — Ingersoll — David & little George, are all in good health — George is only with me. Charlotte — sweet child, I cannot name among our living children — but *she* is not to be forgotten. . . . Mary's three children, Wm, George Tod, and Sarah Ann, are fine, healthy, promising little fellows. Sarah Ann will be a year old on 12: instant, I think. — Julia Ann (Mrs Ford) with her little daughter Sarah Tod we have been looking, a long while — but the weather — roads &c — have interdicted a personal intercourse between us. Little Sarah Tod has been very

[1] His wife.

[7]

sick — her mother writes that she has recovered — she was a year old on the 2⁰ of this present month: — and is thought to be much of a Tod — by some &c — Now dear Sis — do make it convenient to visit us — why not? your Sons, I believe, are all in New York City. — Can you not leave your paradise in the East: for a trip to the wild woods of the West? — Write me, if you should conclude to come *lake-about,* and you shall be met *suitably, at least;* — if not by me. Or if the Pennsylvania rout should best suit your pleasure, advise me of your intention — and I will meet you at Pittsburgh if at home — if not — one of my Sons shall take the place of their father as your gallant.

Feby 11^h Your Sister returned from Warren on Saturday last. She sends her love to you and to your Sons; in which I cordially join her.

Your affectionate brother

GEORGE TOD

George Tod's son David, a first cousin of Mrs. Gardner's father, David Stewart, was Governor of Ohio during the Civil War.

Mr. and Mrs. James Stewart had three sons — James Arrott, Charles, and David. In 1813, Mr. Stewart died, leaving his widow a fortune of seventy-five thousand dollars in addition to the home farm; that she managed it capably is proved by the silver cups [1] awarded her in 1821 and 1828 by the New York Agricultural Society. The eldest son, born in 1806, died of yellow fever in 1829, while returning from New Orleans, and was buried at sea. Charles, who was born in 1808, grew up to be a bookworm; he had a library, and in the eyes of his contemporaries was over-educated; he died February 4, 1849. The youngest son, David, was born September 7, 1810; before he was seventeen, he went to New York to make his fortune. He was placed with Russell & Company, importers, to learn the business, and there he met his future partner, Thomas Paton. They opened an office in Pine Street, and imported Irish and

[1] Now in the collection at Fenway Court.

[8]

Scottish merchandise, chiefly linen; later they moved to Fulton Street, then to Reade Street, and afterward to Dúane Street. Mr. Stewart continued to be an importer until about 1872, but gradually his interests were concentrated in mining. Early in the sixties he became president of the Jackson Iron Company with mines in Northern Michigan; of this prosperous company Mr. Stewart served as president, without salary, for about thirty years. Later, he formed the Stewart Iron Company, with mines near Uniontown, Pennsylvania.

In 1839, Mr. Stewart married Miss Adelia Smith, who was born in Jamaica, Long Island, July 4, 1814. The ceremony was performed by the Reverend Dr. Johnson in the Episcopal Church which formerly stood on the corner of Washington and Johnson Streets, Brooklyn.

Miss Smith was a descendant of Richard Smith, who came from England to Boston, Massachusetts, in 1650, married and lived there till 1655; then he and a number of other Bostonians moved to Long Island and established themselves at Setauket, later called Brookhaven. Benjamin F. Thompson, in his 'History of Long Island,' says: 'The original planters [of Brookhaven] were Presbyterians and well-educated men, who possessed a competent knowledge of the laws and constitution of England, and brought with them the true spirit of freedom and independence.' He gives a list of fifty-five men, who with their families composed the settlement about 1657, and says that most of them, if not all, came directly from Boston and its vicinity. Smith must have been more enterprising or more ambitious than his neighbors, for in 1663 he decided that he wanted a township of his own, and purchased one nearly ten miles square to the west of Brookhaven, which was thereafter known as Smithtown. For some reason, probably because horses were rare when the town was settled, Mr. Smith used to ride a large bull, and his descendants were known as the 'Bull Smiths.' The historian states that 'not a few strange stories are related concerning this famous progenitor of the Smiths of Smithtown, the records of which have too much the semblance of fiction to be worth perpetuating.'

An uncle of Miss Smith, Wilmot Oakley, was the scout who led the army of Washington in its retreat from Long Island; Mrs. Gardner's great-grandmother, carrying her six months' old daughter in her arms, crossed in a whaleboat to the Connecticut shore with the other fleeing colonists.

At the time of his marriage, Mr. David Stewart was already a successful business man, and the wife he chose was a practical woman with strict religious views. They first lived at 20 University Place, on the corner of Eighth Street, New York, then one of the best residential parts of the city. There, on April 14, 1840, Isabella Stewart was born. A second daughter, named Adelia, born April 6, 1842, died April 2, 1854; there were also two sons — David, Jr., born January 28, 1848, who died of a malignant tumor October 5, 1874, and James, born December 18, 1858, who died April 15, 1881. Neither brother married.

Mrs. Gardner talked little about her childhood and her family. She admired her father, was loyal to her mother, and loved her brother David. But her great affection was for her grandmother Stewart, who undoubtedly spoiled her. Her mother's discipline was more strict. When little Isabella wore new shoes to church one Sunday, and because they hurt her feet took them off and walked home in her stockings, she was well spanked. Among her earliest books (still at Fenway Court) were these virtuous classics — 'Line upon Line' and 'Peep of Day,' which were presented to her November 4, 1845. The long summers spent on her grandmother's Long Island farm were periods of great happiness, never to be forgotten. The work was done by slaves, and over the pickaninnies the little white girl was an absolute monarch. She was a swift runner, and playing horse was her favorite game; using the whip on her black steeds she thoroughly enjoyed; and her childhood pleasure in driving and lashing others was never outgrown. But also at Jamaica, she was humiliated by one of the few defeats she ever experienced. The circus came to town; having seen the parade, she longed to view the marvellous sights under the big top, and set out independently to do so. Unfortunately, she was seen running away, and the darky butler was sent after her; he was middle-aged and fat, she was very young and slim. The race was hers till the finish. Just as she was crawling under the canvas, the butler grabbed her by the leg and pulled her back. The ignominy of that moment! Not only the defeat, but the manner of it was a painful disgrace. On July 26, 1848, when Isabella was just over eight years old, her beloved grandmother died at the age of seventy.

Her education as a child was chiefly received from private teachers; but during the season of 1854–55 she attended the school kept by Miss Mary Okill. When asked once if she studied hard at school, Mrs. Gardner said that if it was against the rules she probably did. Among her papers were five certificates from Miss Okill, each entitling Miss I. Stewart 'to a premium on the first of July next ... if she remain till the close of school to receive it.' All but one were given for 'Excellence in Reviews,' and that one, dated January, 1855, was given for 'Six perfect weeks.' The latest in date is for May of that year. Instead of remaining till the close of school, she went for the month of June to Saint Mary's convent. Had there been some unpardonable prank?

Her 'Album' gives the names of her school friends. The two she remembered always were Lillie Oddie, who lived at the corner of Fifth Avenue and Fourteenth Street, and Amy Gerry, whose mother before her marriage was Miss Goelet and who lived in the Goelet mansion on Broadway, a famous house in its day, surrounded with spacious grounds enclosed by a high iron fence. A friend at Saint Mary's chose for the album the following admirably fitting couplet:

> 'Favours to none, to all she smiles extends,
> Oft she refuses, but never once offends.'

The room in her father's house which Mrs. Gardner said she remembered best was the one in which she did her exercises. All her life she was interested in sports. The girls did not play many games, but, in addition to her prowess as a runner, she was a good swimmer, an excellent horsewoman, and took the keenest delight in all athletic contests. In 1909, one of the years when her grand-nephew, George Peabody Gardner, Jr., played on the Harvard hockey team, which went through that season undefeated, she attended every game, although she was nearly seventy, and often went to watch the practice on Soldier's Field even when the thermometer was below zero. This same nephew was a hurdler on the Harvard track team and a prominent tennis player. Mrs. Gardner carefully collected and proudly preserved the newspaper accounts of his triumphs. In Brookline she was a neighbor of the Haughton family, and she followed with enthusiasm the brilliant career of the Harvard football team under Percy Haughton's coaching. Although she was a good loser, she loved success.

Her sister Adelia had died in 1854, and Mr. and Mrs. Stewart were determined that their remaining daughter should have every possible advantage. Some of her schoolmates were going to Paris to 'finish,' and to Paris Mr. and Mrs. Stewart took Belle. Finding a satisfactory school was difficult, as Mrs. Stewart insisted that it must not be Roman Catholic. She had read 'The School Girl in France,' its first American edition published in Philadelphia in 1850, and her daughter was not to be exposed to 'the snares, pitfalls, and innumerable perils of a Popish school.' This careful protection in her youth did not prevent Mrs. Gardner in her later years from forming close friendships with Catholic prelates and from feeling very strongly the attraction of the Catholic faith.

Among her schoolmates was Julia Gardner, of Boston. Miss Gardner, who was of a quiet, law-abiding disposition, was captivated by the brilliant, gay, imaginative, vibrant New York girl, and her little sister Eliza shared her admiration. In Belle's album, Eliza wrote — 'Souvien toi de ta petite Amie, 30 Mar 1857 Eliza Gardner.' A design representing overlapping visiting-cards was a favorite device for decorating the pages of this album, a friend's name being written on each card. On such a page appear the autographs of Julia Gardner and Helen

ISABELLA STEWART GARDNER

Waterston, and each has written 'Boston' in the corner of her card. Most of the girls wrote only their names, but to be from Boston was a distinction to be recorded.

Mr. and Mrs. Gardner had come to Paris with their daughters, and there made the acquaintance of Mr. and Mrs. Stewart. The fathers were both rich business men, who appreciated each other's abilities, and each found the other a boon in this foreign land. Neither cared much for society, and together they could joke about the French language and French manners and customs. Mr. Gardner, to his daughter's amusement, insisted on calling the Bois the 'Boy.' Henry L. Higginson, recalling an episode in his young manhood, wrote: 'The Gardners are high-minded gentlemen all the way through — scrupulous, careful, bold, not afraid of the devil.'[1] The friendship of the mothers was less pronounced. Mrs. Gardner was Miss Catharine Elizabeth Peabody, of the Salem Peabodys, who by way of tribute to their abilities and attainments were called 'The Royal Family.' It was 'Peabody, or nobody,' in Salem.

In 1857, Mr. Stewart took his wife and daughter for a tour in Italy; when they reached Rome, he left them in the care of the United States Minister, Mr. Lewis Cass, of Michigan, while he made a hurried trip to New York to attend to business matters. In Rome, Miss Stewart met Miss Ida Agassiz (afterward Mrs. Henry Lee Higginson) and they and Miss Waterston made up a class to study Italian. Miss Stewart seemed to Miss Agassiz very attractive because of her beautiful figure and lovely complexion; she was so exceptionally quick at her lessons

[1] From letter to Barrett Wendell, November 14, 1919, quoted in *Life and Letters of Henry Lee Higginson*, page 284.

that her classmates realized they must do their best if they wished to keep up with her. To make the lessons lively, Miss Stewart amused herself by mildly flirting with the teacher. In 1923, Mrs. Higginson was again in Rome, and wrote to Mrs. Gardner: 'I first met you taking my Italian lessons with you and Helen Waterston — do you remember it? and I also remember what you said to me (you were I think about sixteen years old), namely, that if ever you inherited any money that it was yours to dispose of, you would have a house, a house like the one in Milan (the Poldi Pezzoli) filled with beautiful pictures and objects of art, for people to come and enjoy. And you have carried out the dream of your youth and given great happiness to hundreds of people.' The season was not right for Naples; Miss Waterston, unfortunately, was allowed to go there, and as the result of a trip up Vesuvius, took a fever and died, but the Stewarts went to Venice, the city which would eventually inspire the material form of the vision seen in Milan. They visited all the sights, even including the Armenian monastery on the island of San Lazzaro, where Miss Stewart got a little volume containing Lord Byron's translations from Armenian and translations of a few of his poems into Armenian.

Toward the end of 1858, the Stewarts sailed for home. As the house on University Place had been rented, they lived for a short time at the Hotel Saint Germain, on the corner of Fifth Avenue and Twenty-Second Street. In 1859, Mr. Stewart purchased the house at 27 East Twenty-Second Street, which was his residence for the next fifteen years.

In February, 1859, Miss Stewart paid her first visit to her friend Miss Gardner in Boston. Fortunately, during part of the visit Mr. Gardner was in New York, and the letters between him and his daughter have been preserved. Mr. Gardner wrote that he was glad they were succeeding so well in entertaining Miss Stewart, and that on her return to New York she would be able to instruct the ladies there in skating, for those he had seen were pretty poor at it. February 14, 1859, Miss Gardner wrote to her father:

... I have been enjoying extremely Belle's visit here, and I think she has also, for we have been very gay, although a great deal of our enjoyment was in a quiet way, small tea-parties, etc. The other day we had a delightful excursion out to Mrs. Forbes's in Milton. The sleigh, Cleopatra's Barge, called for us at about seven o'clock, and we drove out of town in company with some twenty other young people, all well 'bundled up,' and all in excellent spirits. The party was matronized by Mesdames Theodore Lyman, Richard Fay, and Fred. Sears, all of whom did their share toward the entertainment. But the most amusing person was *Mr.* Lyman, who made us laugh all the way out, danced, organized games, and 'kept the fun going' all the evening; and finally sung all the way home; in short, he was the life and spirit of the party. As I said before, we spent the evening very pleasantly in dancing and playing games and had a very merry drive home, notwithstanding a slight rain which wet our faces a little, but found it impossible to annoy us in any other way, we were so well protected against it. I am sorry you were not here at the little party we gave last Monday — it was very successful and everybody seemed to enjoy themselves except poor Georgina Putnam, who had a bad headache and who waited an hour and a half in the dressing-room for her carriage to come. Aunt Helen is kind enough to give a party to-night for Belle. . . .

I look forward with great pleasure to resuming my evening readings with you — it is so long since we have had a chance! . . .

Your affectionate daughter
JULIA

The visitor charmed all the family; Julia's brother Joseph wrote the following sentiment, which Miss Stewart inserted in her Album:

May your own path in life be always strewn with flowers as gay as those which spring up everywhere around you under the vivifying influence of your sunny glance.

JOSEPH P. GARDNER

To MISS BELLE STEWART
February 13, 1859

The younger brother Jack fell desperately in love with her; his little sister Eliza, with the uncanny intuition of youngsters in such matters, said afterward that she suspected it from a walk that Jack and Belle took out the new Beacon Street. At a ball, after one or two preliminary questions, young Mr. Gardner asked Miss Stewart how she would like to make Boston her permanent home. 'If you want to ask that question,' she replied, 'you will have to come to New York.' No sooner, therefore, had Miss Stewart finished her visit and returned to her father's house than Jack Gardner rushed to New York to ask his question again. Young Jack was a very fine young man, whose life was to prove the sincerity and fidelity of his love. He had entered Harvard College with the class of 1858, but left at the end of his sophomore year. (The College gave him the degree of A.B. at Commencement, June, 1898, six months before his death.) The match was highly satisfactory to both families; Miss Stewart had wealth and charm; Mr. Gardner had wealth and position. What Miss Gardner wrote to her idolized friend we do not know, but this was Miss Stewart's answer, calling her friend Julie, in memory of Paris days:

NEW YORK, *February* 28, 1859

Your very welcome letter, my dearest Julie, was received on Saturday, by one of the happiest of human beings. Surely no one has so many causes to rejoice as myself; independent of the *great* event, the *very* kind letters and expressions of satisfaction that I have received from your family make me feel most deeply sensible of the happiness that is my lot.

I am almost inclined to scold you, as a naughty little rogue, for remembering those little idle remarks (I once made to you) in order that you might 'have the laugh on me'; but I have one consolation that bears me up, in consequence of which I forgive you and let you laugh.

I am most anxiously awaiting the time of your arrival here; when I left Boston, we did not imagine it would be so soon? I am very sorry for your sake that New York is so dull now; I fear we will never be able to return but very little of your great kindness to me; however, you must take the will for the deed.

The one drawback to mother's bright visions of the future is the thought of losing me from New York. It has been proposed, as a compensation, that David should grow up very quickly and bring home another daughter; which idea, however, does not suit him precisely, although he has come to the heroic conclusion of giving up living on a farm (a plan in which he formerly persisted) in order that he may, in a degree, take my place at home.

Ever your most affectionate
BELLE

Soon after, Miss Gardner became engaged to Joseph Randolph Coolidge, and Belle sent her congratulations; there seems to be more ecstasy over this event than over her own engagement. The letter, which has no date, was probably written in the spring of 1859, and is so characteristic that it sounds like letters written by Mrs. Gardner sixty years later.

I am so *very, very* happy, my darling Julie, that I don't know what to do! So you are engaged! Oh, it is *too* glorious! And to Randolph Coolidge, of all others! I have just received your note and as the mail closes in a few moments and as I am perfectly crazy, you must forgive me if this letter has no apparent meaning. It intends to express my great joy at the most happy of events.

I am not in the slightest astonished. Do you remember a little talk we had together one night in bed?   .   .   .   .

I have no more time to write. I wish you the greatest possible happiness and am sure that you will enjoy it, for you deserve it. Hoping very soon to see both you and your fiancé, I remain ever

Your most affectionate friend
BELLE

Portrait of Mrs. Gardner's grandmother, *Isabella Tod Stuart* (1778-1848), by Thomas Sully, oil on canvas, 29½ x 24½ in.

Mrs. Gardner in a pony cart (with an unidentified escort)

Green Hill, Brookline

Music Room, 152 Beacon Street, ca. 1895

Music Room, Fenway Court, from the stage, 1902-1914

152 Beacon Street

Mrs. Gardner's Egyptian diary entry for Sunday, December 20, 1874, with her watercolor of the Nile

ALPHA

In October, during a visit to Miss Stewart, Miss Gardner wrote the following letters, delightful in their simplicity and in their expression of filial affection — commoner, perhaps, then than now — and particularly interesting as a record of the ways of entertaining young people which were then in vogue in New York. Her brother Jack, as it happened, was in New York at the same time.

Saturday, October 8

MY DEAR MOTHER,

Although it is late in the evening, I snatch a few moments to write and tell you that I am very well, and having a delightful time. On our arrival we found Mr. Stewart and the servant waiting for us, and when we got to the house, we received a most cordial welcome, Mrs. Stewart actually rushing downstairs with her arms wide open.

The next day, I worked on my carpet bag (in which, of course, I made a dreadful mistake) until about three o'clock, when we all drove over to Hoboken (I am sure I don't know how to spell that wonderful name) to see the grand cricket match. When we arrived the fun was just over, for which we were rather glad afterwards, for we found that it was not a very nice place for ladies. In the evening I played chess with Mr. Stewart, from which I was called off to see Mr. Codington, a little gentleman who looks like a wax doll, and who had come to make a call. This morning Belle and I took a long walk, and on the way bought 'Quits' and the last new publication of M. Athenase Coquerel. We have had a delightful little dinner party this evening given for me. The 'convives' in the order in which they sat at table were, Mrs. Stewart and Mr. Joseph Peabody, Miss Stewart and Mr. Grenville Winthrop, Miss Gardner and Mr. Stewart, Miss Mamy King and Mr. Kruger Oakley, Miss Lily Oddie and Mr. John Gardner. After a very handsome dinner we went into the other room and played games — Fox and Geese, Hunt the Ring, Consequences, etc. Everybody seemed to enjoy themselves very much, and especially Joe Peabody, who to my surprise entered with great spirit into all that was going on, and appeared to be in a very jolly frame of mind. (I heard Lily Oddie whisper to Belle after we came out from dinner, 'I think that Mr. Peabody is splendid!' to which Belle replied, 'Of course he is' (! ! !) I am going to church with him tomorrow morning to hear Dr. Bellows. The Stewarts are as usual all kindness, and they are constantly repeating, 'Make yourself perfectly at home, this is Liberty Hall,' and, moreover, they provide their guests with every comfort and luxury. This note is very badly written, but it is *partly* because I am kneeling on a chair writing with a bad pen. If any of my friends call on Tuesday please give them my most sincere regrets. With a great deal of love to yourself, and Pa, and hoping to hear from you soon, I am

Your affectionate daughter

JULIA

Julia Gardner to her father, from New York, October, 1859:

... I still continue to enjoy myself very much, for the Stewarts have done everything to make it pleasant. Yesterday morning Belle and I went to see the famous picture, the 'Heart of the Andes' by Church — it is said to be the finest painting of modern times, and I think it deserves its reputation, for it is magnificent, and compares well with any Claude I ever saw. Later in the day Mrs. Stewart, Belle, the nurse and baby,[1] and myself, all drove over to Greenwood; — it is a beautiful cemetery, but I was a little disappointed in it, for it is very much up and down hill, and contains very few really *handsome* monuments, though a great many in very bad taste. In the evening we went to the theatre to hear Dot (from Dickens's 'Cricket on the Hearth'). Mrs. John Wood and Miss Agnes Robertson both played, and I was delighted with the performance. . . .

Give my love to Mother and tell her that my carpet bag gets on slowly, but promises to be very pretty; I work on it while Belle reads aloud 'Night and Morning,' a very interesting novel by Bulwer. . . .

Your affectionate daughter

JULIA

Julia Gardner to her mother, from New York, October 17, 1859:

Since I last wrote I have been twice to the theatre, on Thursday evening to Laura Keene's to see the 'Sea of Ice,' 'which was a Grand Spectacle,' indifferently well carried out. On Saturday we went to the French Theatre with Joe Peabody, and saw some amusing little vaudevilles. Friday evening we had a visit from Joe Peabody, Mr. Sanford, and one of Belle's cousins, a Mr. Hicks.

I began this letter yesterday morning, but was unable to finish it then, on account of being obliged to go out early with Belle to Lily Oddie's in order to see the firemen's procession, that went by her house. The procession was a very long one, and consisted principally in a mass of red flannel shirts

[1] Mrs. Gardner's brother James.

and black hats, relieved now and then by an engine or a hose-cart gaudily painted, and decked out with flowers.[1]

The other day we drove out to Central Park; it is beautifully laid out with walks and lakes and arbors, and promises to be, when it is finished, *almost* equal to the Bois de Boulogne.

. . . .

We went last night to the Opera, hoping to hear Speranza make her début in 'Traviata,' but were disappointed, on arriving, to find that Speranza was sick, and that the opera was changed to 'Trovatore,' with Crescimano for prima donna. Somehow or other everything seemed to go wrong. Crescimano sang pretty well, but acted wretchedly, and was not at all attractive in appearance; Amodio came on the stage, and had such a cold that he could not sing a note; part of the opera was left out, the scenery made trouble about being shifted; in short, the whole thing was a failure. Notwithstanding that, I enjoyed myself very much, for the theatre was gay, the audience brilliant; and, above all, I had a very agreeable young man to talk with almost all the evening; our box only had chairs for four, so that he was obliged to seat himself by my side on the platform, at Mrs. Stewart's feet. We are to have a little dance this evening, and Belle and I are going to introduce the Caledoniano; some of her friends have already been initiated by us, so I don't think we shall have much difficulty. . . .

One evening the Stewarts took Miss Gardner to see the minstrels, and Mr. Stewart sent word to the management that he hoped there would be no coarse jokes that evening because Miss Gardner, of Boston, was there. Consequently, throughout the entertainment the performers cautioned one another: 'Sh-sh! Miss Gardner, of Boston, is here.'

The following year the marriage took place. As it was reported in the 'New York Herald' for Thursday, April 12, 1860:

Married

GARDNER-STEWART. — In Grace Church, on Tuesday, April 10, by the Rev. Dr. Taylor, John L. Gardner, Jr., of Boston, to Isabella, daughter of David Stewart, of this city.

[1] When the Prince of Wales visited New York in 1860, a firemen's torchlight parade was one of the entertainments provided for him.

ISABELLA STEWART GARDNER

In those days forests were not destroyed that a transient record might be made of details of dressmaking, floral arrangement, or even the names of bridal attendants, but there were six bridesmaids, among them Amy Gerry and the bride's cousin, Adelia Hudson. Julia Gardner and Lily Oddie were probably two of the others. Like so many young bridegrooms before and since, Mr. Gardner took his bride to Washington, quite the most magnificent place to journey to, if New York was your home. The one incident of their stay in Washington which Mrs. Gardner liked to narrate occurred at the table d'hôte on the day they arrived. She was young and self-conscious; the waiter was a huge, very black darky, of pronounced racial features; the dessert was meringues, and as he passed them to the bride he said genially, with an absurd lisp, 'Have a kith, Mith?'—not even bestowing on her the dignity of 'ma'am.'

Miss Gardner, who had stayed on in New York after the wedding, wrote to her father April 21, 1860:

We went out to the Central Park the other day, and thought that it promised to be very fine, though I imagine that it will be a good many years before it is at all equal to the 'Boy' (as you used to call it). Oh! there is a great pleasure in store for me, if I choose to avail of it, and that is, going to see somebody *shorter!* than myself and that person a man!! — in a word Tom Thumb is here on exhibition, and I have half a mind to go to see him, in order to have the satisfaction of looking over his head without standing on tip-toe. . . .

Jack and Belle have returned and are as happy as possible; four other newly married couples made the journey to Washington at the same time with themselves, and they seem to have been very busy watching each other.

And yet, up to the time of Mrs. Gardner's death, ladies in Boston, who were just too young to be called her contemporaries, repeated the tale that 'Belle Stewart jumped out of a boarding-school window and eloped with Jack Gardner.'

CHAPTER II

THE INTRUDER

IN November, 1859, Mr. Stewart purchased from the Commonwealth of Massachusetts the lot of land on 'Western Avenue or Beacon Street' numbered 152, part of the tract conveyed to the State by the Boston and Roxbury Mill Corporation in 1854. A house for his daughter was started there, but, as it was not ready for 'Mr. and Mrs. Jack' (as they were always called) when they returned from their honeymoon, they first made a long visit to Mr. and Mrs. Gardner, and then established themselves temporarily in the Hotel Boylston.

From the first, Mrs. Jack intrigued Boston. Her ways were different from Boston ways. She was a fascinating, frail, delicate little creature, delightful to everybody, but determined to lead her life in her own way. Because she was not well, she often spent her morning in bed; this was 'not being done' in Boston, and seemed very peculiar. She discouraged informal, early morning 'running in'; all her life she allowed her friends to take no more liberty than she chose to give; yet she was warmhearted and always delighted in giving others pleasure. She was considered shy, and during her early married life her health prevented her from going much in society; she was glad to escape frequently to New York and to stay with her parents until her eager husband came to fetch her. While Julia Gardner was driving through the White Mountains with her parents during this summer of 1860, she received from Mrs. Jack the following account of a week-end spent at the Gardner country place in Brookline.

[23]

ISABELLA STEWART GARDNER

BROOKLINE, *Sunday evening*

MY DEAR JULIE

Joe and Harriet[1] have just started for Longwood, having taken tea with us and as there is still a half an hour before bedtime, I thought I could not do better than write to you, as news of Randolph[2] I knew would be acceptable. We got out here about seven o'clock Friday evening. We had several things to attend to in town before leaving, which made us later than we expected. Everything looked so charmingly here, notwithstanding the weather, that I could find nothing to wish for but the presence of the pleasant people that are now among the White Mountains. We, immediately, went in to see Randolph, who seemed very bright and who was 'pretty well' according to himself. We took our tea in his room, at the same time that he took his, and as he assured us we would not disturb him, we took up our abode there for the rest of the evening. Randolph taught me 'all fours' and beat me, but I revenged myself afterwards by beating him two games of backgammon out of three. Jack read to himself and talked to us during our games, so that it was altogether a little family party. Tell your mother he (Randolph) has been very industrious with his worsted work. He had finished his breakfast yesterday by one o'clock, so from that time until dinner time I passed in his room. He entertained me immensely and seemed very bright. He said he felt much better than he had done and began to talk about going away. . . .

Saturday evening was spent in the same way, with 'all fours' and back-gammon.

For the next two years Mrs. Gardner was much of an invalid. The winter of 1861–62 was spent at 126 Beacon Street; in 1862, Mr. and Mrs. Jack moved into their own house at 152. The summers were spent at Beverly Farms. Her husband was devoted, and they passed the long evenings playing backgammon together. Fifty years later, Mrs. Gardner would still bring out the backgammon board to get through an evening, and could appear to enjoy the game. Occasionally they would drive to Danvers to see their Peabody relatives, although she was sometimes so weak that she had to be carried into the house. As soon

---

[1] Joseph Peabody Gardner (1828–1875) and his fiancée, Harriet Sears Amory (m. Nov. 14, 1860).

[2] Joseph Randolph Coolidge (1828–1925); m. Julia Gardner, Dec. 18, 1860.

as she entered the room, interest centred in her: young and old succumbed to her fascination; though she was not beautiful, she produced the effect of beauty; her neck and shoulders were snow-white, her complexion peaches and cream, her eyes a wonderful blue, and her hair golden.

It was her supreme desire to be a mother, and on June 18, 1863, this desire was gratified by the birth of a son. It was such a terrible ordeal for her that the doctor told her she could never have another child. That mattered little; her joy was complete, since the child she actually had was a son to bear his father's and his grandfather's honored name. Her pain and her fate were very patiently, even happily, borne. The members of the family who came to see her found her lying in bed, very straight and very quiet, waiting stoically for the return of health and strength. All the intensity of her deep emotional nature was focussed on Jackie; she was a devoted, happy mother, caring for little but her baby and the pleasures of domestic life. He was a beautiful baby, with his mother's coloring, her eyes and hair, and she would sit in the window playing with him so that passers-by might see him; to every visitor he must be exhibited; if they had an evening party, the doting parents would take Jackie out of bed at midnight and bring him down asleep to show him to their guests.

On April 10, 1864, her fourth wedding anniversary, Mrs. Gardner was confirmed at Emmanuel Church by Dr. Manton Eastburn, Bishop of Massachusetts. This was the devout expression of her gratitude to God for the gift of a son.

So absorbed was she in her baby that she took little interest in the Civil War, and in later life always said she was too young to remember it. Abolition was not popular in Boston society; Maud Howe Elliott, in 'Three Generations,' recalls that at Papanti's dancing-school she and Governor Andrew's daughters were called 'nasty little abolitionists,' and the older girls would not speak to them. To dominate others gave Mrs. Gardner such pleasure that she must have regretted the passing of slavery. She once said that the only person she envied was the Empress Dowager of China, because whenever she wished she could give the command, 'Cut off his head.' Fascinating as she was in her mirth, she could be terrible in her wrath. To be her friend and to be her servant were quite different experiences. Yet she had a just regard for faithful service, even if she did not choose the usual methods of showing appreciation, and those who remained long in her employ developed an affection for her and a devotion to her which it was often difficult for them to explain even to themselves.

November 4, 1864, she wrote to her mother-in-law in Florence:

BOSTON, *November* 4, 1864

MY DEAR MRS. GARDNER:

I think if you could take only one peep at the poor people of Boston to-day, you would be satisfied and would hurry back to your apartment in Florence, however unsatisfactory it is, and be thankful that you had a place to live in in a country where they have such lovely weather as in Italy. You have no idea how it is pouring, nor how the wind is blowing. It all seems to come from the opposite side of the way and the wind is blowing the rain into our windows at such a rate that I am afraid we will soon be afloat.

And to-night is the night of the grand Lincoln torchlight procession. I hope it won't so happen that they will be obliged to postpone it until the same night that the McClellanites have theirs — next Monday, the night before the election.

Before I go on with my real fireside letter (for I am sitting on the hearth with a wood fire as near me as my paper), I must tell you of the pleasure you have given us by your choice of our dinner-set. Opening the cases was our

[26]

THE INTRUDER

great spree last week, and when we had uncovered one dish and plate of each kind we were perfectly delighted. The dinner-set is remarkably pretty and is, I think, exceedingly elegant. The dessert set has been a study for us — the flowers are so beautiful. In future, when we have dinner companies we will always think of your kindness, and good taste, neither of which has confined themselves to the buying of dinner-sets.

We have had rather a sick time this fall. After my doleful visit to New York was ended, we came home to have a siege with the baby. The poor little fellow was miserable — vomiting, with a high fever for two or three days. At first we were very much worried, particularly as the doctor hinted measles and whooping cough, but it subsided into a bad cold, aggravated by the coming of four double teeth. He looks very well now, and although he is very backward with his walking he is quite advanced in talking and says any quantity of words very distinctly. I am quite well again, although my strength and flesh haven't come back yet. I am very busy, principally with thinking over all that I have got to do; however, I have really accomplished wonders to-day, for I have made myself a bonnet. I found that my best one cost so much that I couldn't afford to have my old one made over by a milliner, so I bought a new-fashioned frame and have turned out quite a respectable bonnet.

I can tell you no news. . . . Give my best love to Mr. Gardner.

Yours affectionately

BELLE

Only a few months later, on March 15, 1865, the baby died. Mrs. Gardner was prostrated; her grief can be conceived only by other desolate young mothers. There was no hope for another child, and she knew nothing could ever fill the void in her heart and her life. For many years the anniversary of Jackie's death was spent in seclusion. In later life, she never mentioned her child, but a miniature of him, inscribed with his name and dates, with a lock of his hair on the back, always stood in a closed case on the writing-table that had been his father's. When his nurse was dying of cancer, Mrs. Gardner went every day to see her, for Jackie's sake, although contact with such an illness was repugnant to her. She acquiesced in the naming of a nephew John Lowell Gardner only on condition that he should never be called Jackie. If her grief was ever completely assuaged, it was not until on her own birthday in 1923 a son was born to her grand-nephew, George Peabody Gardner, Jr., and his wife, Rose Grosvenor Gardner, to whom the old family name was given. Throughout her life, her ever-quick sympathy for her friends was never more deeply stirred nor more affectingly shown than at the death of a baby boy.

The next two years were years of depression and illness. In the spring of 1867, the doctor suggested to Mr. Gardner that if he took his wife to Europe, the change of scene might be beneficial. Mrs. Gardner was taken to the steamer in an ambulance and carried up the gangway on a mattress. They landed at Hamburg on June 10th, and after a few days went to Copenhagen. The sculptures of Thorwaldsen, then more admired perhaps than now, gave her great pleasure. Under photographs of them she wrote in her album this quotation: 'We saw a swan strike the marble rock with his wing so that it cleft asunder, and the forms of beauty, imprisoned in the stone, stepped forth into the light of day, and people of all lands lifted their heads to see these mighty forms.' They sailed up the coast of Norway to the North Cape, to see the midnight sun; after six weeks in Norway, entertained by the manners and customs, and particularly the costumes of the peasants, they spent three weeks in Sweden, and then went on to St. Petersburg. A brief week here, another in Moscow, and a day at Nijni Novgorod could give only a superficial idea of the country, but Mrs. Gardner enjoyed it all. Sturdy, vigorous peasant types always attracted her. A visit to Vienna and two months in Paris completed the trip. The change and the invigorating northern air had greatly improved Mrs. Gardner's health.

When she returned to Boston, it was to make a fresh start. Her nature was too buoyant for her to continue to spend her days repining for what she could not have. Fate had been cruel, but there was much in life to enjoy, and enjoy it she would. Quickly she became one of the most conspicuous members of Boston society. Effervescent, exuberant, reckless, witty, she did whatever she pleased, and the men, the gayest and most brilliant of them, she captivated. Fashion had not imagined the narrow, straight-line silhouette; curved outlines were still considered beautiful. Even the most envious of the women admitted that her figure was perfect, her complexion marvellous, her grace incomparable. Looking back upon those days, she called Boston society delightful because it was so small that every one really knew every one else; its inability to forgive her escapades only amused her.

The 'Assemblies' were held in old Horticultural Hall or at Papanti's on Tremont Street. It was her custom to arrive very late, and her entrance, her arms filled with bouquets sent by her admirers, was the excitement of the evening. An elderly relative, when told of a specially magnificent bouquet of orchids that she had brought to a ball, said, 'Of course only Jack will have given her that!' At one ball she and another popular young matron, who was perhaps the belle of the day, arrived with so many bouquets that the young men laid wagers on which of the two could bring the most. At the next ball, to every one's delight, the other lady arrived carrying more bouquets than ever; a few minutes later, Mrs. Gardner, who would never have made the mistake of arriving first, did the only effective, amusing, and also dignified thing — she entered the ballroom without a single flower.

Her dancing was so good that the first time she went to Papanti's he said to her: 'May I ask where you learned to dance?' — 'At school in Paris.' — 'I thought so.' The young men watched for her arrival, speculating on what she would wear; in the morning would come such a note as this:

Accept my respectful congratulations on one of the most perfect dresses I ever saw — even on you!
— next morning.

Acknowledging a kindness, Dr. Henry J. Bigelow, a wit as well as a great surgeon, wrote:

My DEAR MRS. GARDNER:
No wonder so many gentlemen admire you. I hesitate to put on paper the way I feel — there are so many people about.

I don't think I ever saw so many grapes together before. They are magnificent. The trouble is you excite all these emotions in other people's bosoms and remain so perfectly hard-hearted yourself. I have seriously thought of trying a course of Jacqueminots, now that the price has come down a little, if I believed they would produce the least effect or if I could find out there was ever a vacancy.

As it is, there seems to be no alternative but to sit on the top of Oak Hill and think of the way your dress fits.

Very many thanks for your splendid remembrance.
Most truly yours
HENRY J. BIGELOW

Years after she was told of the legend that it was her custom at the end of the season to burn her ball dresses in the furnace. She laughed her indescribably rippling, musical, amused laugh and said: 'How the house must have smelled!'

'That legend came from Newark, New Jersey,' she was told.

'I didn't know,' she replied, 'that Newark had so much imagination, but if people *like* to believe such things, please don't contradict them.'

One of her favorite quotations was: 'Don't spoil a good story by telling the truth.'

Among her dancing partners, one of the handsomest and wittiest was a man she had met when she first visited Boston in 1859, Richard S. Fay. The Fay and Gardner families had long been friends, and Richard was an intimate friend of Jack; besides being a perfect dancer and an excellent horseman, he was a travelled man with artistic tastes, a talent for water-colors, and a great fondness for music.

In 1851, Mr. Fay's father leased a country seat, 'Moor Park,' in Shropshire, England, to which young Richard came from Bonn for the Christmas holidays. His cousin, Anna Maria Fay, says of him in a letter published in 'Victorian Days in England': 'He is not less grave than he used to be, but I think he endeavors more to make himself generally agreeable, and he is much improved in every respect. He is remarkably elegant in appearance. The repose of his manner accords perfectly to my taste with his fine classical face. I think his mother would like to have him gay like other young men, but I do not think it would suit him.' His gaiety increased as he grew older, and in the late sixties he was the leading beau of Boston. He was also an intimate friend of Mr. Gardner's cousin, Frank Peabody, who went from the École des Beaux Arts to be one of the 'Moor Park' Christmas party in 1851.

It was Mrs. Gardner's rule to select and acquire the best. If she were attending a polo game, she would be escorted to her seat by the best player of the day; the best tenor of the opera, the best painter, the best art critic, the best judge of horses — these, each for a special purpose, were her friends. One of the best business men in town was her husband; and naturally the best dancer in society was pretty regularly her cotillion partner. Before her advent, the belles of the day had received his homage, and these lovely ladies, angered by his defection, vented their spite in criticism of what they called Mrs. Gardner's outrageous flirtations. If such criticism ever influenced her — which is doubtful — she never let it appear to, but preferred to excite more criticism.

Her superior fascinations were not conceded without a struggle. On one occasion two ladies, who felt that their combined charms and wits would surely be a match for Mrs. Gardner single-handed, gave an evening party, inviting a few people for dinner, and others for the music which followed. Mrs. Gardner was to be handicapped by not being included in the dinner party, of which Mr. Fay was the particular star. After dinner, with him secure between them, the hostesses received their other guests. Mrs. Gardner arrived, took in the situation at once, and demurely retired to a secluded seat. Presently she coughed, just enough to attract attention, then hurried from the room. The hostesses said to Mr. Fay: 'Oh, do go and see if anything is really the matter with Mrs. Gardner.' He went, but never came back to report; Mrs. Gardner carried him off in her carriage for a quiet evening à deux.

Such victories the ladies could not forgive. They wrapped themselves in virtue and would have nothing more to do with such an outrageous woman. They decided that their daughters could not associate with her, that her influence was harmful! The girls whose parents were not so scrupulous remember that Mrs. Gardner was very lovely to them, kind, sympathetic, affectionate, delightful; to young brides coming from New York to the stronghold of decorum, she was particularly gracious. At her house they met charming men — James Russell Lowell and John Chipman Gray, who were cousins of Mr. Gardner; Henry and William James, Henry Adams, Henry L. Higginson, Dr. William Sturgis Bigelow, and many, many others. If she could ever have been a harmful influence, it was not because of anything the young girls saw her do or heard her say, but because of what they heard their elders say about her. To-day it all seems ludicrous, when mothers and even grandmothers find it so difficult to defend themselves against the perverting influence of their daughters and granddaughters. When Mrs. Gardner was asked for a subscription to the Charitable Eye and Ear Infirmary, she replied that she did not know that there was a charitable eye or ear in Boston. This remark has been attributed to another lady whose witticisms are famous in Boston, but Mrs. Gardner often said it was her one ewe lamb and she would not give it up. She was never a professional wit, nor a maker of bons mots, but she was so vivacious and her mind was so alert that, as one man put it, 'every one who has ever talked with her declares that she is the most brilliant, charming, and attractive woman on earth.'

The local aspirants for literary fame wrote novels in which Mrs. Gardner, disguised only by name, was the leading character. In the magazines that circulate scandal there were frequent paragraphs about her. A public curiosity was thus developed, which was vulgar enough at the time, but from that thorn grapes were ultimately gathered; when the day came to open Fenway Court to the public, that old curiosity led many into the uplifting presence of such beauty as they had never before imagined. Through thick and thin Mr. Gardner stood by his wife; he had unfaltering faith in her, and enjoyed the admiration that other men gave her. In the gaiety that she always created, he shared. Her readiness for any kind of lark, and her capacity to extract pleasure from any circumstances, her intensely vital enjoyment, made her the centre of the entertainments arranged by her contemporaries and the younger set about her. When she and Mr. Gardner missed the train from Boston that was to take them to a North Shore coaching party, it was she who suggested that they hire a locomotive to take them down. The rest of the party, quite in the dumps over their failure to arrive, were suddenly startled by the screeching of an engine coming down the track, and were thrilled to see the immaculate Mrs. Jack, in a white Paris gown, descend from the cab, followed by Mr. Jack, hugely pleased with the success of his wife's idea.

Every incident in life was an adventure — she did not need to go to outlandish places in search of them; although she was elaborately sophisticated, she retained to the end an element of naïveté, and enjoyed simple things with the fresh enthusiasm of a child. Mr. Gardner once remarked that she had never grown up. She was a will-o'-the-wisp, leading Boston society a merry chase, always pursued but never caught, vexing those whose vanities she piqued and whose conventions she disregarded, but delighting those whose imaginations she fired and whose daring she challenged.

Bernard Berenson, ca. 1887

Mrs. Gardner in 1888

Nephews William Amory, Joseph and Augustus

The Concert, ca. 1662, by Jan Vermeer, oil on canvas, 27¼ x 24¾ in.

Count Tommaso Inghirami, ca. 1512, by Raphael, oil on panel, 35 x 24½ in.

An Interior in Venice, 1899, by John Singer Sargent, oil on canvas 25 x 31½ in., Royal Academy of Arts, London (diploma work). Mr. and Mrs. Daniel Curtis, their son Ralph, and his wife Lisa in the *salone* of the Palazzo Barbaro

The Little Note in Yellow and Gold (Mrs. Gardner), 1886,
by J. A. M. Whistler, pastel on cardboard, 10½ x 5½ in.

CHAPTER III

EGYPT AND PALESTINE

MRS. GARDNER'S brother David died October 5, 1874. Because she could not take any part in the season's festivities at home, she and Mr. Gardner spent the winter of 1874–75 in Egypt. When they passed through London, they purchased the first string of the pearls which were to become almost as famous as Mrs. Gardner's pictures. Beginning in 1884, Mr. and Mrs. Gardner went to Europe every other year; each time they bought a string of pearls, until she had seven. After Mr. Gardner's death, when her desires for Fenway Court made her feel that she had not enough money for other purposes and she talked to her friends of her poverty, one of them said it was amusing to imagine her standing on a street corner, wearing all her pearls, playing her Stradivarius, and begging alms. The Stradivarius was eventually given to Mr. Charles M. Loeffler.

Always sensitive to the 'Spirit of Place,' the following extracts from her journal of the Nile trip show how deeply she felt the spell of Egypt.

When I went on deck on the morning of December 10, I knew that it was a dream, for never had I seen such a colour as was the sea — there is no word for it — and on the horizon was a low stretch of sand and waving palms. I felt that it was Africa, and from that moment everything was interest and excitement. The dragoman Bonnici [later spelt Bonicci] came for us in a boat, but instead of being anxious to get away and ashore we lingered and lingered to watch the mass of screaming, scrambling Arabs, men and boys, each more determined than the others to secure his prey. The next day we went to Cairo, where the dream only became more coloured with Eastern glow. The people had stept out of the 'Arabian Nights,' which were no longer tales that we had read, but were bits of real life happening, with us looking on — and we had truly 'come abroad and forgot ourselves.'

Oh, the grace and beauty of the men, and oh, their gorgeous clothes! From the Princes of Persia to the barber's son, what graceful languor and what perfect postures, as they lean against a deewan or a wall!... Our first sunset in Cairo we saw from the Citadel and it was our first view of the city — a sky that had been prayed for could not have been more perfect. The haze softened every outline and the sun went down behind the pyramids, steeping everything in gorgeous colours.

After the first visit to the Pyramids:

I felt that I was disappointed when I stood close to Cheops hemmed in by the screaming Arab host — but when I got away from carriages and many of the people, and could lie on the sand near the Sphinx, with the silent desert beyond and on every side, and the Pyramids a little away from me — then solemnity and mystery took possession and my heart went out to the Sphinx.

.   .   .   .

I went with my English spinster friend to see the wife of Hassan, her donkey boy aged nineteen. It was very interesting to see how that class really lived 'in my house' as Hassan called the one room which had only a window looking on a court to lighten it, and even that was barred. . . . I made the wife squat by my side and I admired her very pretty face, her clothes, and her jewelry at my leisure. This donkey boy's wife wore gold necklaces and bracelets the like of which I had found much too dear to buy. . . . When I told Hassan how pretty his wife was, he tossed his head and said, 'I no have *him*, if *he* not.'

December 18th they embarked on the dahabeah Ibis:

And we were charmed. With a few touches the little parlour became very pretty, and as we could spread ourselves well over the boat, we were quite comfortable, with our separate dressing-rooms, bathrooms, etc. After dinner we went up to the sky parlour and there, with the many Eastern rugs, couches, plants, and awnings — it was only part of the dream — the lights of Cairo looked at themselves in the water, the palms waved and whispered to us from the bank; the moon looked down on it all, and when the crew, with their turbans and many-coloured robes, squatted in a circle about their little lurid, flickering fire, cooked their coffee and chanted their low, weird songs to the tapping of the tarabuka, it was too much.

Before moving to the Ibis we went to the Mosque of the Howling Dervishes. I have never seen anything so terrible — they worked themselves into a perfect frenzy, some of them almost fainted, and one foamed at the mouth.

Saturday, December 19. A last visit to the Bazaar and then to the Museum at Boolák. It was my first glimpse at the Old Egyptian wonders and it was a revelation to me. I always knew of their great interest, but I was surprised by their high state of art. Some of the statues seem to me unequalled.

Of Memphis she wrote:

Although there is little now to be seen to tell of the past of glorious, regal Memphis, still to me it will always be a memory of surpassing loveliness. The ride through the palm groves, with the earth more green than it was ever painted elsewhere, with the caravans camping here and there by the side of the little lakes, and the graceful women coming and going with the water-jars on their heads, make the picture perfect. I can never praise enough the fresh morning air. The tomb of Tih, the Pyramids, and the Apis Mausoleum astounded us, and all that, with the desert hemming us in, made me very solemn.

On every page are water-color drawings made by Mrs. Gardner.

December 24. What a lovely evening it was as our bird stole so quietly under the banks of Maghagha and folded her wings for the night. I went up as usual alone after dinner and found the steersman at his prayers, his forehead touching the deck and little Alee at the helm. As I lay upon the couch with the fragrance of the frankincense stealing over me, the wake of the moon was a fit path by which my thoughts went straight to Cleopatra — and I forgot it was Christmas eve.

December 26. Late in the afternoon we passed the curious old Convent of the Pulley, but long before we reached it the monks swam out to us begging. I hope they were as innocent of sin as of clothes.

The Coptic Church at Tehneh, the first they had seen, reminded them of Norway. At Girgeh they went to the Latin Convent, where 'it was good to see the I.H.S. and the X over the very picturesque door of the chapel.'

Tuesday, January 12. Our first Egyptian Temple! Denderah! . . . I was rather suffocated at first by its massiveness, and its eighteen giant columns in the portico. And the inner part, the real temple, is so mysterious and

[37]

ISABELLA STEWART GARDNER

dark, with its huge walls in the thickness of which run long secret passages, that it affected me as terrible. And to read of the processions that wound in and out of its halls and of the sacrifices that were offered only added to it. It was very interesting to find Cleopatra and her son Cesareon on the walls with their cartouches.

They visited Karnak by moonlight:

I have never had such an experience and I felt as if I never wanted to see anything again in this world; that I might shut my eyes to keep that vision clear. It was not beautiful, but most grand, mysterious, solemn. I *felt* it, even more than saw it. It was a terrible that fascinated. I never can forget that night and Karnak will always be to me at the head of everything.

At Esneh:

What nights we have! The river runs liquid gold and everything seems turned into the precious metal, burning with inward fire; and then the sun sets and the world has hardly time to become amethysts and then silver before it is black night. And the moonlight nights! How different from ours! Nothing sharp, clear and defined, but a beautiful day turned pale. It was so beautiful, inexpressibly lovely to-night on deck and everything was so still when the muezzin's call to prayer was wailed through the air that the tears would come.

Next day, January 21st:

The governor had just been seizing the conscripts, and when some could not be found, the fathers had been taken as hostages. The soles of their feet had been bastinadoed, and if they still would not or could not tell where their sons were hidden, they were walked naked through the town. About three o'clock we went through the green fields a lovely ride, with a venerable Abraham of a Patriarch in the person of a Coptic Babas leading the way to the old Dayr (Convent) built by the Empress Helena, the oldest in Egypt. It was very interesting and the ride home very lovely, the men and women so like the Old Testament tending their flocks and carrying home their bundles of straw.

At Philæ, where they were delayed from January 25th to February 8th waiting their turn to go through the cataract, Mr. Gardner bought her a 'dear little monkey,' which the crew named Coco.

February 8. Prince Arthur is momentarily expected and the Cataract must be kept clear for him. Every one is in a fury and a grand palaver takes place; the jet black governor sitting on one of our couches on deck, with gentlemen, dragoman, and Shellalee all hard at it, sipping coffee, all talking at once, and I with difficulty keeping from laughing at Coco, who sits quietly examining the skirts of the Sheik of the Cataract which she turns over and over and I expect every minute to see her bite the uncovered legs. Strange to say one can't feel very actively impatient, there is such a delicious laziness in the atmosphere, and at times I even don't care.

February 11. About 10.30 A.M. we were boarded by the Shellalee and started for the second gate. And what a day it was! Four mummies with their bandages more or less unrolled stationed themselves on the upper deck, in charge of the helm. A maniac placed himself on the gangway and jumped up and down, waving a stick and shrieking; and one and all of the tribe, the commanders and the commanded, yelled and screamed at the same time and continuously.

February 22d they arrived at Wády Halfa and the next day went to Abusir.

I had the top of the mountain all to myself, and there was nobody to laugh at me for being absolutely unhappy because our journey was over and our faces were to be turned to the north even in half an hour. I was very glad we had got there so early, for I do hate to be in interesting places with a crowd of people. It was a quick row back and I made myself very comfortable on the shawls and cushions in the bottom of the boat. We got back about 12.30, and with a quarrel with one of those children, the crew, about the oar he was to have rowing down the river, we turned our backs on Wády Halfa — the Ibis in a wretched enough plight, shorn of her feathers; her pride and my delight, the beautiful big sail, being stowed away and everything cleared for action. There were great larks in the afternoon, the crew cutting up all kinds of pranks in their rowing; and when bedtime came and they each had the hole to sleep in that was made by taking up the planks between the rowers and they sat up in their holes in their white garments, it looked like resurrection morn.

Wednesday, February 24th, an evening visit was made to Abu Simbel.

It was not long before we had reached Abu Simbel, where we found the Nellie waiting for the moon to rise. I was so glad to get there before it did, as I wanted to see the effect of blue lights on the tremendous figures, so we invited the Rookers and all climbed through the sand and were rewarded by the weirdest effect. It was very startling the way the strange unearthly lights played about and seemed to bring out the hugeness of the Colossi. Then with candles we examined the interior with its hall supported by eight Osiride pillars, its spirited sculptures on the walls and the holy Adytum with its four seated gods. And then to make it perfect the moon rose directly opposite the Temple, in at the very door, so that all the lights were put out, and the great hall was the strangest thing I have ever seen, with its shadows and ghostly light. The others went off and the Miss R——s and I felt our way into the inner room and, seated on the knees of the stone gods, watched the moon through the distant door of the Temple with occasionally the shadow of an Arab passing before it. Then we went, and I climbed onto the foot of one of the Colossi and we feasted our eyes once more on the wonderful place.

Thursday, February 25. We had arranged to say good-bye to one of the old world's wonders at sunrise. I was the first to be there and almost buried myself in the golden sand as I lay watching the light streak in the sky getting deeper and deeper, and by and by a yellow light began to creep down the rock and over the benign calm of the great Rameses.

Saturday, March 6. Hagar Silsileh. We made visits to both sides of the river. There are a few grottoes on the west side, but the quarries on the east are much the most interesting and are really most wonderful — J. says the best thing he has seen in Egypt. Coco had one of her very jolliest and most mischievous times and capped the climax by taking away dear old Reis Ibrahim's cigar. It was funny enough to see them. He squatted on one side of the tin basin with his breakfast in it and Coco on the other side, and when she couldn't be satisfied by dipping her fingers into the dish, she sat in it, and had to be slapped and tied up.

Monday, March 8. *El Kab.* A nasty day on the river; the dust and wind, a perfect gale. I was feeling almost too wretchedly to move, but we took donkeys and started for the desert, and then what a change! On the arable land they were beginning the harvesting; women and children gleaning, like the Bible. Soon we left all traces of green and what a perfect day it was! The desert, the rocks, and the air were exactly tuned to my nerves. It was the most delicious thing I ever felt. A large amphitheatre of hills bounded the east, with unnatural-looking paths going in here and there where I could get glimpses of such valleys that I expected at every peep to see an enchanted castle. Sinbad's scene of adventure *must* have been hereabouts.

Friday, March 12. A feast of letters and no bad news, thank God. We said good-bye to the Rookers, and then to Karnak for a glorious day. There is nothing like it.

Friday, March 19. [*At Abydos.*] The harvest scenes are full of incident;

there is so much life — people, camels, donkeys, goats, sheep, dogs, cows, and buffaloes, and all such Bible pictures. The one great disappointment in Egypt is the wild flowers. It is an absolute fête the day I see the pretty little white and pink convolvuluses, those dear cunning wee pink flowers that kiss the earth, and the wide-open staring blue ones all at the same time. Abydos is beautiful. By far the finest sculptures we have seen, with very brilliant colours.

At Assiut they visited an American Mission School, and heard the boys sing in Arabic, 'There is a happy land far, far away' —

One of the hymns the dear boys sing those Beverly Sundays. It quite startled and affected me. In this country of woman's intellectual depravity it was good to see the young girls who could read and write.

Good Friday, March 26. A fearful day — what they call the yellow wind. The wind, a gale, the river dashing like the sea, and the air full of sand, so that it was impossible to see anything. We were moored as strongly as possible, our felucca full of water and the waves dashing continuously over the lower deck, and the poor crew and all their effects drenched. A canvas was rigged to protect them a little, and a miserable day it was. It was easy to understand how on the deserts such a storm should suffocate man and beast, for we, surrounded by the water on one side and cultivated fields on the other, could see nothing but the clouds of sand. Muffled and wrapped as well as possible, I sat a little time on deck, to watch a poor woman who came to the river to fill her water-jar. It was a terrible struggle, but it was to be that or thirst — the jar was placed on her head and she disappeared in the yellow cloud. The Maltese story is that there is always a storm, more or less, on Good Friday, but such as this had not been for thirty-six years.

April 2. The Pyramids are looming up on our left and the Citadel of Cairo is beginning to be distinct in front of us. Good-bye to the dear Nile Voyage.

The account of their stay in Cairo is briefer.

Our second week was the fête of the prophet, or Moolid en Nebbee. Saturday, [April] 10th, was the procession of the holy Camel and the Mahmal through the streets — the return of the pilgrims. From that day until Saturday 17th was the Moolid. A great holiday. Tents with everything to sell and all kinds of amusements, fireworks every evening and the Darweeshes howling, etc., continuously in their tents, which were beautifully lighted at night. Saturday 17th the climax and end were reached with the

[41]

Dóseh. The Sheykh of the Saadeeyah rides over the fanatics, who are closely packed on the ground. In the procession before the ride are the pretended saints, who appear to thrust knives into their eyes, cheeks, and bodies and those that were to be ridden over passed already nearly unconscious. After the Dóseh, another Darweesh ate a live snake!

April 26th, they left Egypt to spend two months in the Holy Land. When they arrived at Port Saïd, Mrs. Gardner was quite ill with fever; and frequently during the trip through the Holy Land there were delays and postponements because she was not well enough to travel. Landing at Joppa she describes as —

a beautiful sight and very exciting. I am so faint that we go straight to a hotel. With the shawls and pillow a bed is made for me on the piazza of the hotel. A Mohammedan graveyard in front. As it is Thursday, the families are spending the day among their dead. One party comes to bury a child, and the waves beat grandly just beyond. About noon I am moved to the tents which are ready, and I feel most comfortable in my own bed, with the pink and white chintz lining of the tent hanging about me. We are quite pleased with the look everything has — nice rugs, etc. Mr. Hurd brought me a bunch of wild flowers. Two poppies grow at the very door of my tent.

The wild flowers that she missed in Egypt she found in profusion in Palestine, and many specimens were pasted in her journal. It was finally decided that she should be driven to Jerusalem, and not undertake long rides till she was stronger. As they neared the city, a thunderstorm came up, and 'everything in darkness, thunder roaring and the lightning flashing on the walls and towers, we were landed at the Gate of Jerusalem.' The following day, Sunday, May 2d, 'Sick and weary. Dragged myself to the Holy Sepulchre and then to bed again. *Decidedly not disappointed!*' The next few days she was 'wretchedly sick and miserable,' but she visited several sacred shrines and was deeply interested in the pilgrims and the services of the different conflicting sects.

EGYPT AND PALESTINE

It is hard to realize that we are living in Jerusalem; it is a fact that seems to *grow into one*, however, and to be living here is like nothing else in the world. . . . The most strikingly disagreeable thing in all Jerusalem is being escorted about even the Christian relics and hallowed places by Mussulmans who are the owners. I wonder there are no more Peter-the-Hermits. . . . The Jews are ugly, dirty, and not even picturesque; the Jewesses beautiful. The latter wear brilliant clothes and white veils embroidered with colour and sometimes gold. The men wear their hair in a curl over each ear, like the Polish Jew, and cut a sorry figure in their greasy long coats.

She never appears skeptical about the identification of sacred places; on the contrary, she enjoyed belief in them.

Sunday, May 9, we breakfasted and started for the Jordan. Mustapha, my little chestnut, very good. We passed over Mount of Olives, the road by which David fled when Absalom rebelled. Then down through the wilderness of Judæa (the scene of the Good Samaritan) to Jericho for the night.

She bathed in the Dead Sea, drank at the River Jordan, and, on the way back to Jerusalem, stopped at Bethany to see the tomb of Lazarus and the house of Mary and Martha. At Hebron they found the Mohammedans very fanatical: 'the children insulted us in every way, and the men looked as if they would willingly and with pleasure tear us limb from limb.'

When Mr. and Mrs. Gardner and their equipage started north, they spent the first night at Bethel. The next morning, May 20th,

we awoke to find we had been robbed; we had taken every precaution inside, and outside were the guards. But they were the fellows who *done* it, most likely. We had down the Sheykh and gave them an hour to find the things, in which time most of them were produced, but not all. We told them 'the things and a thrashing or we should go to Jerusalem, and then woe to them.' They couldn't find the things, so we turned our faces south, lunched again at the Old Khan and re-arrived about 3.30 at Casa Nova. J. went to the Consul about the robbery and the next morning about 5.30 we were on our second start.

ISABELLA STEWART GARDNER

The rest of the diary is more concise, but almost always mentions the chief Biblical occurrences at the places they visit, and always there is keen enjoyment of natural beauties, and great interest in the native peoples. They spent several days at Carmel, resting.

Our tour in Terra Santa nearly over, for soon it will be merely Syria. So far delightful. Our entire force consists of Bonicci, old John (who is such an intense, good old Catholic), the cook, head muleteer, four under-muleteers (one a druze, one a beauty Daavis, one a poor woe-begone, one Rachid), eight horses, five mules, and two donkeys. The flowers of the land are only equalled by the birds of Egypt. Many simple wild flowers, and besides, roses (red and white), azaleas, hollyhocks, anemones, pinks, marigolds, honeysuckles, poppies, cyclamen, morning-glories, and oleanders. And such thistles — twelve feet high! And the prickly pear hedges! . . . Continually meet the shepherds *leading* their flocks, and the music from their pipes comes to us from all the hillsides. It is odd enough to see a man (gun on his back) walking quietly by the way playing a low tune to himself.

June 6–10. Resting at Tyre.

June 10. Left Tyre at 6.15 and arrived at Sarareah about a quarter of eleven. Lunched under a tree, waiting for mules — and the strangest of days began by visits from many of the populace, Metawileh. Tents pitched in beautiful place, hanging over the valley, and all afternoon troops of natives to see us — finally the Bey's wives and family, and it ended in my being taken to walk by them — the principal one a stunner (they petted me within an inch of my life) — shewn through the town, into many of the houses, etc., and finally was brought home by two sons of Bey, one of which spoke French. Altogether the funniest experience of my life.

Friday, June 18. Ahmet goes to Damascus, gets our letters (thank God — good news), and brings report from Consul of real Asiatic cholera having appeared and people leaving; so decide not to go.

Saturday, 19. Start quarter to six for Welyon hill over Damascus, arrive there 9.15, breakfast and feast our eyes, then pluck up strength of mind and turn our backs. [That night the tents were pitched at Ain Fijeh.] Perfect gypsy encampment under great walnut trees. Pomegranates closing in behind us. The river, tearing and roaring by, and almost over our heads a great orange mountain. Over the spring, a ruined temple.

They reached Baalbec on June 21st — 'Beyond words!'

EGYPT AND PALESTINE

On the 28th they sailed from Bassoul on the Austrian Lloyd Espero.

Friday, July 2, from Chesmey on Mainland, came on board the grand vizier's family. Such a mess! Balloon women, boxes, bottles, baths, sheep, goats, bedding, and the whole boat pervaded with perfumes of the heaviest sort. [That evening they arrived at Smyrna.] Some fuss was made about quarantine, but at last we were allowed to be considered all right and to go ashore. . . . Saturday . . . in the P.M. about seven went to Captain Paolo's to get an ice-cream and saw a Chinese troup perform. The next day troup and English woman manager were all at church in front of us — very devout and clean.

They reached Athens Friday, July 9th. 'Can't quite believe I am in Athens.' The days were hot, and they made it a custom to be 'up and out a little after five. Deliciously pleasant. Took rolls of bread in my pocket and ate them with the coffee between the pillars of Jupiter Olympus.' They saw everything as they did everywhere and were much interested in the numerous small churches. July 16th, they arrived at Constantinople. 'Most beautiful and very like New York — i.e., before we came near. . . . J. went for the letters and found the two terrible telegrams about poor dear Joe.[1] He had died on the night of June 11.' On Sunday, the 18th, they went to the English Church and in the afternoon drove to the old Seraglio, where they visited the Treasury 'full of such diamonds, pearls, rubies, and emeralds as I have dreamed of. . . . Saint Sophia a little disappointing, and the turning to Mecca very distracting to the eye. Dome really wonderful. The exterior of church very unattractive.'

This is an honest opinion, unaffected by the enthusiasms of art-historians. Mrs. Gardner could not have been the genius

[1] Joseph Peabody Gardner, 1828–1875.

she was if she had not been independent in her judgment and firm in her convictions. More than once her honest expression of opinion did violence to an old friendship, but she could and did judge impartially, disregarding the personal element, the element of friendship, and, when she found it impossible for a friend to do so, her opinion of the friend suffered. On the other hand, she was perfectly capable of overvaluing the performance of one in whose success she was interested, and of trying to persuade her friends and the public to share her expressed opinion. Yet her own unconfessed opinion was probably accurate.

The week Mr. and Mrs. Gardner spent at Constantinople was one of strenuous sight-seeing. Mr. Hurd was there. He and Mrs. Gardner went out in a caïque on the Bosphorus by moonlight. Eyoub and the Sweet Waters of Europe were visited; also the Seven Towers and the old walls, and Belgrade Forest and the Reservoirs.

July 23d they left by boat for Varna, and spent nearly a week reaching Vienna, going up the Danube from Rustchuk to Bosiash, and staying two days in Buda-Pesth. In Vienna she received a letter from her father, with the news that he had bought the house at 322 Fifth Avenue, which was his residence the rest of his life. Vienna seemed to her much changed, apparently from its appearance in 1867, 'great number of fine new buildings, Saint Stephen's beautiful; also Canova's monument to Archduchess Christina.'

From Vienna they went to Linz, Salzburg, Munich, and Nuremberg, where they bought from A. Pickert eleven late fifteenth-century pieces of stained glass, eight large ones and three quite small ones. The price paid was thirty-four hundred florins. These are the first objects purchased abroad that Mrs. Gardner retained in her collection at Fenway Court.

On August 14th, they arrived in Paris. There the journal ends.

CHAPTER IV

NEW INTERESTS

DURING the next ten years Mrs. Gardner was groping after some activity that should satisfactorily engage her energies and abilities. When they returned from Europe, she and Mr. Gardner took into their care the three orphan sons [1] of Mr. Gardner's brother Joseph, news of whose death had reached them in Constantinople. Their mother had died in 1865, three weeks after the birth of her third baby; since that time their training had been in the hands of an English governess. It was therefore no easy task and no small responsibility that Mrs. Gardner was assuming, and her willingness, for her husband's sake, to take charge of three temperamental boys gave evidence of a kind of character with which few of her society acquaintances had credited her. In the performance of her duty to these boys, she was faithful and conscientious. Not only did she take them, beautifully arrayed, to concerts and to church, but, fond of all sport as she was, she took a keen interest in their sports, in their learning to ride, to swim, and to sail; a mother could hardly have taken greater pride in their achievements or kept with greater care the mementoes of their youth. She read Dickens aloud to them, beginning with 'Pickwick,' who so delighted them that 'Oliver Twist,' 'Nicholas Nickleby,' 'David Copperfield,' and others followed; when the oldest boy went to Harvard, the Saturday evening reading was the treat of the week-end at home. After the family Christmas in Bos-

[1] Joseph Peabody Gardner, 1861–1886.
William Amory Gardner, 1863–1931.
Augustus Peabody Gardner, 1865–1918.

ton, Mrs. Gardner took the nephews to her father's house for the New Year gaieties in New York.

At this period Mrs. Gardner took an active interest in church work. Since 1870, the Church of the Advent had occupied the building on Bowdoin Street now known as the Church of Saint John the Evangelist. Bishop Grafton, of Fond du Lac, was the rector in the seventies, a man of energy and piety, whose influence was widely felt. Mrs. Gardner was a member of the Altar Guild and gave the reredos for the new church on Brimmer Street.

The summer of 1879, spent by Mr. and Mrs. Gardner in England and France, was virtually a cathedral pilgrimage. Bent on the education of their nephews, they had taken Augustus with them, and in London were joined by Amory, who had stayed behind to take his Harvard entrance examinations. Although their friends may have thought that Mr. and Mrs. Jack travelled only for amusement, each of their early journeys had a definite purpose; each one was undertaken to secure first-hand contact with some novel phase of life, past or present. Humanity — all humanity — interested her and made her willing to undergo the discomforts and hardships of travel. The ocean passage she regularly spent in her berth, living on champagne and biscuits. Noisy trains and the whirling countryside made her ill; shut up in a compartment by herself, with curtains drawn, she stoically endured in solitude. Mr. Gardner, on the contrary, was a good traveller, enjoyed company both on boats and trains, and in later years they often invited a young man to make trips with them so that Mr. Gardner might have the pleasure of an agreeable travelling-companion. In

1879, after a stormy crossing, they reached Liverpool in the morning of May 28th and went immediately to Chester. One day there, Mrs. Gardner said, compensated for all the agonies of seasickness.

The next day they went up to London, where everything was done to give the two boys a good time. Little attention was given to art collections and picture galleries; only one visit was paid to the National Gallery, where photographs of Moroni's 'Tailor,' Reynolds's 'Angel Heads,' Landseer's 'King Charles Spaniels with Hat,' and Gainsborough's 'Mrs. Siddons,' were bought. At Grosvenor House, however, Gainsborough's 'Blue Boy' made such an impression that, when Mrs. Gardner began acquiring masterpieces, this was one of the few pictures that she craved; long negotiations were carried on for it, but the owner would not sell. Many years later, when it was for sale, Mrs. Gardner's collection was formed, the English School had no place in it, and the American passion for collecting, started by her, had raised the value of the 'Blue Boy' to a fantastic height.

Her old friend Henry James, who was in London at the time, arranged a visit to Hatfield House, and wrote that he hoped she would bring 'those brilliant boys.' In another letter he wrote to Mrs. Gardner that her 'appreciation of this dear old London under these persistently inhuman skies is one of the most magnanimous things I know.' There was not a drop of pessimism in her nature; weather never disturbed her; if rain and fog were characteristic of a place, she would want to experience its rain and fog.

Westminster, Saint Paul's, and other London churches were 'done'; the Cathedrals at Canterbury, Litchfield, Winchester,

Salisbury, Chichester, Peterborough, Lincoln, York, and Durham were visited, and many other famous churches of architectural or sentimental interest.

Between cathedral visits, they went to the Ascot races — in Mrs. Gardner's album is a picture of Isonomy, winner of the Cup — to the Oxford-Cambridge cricket match June 14th, to the Musical Union Matinées, to the funeral of the Prince Imperial, to a performance of 'Trust' by Bronson Howard, just closing a run of one hundred and fifty performances at the Criterion Theatre of which Mr. Charles Wyndham was lessee and manager.

In France they visited royal residences, quite as ordinary tourists do, and the Cathedrals of Paris, Chartres, Rouen, and Amiens, the Abbey of Saint Denis, and the great church at Abbéville. Of each church and cathedral she bought photographs enough to represent the salient points of its architecture; these she humanized by pasting beside them in her album wildflowers and ivy leaves from the churchyards and the coats of arms of the different sees and their great bishops.

Besides being devoted to the Church, Mrs. Gardner was cultivating tastes which escaped the notice of her critical, frivolous friends, whom she continued to distance as a social leader. Before she turned her energies to collecting works of art, it might have seemed that music was to be the great interest of her life. It always stimulated her emotionally, but, because she did not wish to be merely a sentimental amateur, she worked hard to acquire a knowledge of it and a sound basis for an intelligent appreciation of it. In order to have a satisfactory music-room, Mr. Gardner, in May, 1880, purchased the house next door,

150 Beacon Street, and made it part of his own. The original house had been 'different' from all other Boston houses; its little yellow drawing-room seemed more like Paris than Boston; although the furnishings of the house were simple, Mrs. Gardner arranged them in a way which gave it individuality and charm. As the floors of the newly acquired house were on different levels from those in the original house, little flights of steps were built to connect them; this device, which sounds so obvious, seemed at the time immensely clever and original, and added one more detail to differentiate her house from other Boston houses.

In the early eighties Boston was truly a provincial city, and life was simple. Boston's jaw dropped, Boston's eyes bulged, when it heard that besides a butler the Gardners kept two footmen, and when it saw Mrs. Gardner drive out with two men in livery on the box. Till then a coachman had sufficed. Mr. Gardner managed the household and engaged the servants; he was a perfect host, and the Gardner dinners were the best in Boston, rivalled only by those given by Mr. and Mrs. Martin Brimmer. Mrs. Gardner's dresses were more beautiful than any one else's, her jewels more dazzling, and her turnouts smarter; her carriages were made by Binder in Paris; her horses, small but swift, were always driven at top speed; and she was mistress of a house undeniably more fascinating than any one else's.

To furnish this enlarged house, more pretentious things were bought than Mr. and Mrs. Gardner had previously purchased. Among Mr. Gardner's carefully filed bills for pictures and furniture, the earliest includes two framed engravings, titles not stated, bought in May, 1861, from Williams & Everett; then the following:

December 23, 1861, from Goupil & Co., New York:
Studio of Raphael, colored,	$12.
Frame	4.
Marie Antoinette	4.
Frame	3.

December 23, 1862, from Geo. Howorth & Son, Agents for Mr. Pratt:
Two Sea Views	$20.
Varnishing and cutting and surface cleaning	2.
Two frames (paid for same)	1.25
Cartage	.25
	$23.50

December 26, 1863, from Goupil & Co., New York:
Engraving, Gluck à Trianon	$22.
Frame and boxing	14.
	$36.

These December purchases suggest the probability of Christmas gifts. The engravings of Marie Antoinette and 'Gluck à Trianon' still hung in Mrs. Gardner's bedroom when she died; the two sea views were used as over-door panels in the drawing-room of the enlarged house, and later, at Fenway Court, were hung in Mrs. Gardner's private apartment.

In Paris, October 21, 1867, Mr. Gardner paid one hundred francs to Persenet for a copy of a painting by Boucher, and the next day bought from Béfort, for five hundred francs, two decorative panels; several other pictures were bought in the sixties and seventies, often at Leonard's for small sums, and neither the name of the artist nor the title of the picture appears on the bill. In 1873, a small landscape by Jacque was purchased from Doll & Richards; this is the earliest purchase that still continues in the Fenway Court collection. In 1875, the stained glass, already mentioned, was purchased in Nuremberg; in 1876, a little Diaz.

Mrs. Gardner's ambition to own fine things was developing, and her eagerness for knowledge was constant. In the spring of 1878, she attended a course of lectures by Professor Charles Eliot Norton, and on April 6th she bought a painting by Mrs. Sarah Wyman Whitman, called 'Dawn, Newport.'

At the auction sale of paintings and drawings by William Morris Hunt, held February 3, 1880, Mrs. Gardner purchased four charcoal drawings and a painting of Gloucester Harbor. When Mr. Hunt's daughter, Mrs. Horatio Nelson Slater, arranged a gallery at the Boston Museum of Fine Arts as a memorial to her father, Mrs. Gardner presented this painting to the Museum to be hung in the Hunt Gallery. Hunt's influence in the artistic evolution of Boston is well known; he persuaded his friends of the merit of the Barbizon School. Excellent collections of the work of Jean François Millet were made by Martin Brimmer and Quincy A. Shaw, but Mrs. Gardner never bought a Millet painting; he was perhaps too literal, too much of a peasant to appeal to her rather eighteenth-century, romantic taste. In April, 1880, she bought a lovely landscape by Corot, and then the enlargement of her house gave fresh impetus to her buying. Early in October, she bought from L. Marcotte and Company, of New York, three Gobelin tapestries for sixteen hundred dollars; these are probably the Noah series. At the same time she bought her two chiffoniers, said to have been used by Napoleon at Elba. A month later she and Mr. Gardner were shopping in New York again. This time they bought 'three antique tapestries' for three hundred and twenty-five dollars, the Genoese velvet portière, now hanging in the doorway to the Dutch room at Fenway Court, and the flag of the First Regiment of Napoleon's Imperial Guard. In December, she bought at Leonard's the elaborate bronze knocker representing Neptune between two of his steeds, which is now attached to a door of the Dutch Room.

But Mrs. Gardner was not at this time planning to form an art collection; she was merely creating an agreeable environment for her own life and for entertaining her friends, among whom were the ablest, most gifted men and women in the community, such as James Russell Lowell, Oliver Wendell Holmes, and Julia Ward Howe. These people were themselves too big to pay attention to unkind criticisms, and they recognized the genius in Mrs. Gardner. A very tender, affectionate friendship was shown her by Mrs. Howe. Like so many others, Mrs. Howe felt that the commonplaces of address were too cold to express her feeling for Mrs. Gardner, who inspired the kind of love which must have a personal, pet name for its object. To her, Mrs. Gardner was 'Kipourà,' a name derived from the Greek word for gardener; to many she was 'Queen'; to one she was 'Piccolina'; to another 'Bianca'; to another 'The Presence'; and to others 'Y,' the initial of Ysabella, a form of her name she particularly liked. As needy foreigners were always appealing to Mrs. Howe, to whom no appeal was made in vain, she was constantly inviting Mrs. Gardner to meet some struggling wayfarer, who hoped for help, always carefully explaining in the invitation that she had promised nothing and had encouraged no hopes. But besides the needy, the distinguished visitors to Boston sought out Mrs. Howe, and Mrs. Gardner was regularly asked to meet them. To this friendship was due one of the exciting little incidents of which Mrs. Gardner's life was full. As she told the story, she drove out one evening to the Perkins Institution for the Blind in South Boston, to see the Howes, and for their amusement she wore in her hair her two large solitaires named 'The Rajah' and 'The Light of India,' which she had had set on springs so that they waved above her forehead like antennæ. A street-car strike was in progress, and on her way home, rather late, her carriage got into the middle of a yelling mob. The thought crossed her mind that if the blazing diamonds irritated some angry eye, the result might be unpleasant; but, before any definite fear had taken shape, a heavy hand was laid on the carriage door, and a vigorous voice said, 'Don't be afraid, Mrs. Jack, I'll see you get through all right.' When they had emerged from the mob, Mrs. Gardner leaned forward and said, 'May I ask to whom I am indebted for this courtesy?' — 'John L. Sullivan.' He was the heavyweight champion. If Mrs. Gardner ever experienced fear, she was never known to show it — except fear of the dark. To be in an absolutely dark place was intolerable to her; if she knew that in a melodrama there was to be a moment of complete darkness in the theatre, she would use a flashlight or would manage to get out into a corridor till the stage was lighted again.

Mrs. Howe's nephew, F. Marion Crawford, came to Boston for the winter of 1880–81, and spent the following summer as his aunt's guest at Newport. There he wrote 'Dr. Claudius,' his first novel, the manuscript of which he gave to Mrs. Gardner. Crawford was then twenty-eight; he was fond of music and had an excellent voice, but was just reaching the conclusion that his gifts were not equal to the requirements of opera. Italian was as much his native tongue as English, and he introduced Mrs. Gardner to Dante; together they read the 'Divine Comedy,' and the two copies which they had used were interleaved and bound by Tiffany according to a design invented by Crawford. It was so much to be expected that it was amusing to find the bill for a photograph of Dante purchased January 21, 1882; although Mrs. Gardner had an extraordinary visual memory, and an extraordinary visualizing imagination, she liked to have at hand visible representations of the people and objects that interested her.

It was at Mrs. Howe's in 1882 that Mrs. Gardner met Oscar Wilde, and a year later, the younger Salvini. In 1889, Mrs. Gardner was one of the guests at Mrs. Howe's seventieth birthday breakfast.

The following letter from Oliver Wendell Holmes reveals the pleasant, neighborly friendship which existed between him and Mrs. Gardner. To old and young she was equally fascinating.

BEVERLY-BY-THE-DEPOT
September 26th, 1880

MY DEAR MRS. GARDNER,

The canopied chair *was* a surprise!

It looks like a Catholic shrine, and I should hardly be startled to see the Madonna sitting in it some fair morning.

I have dreamed of something like this for the past twenty years. I think I have seen one, once before, but I am not sure that it was not in a dream.

I confess I like a lady's promise, even without fulfilment. It gives us some pleasant moments and it is a reed on which we do not expect to lean very hard. Has not Virgil told us that woman is

'Varium et mutabile semper'?

[57]

ISABELLA STEWART GARDNER

Does not Scott say of her pledges

> 'Woman's faith and woman's trust —
> Write the characters in dust.
> Stamp them on the running stream,
> Print them on the moon's pale beam'

and more and worse than this?

I shall denounce them henceforth as slanderers and libellers of the lovely sex. For a promise so gracefully made and so promptly and fully carried out should redeem it from the malicious wrongs of the Scotch minstrel and the Roman poet.

I thank you heartily for the welcome gift, and as they say at dinner parties 'beg to conclude with the following sentiment':

> May you still blossom in perennial flower
> While I sit ripening in this leafless bower.

Gratefully yours

OLIVER WENDELL HOLMES

In December, 1881, Henry James, who was making a visit in New York, wrote to Mrs. Gardner that he had been to a 'pleasant feast,' at which the three ladies of the party begged him to tell them about her — they had heard she was so 'original.' He adds: 'I gave a sketch, with a few exquisite touches, and then they sighed and said to each other: "Oh, if we only knew how to be like that!" But they don't!'

CHAPTER V

THE ORIENT

IN February and March of 1882, Professor Edward Sylvester Morse, of Salem, who had been Professor of Zoölogy from 1877 to 1880 at the Imperial University, Tokio, gave a series of lectures on Japan at Mrs. Gardner's house. His Lowell Institute lectures had stimulated Dr. William Sturgis Bigelow and Mr. Percival Lowell to go to Japan, and these lectures at her own house fired Mrs. Gardner with a desire to see the Orient. In May, 1883, Mr. and Mrs. Gardner started on their trip round the world. The carriage that took them to the railroad station was followed by two others filled with flowers, farewell offerings from Mrs. Gardner's admirers. They reached Yokohama June 18th; the following extracts from her letters and her journal tell the story of this year in the East.

YOKOHAMA, *June* 30, 1883

We are still here, dear friend, and it is so fascinating that I well understand Sturgis Bigelow who cannot tear himself away. It is a bewitching life and I am wild with excitement. We make use of the comforts of this charming hotel, but almost daily we run up to Tokio, which is of course much more delightful being so much more Japanese. All the embassies are there and the people like Bigelow, who have taken houses. Yokohama is given over to many foreigners who live here charmingly, but without local atmosphere, and who are here for money-getting. The bankers also live here and dear old M—— W—— and G—— are darlings. We are going to breakfast (tiffin) with them in half an hour, after which some sort of excursion. We are leading a perfect holiday life, and it is a most delightful one. And the few Europeans that we see are entirely devoted, doing everything they can think of (and their brains are fertile) for us. Sturgis Bigelow (my (our) doctor's son) never seems to have us off his mind for one moment and is constantly turning up here for tiffin or dinner, or else telegraphing to us that we must go up to Tokio for this or that or the other, and consequently we have tiffined and dined together in every conceivable place and style; and I should say that we have drunk gallons of the canary-coloured tea out of their dear little cups and have eaten pounds of sweets, as we three have sprawled about on the soft, clean mats, in the funny little shops, looking at curios. If the Japanese were only handsomer, they would be perfect. Such charming manners, so gentle, tempers never change whether you buy all they have or don't take a thing — and their clothes are delicious, so soft in colour and fabric. Bigelow wears the Japanese garment always when in his house, and shoes are such an unheard-of thing on the pretty mats that I kick mine off on every occasion. We dined with Bigelow yesterday. He had a Japanese and wife to meet us. . . .

YOKOHAMA, *July* 30, 1883

MY DEAR, DEAR FRIEND: . . . Your lovely letter has just arrived. . . . How I laughed at your idea of housework being good for women! I am afraid you would disapprove of my life now altogether. It is such everlasting play. We have been away for a week, at Nikko. It was two days there and two days back, and it was hot, and one of the horses died, and the coachman got drunk, but it was all paid for by the glorious beauty of Nikko. Its very name means 'Sun's Brightness.' It is mountains, valleys, trees, waterfalls, lakes, and in such a setting (with a driveway of sixty miles with a double row of grand old Cryptomerias) are the famous temples, that bring pilgrims from all Japan, because there are buried the two greatest Shoguns, and pilgrims from all the world, because there man has done his best to rival nature. — We got back a day ago, in time for our letters and I am writing this hurriedly to catch the mail. It is *very* warm. I look out of the window, fan, read scraps from the newspapers, write until my fingers stick to the pen, and wish it were five o'clock. Rosen is coming down then and we go on a water party. When we got back from Nikko, the people here really seemed like old friends. Bigelow came rushing down from Tokio and stopped for dinner, and since then from him and Rosen have come notes and pink telegrams (all is couleur de rose you see) proposing all manner of things. But Fenollosa's fresh, enthusiastic greeting was unlike anything else. You must know him. . . . There is to be a great water fête on Wednesday if it doesn't rain. Rosen is to have a house-boat and great party, and we shall go. But it may rain. — Dear one, good-bye. Always write, answer all my questions, take great care of yourself, give my love to your mother, and tell me all your plans. Why do I not see your mother's life by you? How upside down that phrase seems?

Thursday, August 2. We have just got back from Tokio, where we passed last night. We stayed up there for the river fête. We went with Rosen.

THE ORIENT

His boat being decorated with lanterns covered with the Russian eagle, and the dinner on board delicious. The sight of the whole thing was fairy-like. We are now off for an inland trip of a few days. Love and love, my very best.

Always affectionately yours

I. S. G.

Baron Rosen was First Secretary at the Russian Legation. After the World War and the Russian Revolution, he came to the United States to support himself by writing. In need of backing for the publication of his book 'Forty Years of Diplomacy,' he turned to Mrs. Gardner, and she, although an invalid, pulled the strings that secured him the necessary aid.

KIOTO, August 24

MY DEAR, DEAR GIRL,

I am in despair about writing to you. I have just read over again one of your delightful letters and the thought of sending you one of mine, so heavily weighted as it must be, is almost too much of a burden to have on my poor conscience. I *do* know (which fact you will hardly have suspected) how stupid it is to have to read about places one has never seen, unless an unusual pen has told the story. But I enjoy these lovely places so much that I forget and try to tell about them. If you could see this beautiful city, you would love it too. It straggles over a valley to the foot of densely wooded hills that make an amphitheatre about it. On one of them is our hotel, in among the thick trees, verandahs to each room; the whip-poor-wills, the locusts, the nightingales, and the cooing doves make me think I am buried in some secluded spot; but at night when every one puts on his or her best clothes, I can hear them laugh and talk down below, sing and play on their samisen and the whole town is a thicket of lights. Now it is after tiffin, the siesta hour. I am writing on the shady verandah and am unconsciously listening to the bells and prayers (chaunts as it were) that come from time to time from the many Buddhist temples that are all about us. — We came up here from Kobe about twelve days ago and have been 'doing' the sights ever since, and to-morrow we go, by the way of one or two places, back to Kobe, and then the steamer to Shanghai and good-bye to this most pretty country. Of course I have missed all our Tokio friends vastly, but I have not had time to think; there has been so much to do. I want to promise

[61]

myself a quiet fortnight with you somewhere next summer, just to sit still, in rather a *cool* place, and hear you talk. It has really been very hot, although much cooler here than in Kobe, and Kioto certainly agrees with me very well. On our way up here, we stopped at Osaka, to see the wrestlers! Famous fellows — and it was such fun. It was more or less al fresco, with mats overhead to protect from the sun — the mass of the audience on the ground squatting, the swells in boxes raised ten feet above, the whole in a circle round a small square sanded place in the centre, that had a canopy over it, and there they wrestled. The audience was a wonderful sight. Brilliant rugs and blankets hanging over the fence of the boxes, and what clothes there were (VERY VERY few) were many-coloured, and every human being had a fan that was in constant motion. Fans serve every purpose among this flighty people. The umpire, whose word is law, starts the match by a movement of his fan (of a peculiar shape). And people who wish to make bets write on a slip of paper which they put in the folds of their fan and throw that into the arena. A man there, on purpose, reads what is written and the bet is or is not taken up. The wrestlers are generally very big men, great swells — they sit in a circle round the arena on brilliant coloured cushions and use enormous fans. I was immensely amused by a man in the box next to us. He was a great swell, servants and all that — his beautiful clothes were carefully laid aside on account of the heat, and there he sat, smoking a most beautiful pipe with nothing on but a waist cloth and an European straw hat. We didn't even notice his want of clothes, as everybody is almost always in that undress. He had a dear little boy with him, who would have been stark naked but for an amulet bag of such beautiful damask that was fastened by a fold of red silk, round his neck and that went in bow and ends nearly to his heels behind. This man was intensely interested to know which wrestlers I thought would win and asked me each time. Once I couldn't form any idea, so he coached me and said it was a sure thing for the small lithe man against a huge great fellow, so I interested myself properly in the little one — and when he threw the big one most cleverly and wonderfully, I thought my friend would have convulsions of delight, as I clapped my hands and called out. Please don't be shocked, dear, at all these dreadful proceedings. 'When in Turkey, etc.' — I shall go to see the Missionaries when I go back to Osaka, to atone. And I am really interested in the work they do, for the poor Japanese *sorely* need help; but how beautiful are their Buddhist temples. When I get into one I never want to come away — I could lie on the mats and look forever through the dim light.

We shall get the mail next week. Thank you now, dear, for the letters I hope for. We have been living for the last three weeks in an atmosphere of lotuses, both white and pink. If my envelope were nearly two feet square I would press a leaf and flower and send them to you.

THE ORIENT

Keep on being good about writing, look upon it as a *duty*, tell me everything and believe me always with love

Yours

I. S. G.

September and October were spent in China. From Shanghai
Mrs. Gardner wrote:

... This Anglo-Oriental life is very full of ease and comfort. And the heat
is too great for thought, word or deed, so I shall not attempt to see or do
anything here until we get back, five or six weeks later, from Peking. Mrs.
Low and I drive about six, people to dinner about eight, the rest of the time
— nothing. I shan't hear from you until Peking, where the letters will be forwarded. Then I shall have a treat, I hope — and hear that you are perfectly well. How I should like to be cold just once! Kind remembrances to
your mother and very best love to yourself from

Yours meltingly

I. S. G.

Shanghai is too European for local colour — There may be a long gap
between this and my next. It won't be my fault. I shall write all the same,
but it takes forever and two or three days to get from Peking, even for
letters. So think of me always, dear, and write and write and write.

On the way to Peking she wrote:

Last night I saw a Chinaman in a boat near by light a little lantern on a
little boat and send it adrift down the stream to be carried — whither?
And I sent off an imaginary one to you, full of happy wishes. It was such a
beautiful moonlit night and it was so quiet and pleasant, moving along on the
water. We are coming up the Peiho. We are very comfortable in two small
house-boats; Jack and I in one, and the servants and cooking in the other.
I was obliged to leave Mary at Shanghai, as a foreign servant was an impos-
sibility on this trip, and I have a Tartar woman for maid with head, arms,
neck, hands, all decked with silver. ... I shall write a line from Peking —
how I do hope to get letters from you.

Remember me to 'your honoured, loving one' — Chinese for Mother
(isn't it pretty?) and 'Pan-Sam' — 'I respectfully beg to kneel and knock
the head.'

Peking, September 21

We got here yesterday P.M. The ride up from Tung-Chow was odd enough.
Such strange sights, processions, people, and such dust! At last we had the

[63]

picturesque Walls before us and were riding through the high, many-storied gateway into the Tartar Town. We have come to the American Legation and are staying here. Pleasant and pretty. The mail goes out now and does not come in until to-night. Don't forget me, and send me everything you can.

At Peking, on September 25th, they received the news that Mr. Gardner's mother had died in Brookline on September 21st. This affected to some extent the social side of their stay in Peking, but not their sight-seeing. Every notable spot was visited.

After getting back to Shanghai, she wrote to the same friend, October 19th:

Thanks, thanks, thanks, beautiful friend and dear. Our letters have been dancing a very Danse Macabre, but at last here they are and I hold in my hand two of your delightful ones. They are such a treat. . . .

Here we are back again at 5 Sia Jow Road at the Lows'. The way the *foreign native* lives is such a good one. Breakfast in one's rooms and only little notes of 'how are you this morning' until 12.30, then clothed properly ('ploper' as the Amahs say) we all meet at tiffin. And here am I sitting at my open window on the broad upper verandah and the pretty, green shaded little park before me. What if it is pouring, I have seen so little rain! We got back yesterday and had such a pleasant voyage down from Tien-tsin. The process up to Peking was only reversed when we turned our backs towards it and our faces towards Shanghai. So I won't tell the same story over again. I am always so sorry to leave every one of these bewitched and bewitching places, and I seemed sorrier than ever when I craned my neck out of the mule litter to catch a last glimpse of the walls of Peking. The pigeons were all whirring through the air with their strange æolian-harp music, made by the whistles in their tails! I was glad to see two rainbow-clad beings 'chin-chinning' each other under the shadow of the Great Gateway, with such graceful politeness, not heeding a small boy with his pigtail (such a wee one) wound round his head, who was banging into them with a load of golden persimmons.

. . . .

This is the hour just before dinner. At the word 'persimmons' above, tiffin was announced, and after that Mrs. Low took me to a silk merchant's.

THE ORIENT

We picked out what we wanted there, and whilst she did the bargaining (talkee too muchee ploper fashion) I gave my attention to a heavy swell. He had come in to buy his clothes. And such clothes! He was as excited over them as a young girl over her first ball dress. It took very 'too muchee' time for him to decide whether he would have the drawers of a light yellow green, the under long flowing robe of the tenderest 'blue-after-a-rain,' and the short coat of mauve — and just as I thought it was settled, his arms bared to the elbow, his foot with its shoe kicked off, dancing with excitement — just at the critical moment of having the three brocaded silks folded, he suddenly dashed them away from each other, seized a superb ruby red instead of the mauve and began a new combination that at last contented him. He was a handsome creature to begin with — I don't dare to think of him when he once gets into these beautiful things. — We came home to five o'clock tea. Many kind people came, and as usual (of late) it was a sipping of tea and declining charming invitations to dinners — for of course, we say 'No' to everything of that kind now. But people are so kind, that they always manage to do something for you somehow. And when we have said no to a dinner, it generally turns out that at any rate I must tiffin with them 'quite alone' and go to see a silk factory, or a silver shop, or a hospital afterwards. And then I come up to my room and think if I have ever done my duty to strangers, and vow that the next one who turns up in Boston *shall* go to Hovey's! Really people are *so* kind and good and delightful. Mrs. Low's Amah has 'a No. 1 bad husband, the gardener is too muchee plenty sick and the No. 1 mafou he makee die' — but maskee; all goes on with greased wheels and this is the only way to live. Please, dear friend, write to me everything you can think of. I am so afraid I have lost one of your letters. A mail seems to have been skipped. Now the winter is coming back I shall be trying to think of you in the midst of Boston society. Tell me all about it. Keep my place for me and we shall have such good times together one of these days. I am so glad of the plan for writing a California story — a fresh land and very fertile.

Kind greetings to your mother and much love to you from always

Affectionately yours

I. S. G.

I haven't said one word about Sir George Bowen. Dear old man — Governor of Hong Kong. We met in the ruins of the Summer Palace, and came down from Peking together. I could make you laugh — but maskee. There are no words for the horrors of Ischia — and Java.

In her journal she says that while she and Mr. Gardner were

lunching on a terrace in the park of the Summer Palace, two Englishmen appeared, 'who turned out to be Sir George Bowen, Governor of Hong Kong, and Mr. Brazier, of the Customs, who were on their way back from Nankou, where they had been robbed of almost everything. Fortunately, Sir George saved his extra suit, but Brazier was rigged out in a wadded Chinese jacket he had had to borrow.' Several days later, during the trip from Peking to Shanghai, she added: 'Sir G. B. a nice old man, has read much, but a little silly, and not so quick as in his youth, perhaps. Remembers and repeats stories and poetry. I watch him sometimes as he sits saying over to himself some verses or other. If he can't quite get them, we never hear them, but if he manages them all right, he is sure to spout them.'

VICTORIA (HONG KONG)
Sunday, October 28, 1883

... We arrived here yesterday, and such an arrival! Never to be forgotten, never to be described! We left Shanghai at 11.30 P.M. Wednesday, so the voyage was not a long one, and the waves treated us well. Fortunately, we began to see the rugged, sharp hills quite early, and about 5 P.M. turned our heads towards the Pass that brought us up to this wonderful harbour. It was sunset, the clear-cut hills were every colour from bright red — pink — orange, to pale blue, all reflected in the water; then the light faded, night came so slowly; and one by one the stars, in the heavens, in the still water, and in the city came out and it was all a-twinkle. The city has its feet in the water and its head on the Peak. We were taken ashore in a way that would have made you shiver. Two sampans were filled with us and the luggage amid the Asiatic Scream and Yell the like of which is not. We were in the hands of the Hakka, the boat population. The mother of the family rowed us, with the baby tied to her back, and with every swing of her body, the baby's head whacked the gunwhale and it yelled. And then such thieves as the coolies were who laid hands on our boxes *before* we landed. They fairly boarded us. At last we were turned loose in two large empty rooms in a wild hotel, fortunately with a great verandah, and we have shaken into place. There is nothing like Hong Kong. Some say it is 'like Gibraltar, only better.' Some say 'like Madeira — only better.' Some say 'like Naples' and I know — 'only better.' We went up to the Peak this afternoon and turned to say to each other 'that this alone paid for the whole journey from home!' We tiffined at the Forbeses' (Russell & Co.) and go there to stay when we return from Canton. And the home letters were sent up from the office, and *there* was a treat! But before I say thank you for this last, I want to say that the lost budget was found (of the mail before this) and in it your dear little letter. . . .

I must say good-night, for to-morrow promises to be a full day. Our dear old friend Sir George (the Governor) is to give us tiffin and if the weather is fine we are to make a little excursion in his steam yacht. And then all our preparations are to be made to start the next morning for Canton. There are many chances that we shan't get into the city, on account of all these late rows. But one can but try, and a pleasant Vicomte de Baré and a friend of his are going to share the danger and profit with us. So, if I were a literary lady I might perhaps write 'A *Run* through Canton,' for we can scarcely let the grass grow under our feet. I went to the Cathedral service this morning, and to hear the beautiful service chanted by the beautiful voiced choristers in this strange land made me cry.

HONG KONG, *November* 3, 1883

It will probably be Christmas-tide with you when this gets to you, so I send a little Chinese rice paper picture and you must pretend it is a Christmas card. At any rate, dear friend, it takes with it very best wishes to you and yours for a 'Merry Christmas and a Happy New Year.' I have just mailed one letter for you, but it may be a long time before I get another chance to write, as our plans are so vague. We have had our run through Canton and I live to tell the tale, but we have just got back, and I am too tired to do more than say so. We found we were going up the Pearl River on the very boat that first caused all the row. The arms, stacked in the saloon, were loaded — and the threats had been so dire that there was an extra guard patrolling the ship and winding in and out among the Chinese passengers all the time. And instead of going up to a wharf, we anchored in midstream surrounded by the gunboats. Opposite was Shameen (the foreign settlement) very much in ruins, and the whole settlement encircled by the tents of the Viceroy's troops, who were there as protection. A narrow canal divides Shameen from Canton; there was an incessant noise of firecrackers and music from the Chinese town (we were at the house of Russell & Co.), and the racket made a good accompaniment to pros and cons that were being discussed, as whether we should be able to go into the city or not. And we went to sleep under the protection of gunboats — a strange sensation. The next morning we went to see our Consul and he agreed to go in with us, so off we started, and we walked just as fast as we could from nine until twelve o'clock — *without any annoyance whatever*. We became so bold that after tiffin we, a guide, but no Consul, started again, this time in uncovered chairs, and we never came back till dark, and the wonderful sights and sounds I can give you no idea of. The streets are never more than twelve feet wide, generally about six or eight. They are matted over, and there are huge red, yellow, green, white, and gold sign boards hanging out at the sides of each shop. The shops all open in front; the streets a mass of people, apparently compact but ceaselessly moving, and one gets through, how? none can tell. And above it all — a din. In the midst of it all I heard a gong clanging. And soon appeared driven up and down the street a thief, naked to the waist, who was followed by the executioner who, at each stroke of the gong, thrashed him with the bamboo. His shoulders were purple, jellied, and bleeding! We went on from one scene to another until night, when the Chinamen shut up all their shops with great shutters and lighted the little joss sticks in the little outside niches in honour of the God, who was to care for it all at night. What a picture your pen would have made of that day! And then through it all was the spice of fear. I never was so frightened as for the first half-hour, but got accustomed and ended by total forgetfulness of all danger. We were two and one half days in that extraordinary place and left yesterday morning for Macao. When there I gathered a leaf at the grotto of Camoes, and we went to see them play Fan-Tan in the evening, and this morning came back here. We shall be with the William Forbeses here, in their delightful house for a few days and then to Singapore or Bangkok. With kindest remembrances to your mother and ever so much love to you, dear, I am as always

Affectionately yours

I. S. G.

'The Governor and Lady Bowen request the pleasure of' our company at dinner on Monday, etc. — which we decline.

We have just decided to go by French Mail on Tuesday to Singapore.

PALAZZO SULL'ARROYO
SAIGON, November 12, 1883

This is the very oddest gîte . . . that I have ever had. We were on our way to Singapore by Messageries Maritimes and our two travelling friends, de Baré and Fontmagne, were fellow passengers. But they were to get off here and go to Cambodia to see the wonderful ruins of Angkor Wat. They said so much that we were finally bitten with a strong desire to see for ourselves. And here we are also, and to-morrow we four start for Cambodia by boat. We go as far inland as we can by river and then take to bullock carts or even elephants! The ruins have only been discovered a few years, and

[68]

now stand near the head of the list. I wish you could see them; what fun it would be if you could be camping out in this great palatial suite that we are living in. Owing to all the valiant French officers, who are crowding to Tonquin and to doubtful glory, there was not a furnished room to be had in all Saigon in or out of a hotel. We found at last these great empty rooms, huge verandahs at each side; our footfalls echo and the sneeze of M. mon Mari makes me jump. But it is cool, airy, and great fun. We are on the Arroyo — a sort of canal; a row of Chinese houses on the opposite side of it. They (the Chinese) are not the natives here, but they light upon all these southern countries and are like ants for number and thrift. All day long they are busy in the shops, and all night long they twang their guitars or do some banging, clanging, firecrackery thing to frighten away the evil spirits.

At 8 P.M. the next day they started up the river; on the morning of the 15th, at 10:30, they arrived at Pnompenh, in Cambodia. The account of the next few days is taken from her journal.

Everything en fête. All the King's boats draped with flags. Our steamer was obliged to make a sweep and go past the whole city. We breakfasted and heard that we were in great luck. It was the last day of the boat races. About two o'clock we four went ashore — first to see the R. C. Archbishop who has lived here thirty-two years. Then went to a pagoda whilst de Baré stopped at Protectorate. Then we all went to M. Rogge, agent of the Hong Kong-Shanghai Bank, and with him to King's Pavilion. There we saw the very most wonderful sight: a huge dragon boat with chairs in it for Europeans, on which we sat. In the inner room, princes; in a boat at our left, some of the hareem; in a boat behind us, the first citizens of the place. Soon the door from the Pavilion opened and the King appeared, small and nice-looking. Plain black clothes tight to his throat. A sort of Scotch cap of black silk with diamond buckle on one side of it. A large emerald pendant, and a belt with diamond clasp. Also chains. He had with him his favourite child, a little girl, dressed in a beautiful dull yellow sarong. Six gold chains over her body from left shoulder to right hip — nine gold bracelets on each arm and two on each ankle, and a good arrangement around her hair. (I say nothing of a horrible contrast between the 'savage' Cambodians and the dreadful Frenchwomen in cheap finery.) The two walk forward under a yellow umbrella. Mary was standing outside, so up he went to her, shook hands, invited her into the boat. Then went on the most extraordinary and exciting races I ever imagined. Very long narrow dug-outs with forty, forty-two, forty-four men paddling, a frantic person exciting them by singing and dancing, a man in the bow waving a pole to beat the stroke. Two boats raced at a time. Later came the Malay boats, much the same shape, but the men stood and rowed forwards, instead of paddled. The whole thing like a wild dream. They might have been Feejee Islanders. When it got dark, H. M.'s gunboats were strung with white lights and then began a procession of small boats, illuminations, representations of pagodas, etc., from forty to fifty. Strange Eastern music and singing and the full moon. About eight we dined at M. Rogge's, and after ten went back to the steamer and slept on deck. What a day! . . .

Saturday, 17. Up at five; soon after arrived at Taona, and such a scramble as it was getting ready and getting aboard the small boats. We left Mary on board the Phnoc Kien, and started in five small boats, M. Fontmagne, J., and I in the one with a cover. In about two hours the boats could go no farther, so bullock and buffalo carts were got ready with much talk and wait, and off we started again. Such odd boating, sailing along over tree-tops, in among them. Such odd little villages, yellow-robed priests on their morning 'beg' along the shore. And in the carts the same thing until Siamrap. There a 'sala,' an empty shed, bamboo floor (Mr. Hunter was and is invaluable) — careful walking. We had breakfast from our store; the Governor sent us pomeloes and cocoanuts and asked us to go to see him. After breakfast we went a procession, ourselves, the Governor's brother and nephew, and seven Cambodians, with our presents! The Palace (?) had a brick wall, an open theatre, and a hall of audience. The hareem peeped at us through doors and chinks, the Governor came in, promised us elephants (he had given us boats, bullock carts, etc.) and gave us cocoanut milk and took our presents. Then we started again in carts, I lying on my back, through a wonderful forest, in two hours arrived at Angkor. Just in time, a severe shower. Sala, where we and luggage were sheltered. The great temple opposite. Such a scene. Tropical forest all about us, buffaloes and their men wandering about. Directly on our left the four great stone gryphons, a huge tree, leaning on them in fascinating group, two natives. M. de Baré sitting at the table making out the ménus for all the dinners that we are to have here. The others putting up the beds; a little fire lighted near by, water boiling, chickens and ducks lying about, another fire lighted underneath the end of the Sala, and the 'nephew of the Governor' squatted à la turque, in red and pink. Then we all went to see the ruins, walked leisurely through, but had no time for examination. Then back for dinner, great fun. Fires, cattle, and carts grouped about. Early to bed. Moon rose, occasionally glimpses of gryphons, camp-fires, carts, natives, etc.

The menu of the dinner that evening was —

THE ORIENT

Ruines d' Angkor-Wat

Siam

Dîner du 17 Novembre 83

Pot au feu

Sardines   Beurre

Mortadella

Pâté de perdreaux

Homard

Asperges

Canard   Haricots verts

Confitures   Fraises

Vermouth   Vin de Médoc   Sauterne

Champagne

Sunday, 18. Up at five, coffee, and off on elephants and in bullock carts about 6.30. About three quarters of an hour to Angkor Thom's gateway, great moats and wall. Then a tramp through the jungle to see the wonderful ruins. The forty-eight great towers, high, and with each side carved with huge Buddha heads; in and around them and everything the Banyan tree (the Sacred Poh) has tied its roots and stems. Such a scramble and climb through the jungle, and every now and then we came upon great ruins, Bapone and Pimean Akas. And ended by the Leper King, Sadait Komlong. At 10 A.M. we got to the bamboo plated house of Prapone, an old Siamese, who has lived there forty-eight years. Such a pleasant place. We had siesta, breakfast, a visit from his wife, sixty-two years, a present to me of an Indra, etc. We left there at two. Elephants from the Governor. Stopped at Observatory, walked up the hill. Got back to Sala about four. Had tea, rested, and before dinner I went for another visit to the Temple. Dinner at 6.30. Afterwards Mr. Hunter told wonderful stories of capital punishments. Ten women beheaded at one time. A strange story of the King's sister and a young Siamese. In the Palace every one wears a particular colour for particular day; i.e., red for Monday, blue for Tuesday, etc., etc., but never yellow (priest) or white (mourning). One of the King's wives has charge of his clothes, and each morning sends him the proper coloured dress in a gold vase. A small Cambodian, naked to the waist, fans me as I write. Within

[71]

the walls of Angkor Thom have already been discovered one hundred and twenty ruins, and there are many more as yet undisturbed.

Monday, 19. Up rather early and off for the Temple about a quarter to eight. Examined the Gallery of Sculptures — wonderful bas-reliefs. De Baré and Fontmagne hunted for Buddha plunder. Took long, last look and back to Sala for breakfast about 10.30. Siesta, then elephants and bullock carts and away. Got back to Banyan tree where we left the boats. There dined, and then sat about on logs and cushions, smoked Mexican cigarettes, talked, Cambodian slave boy fanned me, the wife of the nephew of the Governor brought me a Jack Fruit on a wonderful dish. The natives squatted round fires. Finally we started in our boats and had a very narrow escape. An elephant of the Governor's had gone mad and escaped and was just plunging for the river when our boats got there. Two moments later, and he would have been in the water and there would have been an end of us. No native boats go up or down the river at night, on his account. He has already killed several men. The steamer was waiting for us, steam up, so we got on board and immediately off we started, down the Lake.

Tuesday, 20. Cool night on deck. A warmer morning. Champagne at breakfast. Arrived at Pnompenh at three. Went to M. Rogge's and were most comfortably put up. About five o'clock called at the Protectorate and then went to see 'le Père Sylvestre' — such a funny old priest. 'J'ai vingt espèces de fruits dans mon jardin, j'ai au moins dix variétés sur ma table tous les jours. Tenez, voici un orange!' And that was all we saw of his twenty varieties. We went to the convent school. The women at prayers, Père Sylvestre *'stopped all that nonsense'* and sent for silks for us to see. Dinner at M. Rogge's.

Wednesday, 21. Coffee, milk (*really*), bread, toast, butter and eggs in our room about seven. At 8.20 we all started in 'Malabars' to see the Palace. We began by a machine shop, where man power took the place of steam. An electric machine had been sent from England, and there it stood (under a thatched roof); of no use, because some important part was wanting or broken. In one corner of the room a white ant construction had begun. At the mint we saw them making dix centimes, man power. And there we stood in the flesh and saw them stamp coins in the name of Norodom I Roi du Cambodge *1860!* With our own eyes on this November 21, 1883. Then we went to the stables, where were six pretty dear little ponies (Java-Sandalwood Islands). Then we got into the Salle du Trône — a really perfect room of its kind, good size and shape, gaudy and brilliant — twenty consoles with mirrors, on each side, between as many windows — a double row of square columns down the length of the room a little at the sides, many chandeliers, a low throne with the white umbrella over the middle and small gilded ones at the four corners, and at the very end of the room a superb structure something like a boat with a throne on the top of it. Both thrones in pure Cambodian style, gilded and semé with bits of glass that gave a most brilliant effect. 'The Palace' is really a village, or collection of many buildings, a wall about it all and a great chief entrance with many roofs and points and an arrangement of posts, painted green and gold, from which the King mounts his elephants. Also went to the Temple, and as another proof of 'the Chinese wedge' it was a mite of a China boy who unlocked the door. Great preparations are going on near by for the cremation of the heir who died a month ago. We went through the chief building — catafalque — very high, covered with white cotton semé de fleurs en or, and everywhere bright colours. Outside, rocks are being made of bamboo, also giants, etc., all to serve during the fêtes that take place at the time of the cremation. Back for breakfast at eleven. Then saw some Cambodian manufactures, silk, and silver, and bought a silver elephant, etc. Siesta, and then a little dawdling by the ever interesting window, looking at the decent way the natives bathe, and at the constant shuffling together of brilliant colours — entre autres a priest in yellow with a blue umbrella! And a strange bronze creature with the brightest of yellow-green scarf over his shoulder; a long bamboo stick, which he waved about as a wand. All to the clanking of the prisoners' chains, who ceaselessly make, mend, sweep, and clean the roads, fastened together, sometimes by a long chain that goes from an iron hoop collar about their throats. A note from M. Fourès du Protectorat, saying that the King is not well enough to receive us. So we go for a drive, in the King's carriage, however, to try and see the second King. By that time it is six o'clock, and he, who is very timid about his appearance before foreigners, said 'it was six o'clock already and he had no time to dress. Could we come to-morrow at four?' Home, hurried dressing, and then to the Protectorate to dinner — also in the King's carriage! A charming house. During dinner Cambodian music in a neighbouring Temple. I ate my first peacock! After dinner a little tiger was brought in for us to see, a dear, wild, savage little thing, growled all the time and his Anamite held and stroked him.

Thursday, 22. Pasted photos all the morning. M. de Fontmagne went to see Père Sylvestre, de Baré wrote his journal, J. *rested*. The compradore brought Cambodian silks and sarongs, which we bought. Siesta, then dressed for the Kings. About 3.30 we all went with Mr. Hunter, except Fontmagne, to see the second King. J. and de Baré in evening dress, the latter with his gilded waistcoat buttons and his blue and white ribbon. I, in my dirty old white and black foulard and black lace bonnet, but to make a glitter, my diamond and pearl dog collar, my two white diamonds in my bonnet strings, and my yellow diamond on the front of my dress! The entrance to the

Palace(?) of the second King is through a red-brick archway of which only the sides remain. Débris everywhere. We waited under a tree, outside the inner gate, and suddenly appeared through the gate a neat little man, purple stockings on his pretty little legs, and shining black shoes, 'sarong' trousers of gold coloured silk, a frock coat with gilt buttons, white shirt, collar and cravat and a gold belt with diamond clasp. It was the second King himself. So we were presented, then and there, under the tree, and started altogether for the hall of reception. He and I ahead. A funny little room. He monstrously polite, giving us all chairs. A few minutes' conversation, Mr. Hunter interpreting, he yelled 'Boy,' a Chinaman appeared with cigars on a red gold stand, later with glasses, and another Chinaman uncorked a bottle of sweet, pleasant wine. He lamented the damage the inundation had done his grounds; we admired Pnompenh, told him where we had been and where we were going — then adieu. Soon after we got back, M. Fourès came to take us to see the first King. When we arrived at the Palace, we knew the King had already arrived at the Iron House (the Reception Hall) as all the people were grovelling about in the neighborhood and bending down as they passed in front — four sentinels. I walked up the path with 'the Protector,' and there was the King standing, waiting, at the head of his steps. Presented, seated in proper places (European furniture, gilded sofas, etc.) round a table. The King at one end of it. In front of him on the table red gold bowls, a beautiful box studded with diamonds, and within it, an exquisite gold and diamond match box. The cigarettes were covered with pond-lily leaves and made by the wives. M. de Baré asked if we might see the Palace, so we all started on a tour of inspection with the King and M. Fourès just outside the door. I alone was presented to five wives, and shook hands with the Siamese Princess (the last in favour) who wore a yellow scarf and a large flower in her ear. They were all squatting on the ground. The King pulled the Princess up by the arm, said something to her, and we shook hands. We saw the dining-room and then had a walk through the garden, very beautiful, and saw many buildings — a particularly pretty one, open on all sides with a little theatre in it. A clock in tower chimed and struck six — instantly Norodom I pulled out his watch — alas! he had forgotten to wind it! There was a great misunderstanding and difficulty, for the King had arranged with Mr. Hunter that the Fourès reception over I was to have been taken to see the female apartments, everything, in short; but unfortunately the Fourès complication disturbed and broke up all the arrangement. Dinner, toasts of thanks, good wishes, etc. Afterwards Mr. Hunter came. He had just dined with the King, who was much put out that the thing had not worked as planned. He apparently does not love the Protectorat de France. Norodom asked about my yellow diamond, said he had no such thing. He was dressed with sarong, blue stockings, white

[74]

jacket, belt with diamonds, black silk cap with diamond buckle, gold chain with emerald and diamond pendant and a superb sapphire ring.

Friday, 23. Up at six. Ready to start at 7.15. Mr. Hunter arrived with sketch of Angkor Thom and flowers for me (yesterday he gave me beautiful little Vishnu and native iron). Said good-bye to him and M. Rogge — wonderful kindness from them both. Back again to our old quarters on the Phnoc Kien.

Angkor Wat remained one of the great experiences of her life; she often talked of it, and urged people to go there. In 1922, when friends sent her postcards showing the new finds and the changes made by the French authorities, who had cut down trees so that the roots should not spoil the terraces, Mrs. Gardner was sure it could not be as interesting as forty years before.

After her return to Boston, some of her incorrigible friends planned a little dinner for her and, in order that she should not have the field entirely to herself throughout the evening, they decided to read up on some inaccessible place that she could not possibly have visited, and insist on talking of nothing else. The place they selected was Cambodia. As soon as it was mentioned, Mrs. Gardner said: 'Do you want to know about Cambodia? I can tell you all about it.' When a devoted friend of Mr. Gardner was told that Mrs. Gardner had dined with the King of Cambodia, he said: 'And one day she'll dine with the King of the Lower Regions!' Certainly there never was a day when she would have declined the invitation.

In 1910, when the marvel of inaccessible places had much diminished, Joseph Lindon Smith wrote from Singapore on November 14th: —

We have been to Ankor Watt! ! ! ! ! ! ! ! too wonderful! ! You know it and know how impossible it is to describe. We were there over a week, Denman

Ross, Louise Nathurst, and I — and I painted like mad, and got five pictures done. Denman proposes a club called the 'Ankorites' — only those who have been there may belong; we wish you to be the President — no dues, and no salary.

November 28th, they sailed on the Ville de Cadix for Sourabaya, Java. 'The Captain gave me his room. A boat for merchandise — never clean; a dog, a monkey, chickens, pigeons, augh!' De Baré and Fontmagne accompanied them.

December 5th she wrote in her journal:

Then poplar trees in long rows peer out of the mirage, then large boats, steamers, and we are told that this is Sourabaya — but never a Sourabaya to be seen. Some pretty native boats, very narrow, with lateen sail. We and luggage get into three of them and sail away — visit the Customs, where they politely take de B.'s gun and don't even look at luggage and we start again in boats for the 'Hôtel des Indes.' Down a long canal, full of boats, on one bank the better class houses, bungalows; on the other native places consisting of one room, bamboo, with bamboo fence about. Men and women (natives) in sarongs, and most of them bathing. Finally arrive. And such a hotel. Apparent to the street, a verandah in front of an open room like a hall. Walk through that, and a large open court. In the middle of it a dining-room, on one side a long row of rooms, verandah in front. Opposite side bathrooms. And everywhere people (Dutch) in the strangest clothes since Eden. The men in pijamas, the women (ladies?) in sarongs, no-heeled slippers, loose white jacket (absolutely nothing else), and hair down their back. Everybody drinking tea. We get settled in rooms. Large, red-tiled floors, thick walls, whitewashed, large doors with screens in front of them. On verandah, in front of every room, large chairs and great table with the cups, teapot, knives, forks, and spoons, and tumblers. And behind the door hangs the white jacket, trimmed with red that our 'Boy' wears at dinner. We ordered tea, and drank it with slices of bread and thin cheese. Horrible dinner, everything served at once. Then rain, then bed — no sleep. People next door sat up until 3 A.M. talking and laughing. Mosquitoes! At 4 A.M. life began again — children with drums. We went out before dinner to see the people in the streets. Eve of Saint Nicholas. Lotteries in all the shops for children.

Thursday, 6. About 6.30 could stand the noise no longer and came out on a most wonderful scene. Every one out on the verandah in nightdresses, girls quite grown in sort of chemise, some taking coffee, bread and cheese.

I took mine, and looked at the native venders. Only European objects of fifteenth class. Pieces of print, white cotton, thread, imitation flowers, toothbrushes, sleeve protectors, etc., etc. On my chair was a large bunch of pink roses de B. had presented. We lounged away hours. Then J. and I went to some shops — bought a kriss — then later de B. went with us to find out about train for Solo — I in white loose pongee wrapper and no hat! And it didn't seem at all strange. Such a strange hotel. The Javanese servants, in loose white trousers and sarong, loose jacket, and handkerchief oddly tied on head. One of them cleaned some furniture in the open court all the morning. Another caught scorpion. A third went off furtively to a large flower jar and nibbled a piece of bread he had secreted there. At one o'clock 'rystaffel' — tiffin, mainly rice with twenty-four different things added. After that had my hammock swung and lay in it until after four. Then came the tropical rain. Afternoon tea, bread and cheese. People in frightful dishabille, the servants catching the water in old oil cans and taking the opportunity to clean the court.

At Soerakarta they were taken

to see the house and gardens of the Independent Prince. Beautiful house with very large open room, white marble floors, twenty crystal chandeliers. The garden full of devices, and cages with beautiful birds, also a bear, some monkeys, and a little summer house high over all, with charming view of river. Then the Prince sent word he would like to see us. So we went back to the great room and behind it in a smaller room, but much the same and raised we saw him sitting with one of his brothers. We made the three bows in the proper places and sat down with him. A nice young fellow, with beautiful diamonds. All the attendants and people outside on the ground (prone) and in the apartments five women squatting holding sword, betel box, etc. From there went to see the imperial tigers and elephants. And while looking at the latter, a native Prince at the head of suite, went in to see the Emperor, stopping at the door to take off his jacket, and was quite right, being much better looking in his brown skin. His suite were on the ground whilst he disrobed, and then folded the jacket and put it on a salver. From the hotel verandah we saw a native dancer, to funny 'bamboo' music. And native princes and umbrellas, all day, passing by. Dined half an hour earlier than usual, and at 8.15 went to the Resident's. He sick with fever, so second Resident, our friend of the morning (M. Saesson) and the Captain of the Guard went to the Kraton and were presented to the Emperor. A very large and handsome palace in shape of open rooms, marble floor, chandeliers, etc. In the second one, which was behind the first, was the Sultan who sat on sofa with sarong, bare feet thrust into red slippers, embroidered with gold, white jacket with diamond studs, and black jacket over it. Handkerchief on head. His son in sarong, head handkerchief, and cotton jacket tight in throat with three buttons at collar of precious stones. A diamond decoration on his breast and a chain of white flowers about his neck. He is sixteen, already has six wives and one and a half children! The whole performance was most interesting and singular. Dim lights, rain pouring in the outer courts, his women squatting about on the floor, one with his cuspidor, one with sword, one with shield, one with cane. Also women dwarfs in attendance. A large orchestra in the shadow, that played most strange music and with a strange fascination. The whole thing under one's breath, and as if something were going to happen. Twice eight or nine soldiers came in in procession, once with tea; once with wine, liqueurs, etc. No conversation except between the Resident and Emperor. (The latter and his family pure Aryan race.) In perhaps three quarters of an hour we left. After we had got to bed, J. was awakened by the Prince's photograph, which arrived.

From Batavia she wrote, December 18th:

We have been into the interior, have tried the funny railroads, the funnier posting, with six little rats of horses, who go along on the full run, with a coachman and two grooms constantly yelling and cracking whips. It is a thing with a great deal of 'go' in it, I assure you. The hotels are the same all through the country, the Dutch the same all through the country, the Javanese and their pretty kampongs buried in palms, the same; the grand ruins really grand, and on all sides looking down on us the terrible volcanoes. We arrived here to-day; we have dined and are sitting on the great verandah; the men of the party looking up a train that we are to take in the morning for an excursion. And the next day we go to Singapore. There our letters must be awaiting us. How I hope so. They will be my Christmas presents, and what would a Christmas be without even letters from the dear ones from home! Will you be thinking of me? With love to you, dear friend, and kind remembrances to your mother I am, as always

Affectionately

I. S. G.

SINGAPORE, *Sunday, December* 23, 1883

At last we are here, and I have your letters, dear friend, and how glad I am! It is simply to say *that*, I think, that I write, for in a few moments to church we go; and I mailed a huge document to you in Batavia. Our voyage of two and a half days here wasn't bad. We passed through fields of pumice stone floating on the sea, results of the earthquake in Java last August. We picked up some pieces. Lately, we have been hearing from every one accounts of that — one does not know what to call it — most interesting, most marvellous, most appalling. The West Coast of Java, with its towns and all that it had, is obliterated. The sea now calmly splashing above it. . . .

December 31, 1883

The last day of the year! We are still in Singapore. We have said good-bye to our travelling companions, who have gone to Bangkok. We go on to India next Wednesday or Thursday, by the Rice Ports. We have spent so much time over Cambodia, Java, etc., that, owing to the time it takes to go to Bangkok we must give it up, for, of course, India must be seen. I am sorry to say our friends have the French element so strong, that because India is owned by the English, they don't care to give it more than a passing glance. Two Americans have the room next to us, and I feel that you know them — Mr. and Mrs. Waters — so I say nothing, but please tell me about them. She speaks of her writings, and I haven't the most distant idea what she ever wrote, so that I feel I am in the presence of one of our great geniuses, and that I am unworthy. But seriously, she is very kind, pleasant and much talkee. Before our friends left we went together to Johore and spent the day with the Maharajah, who gave us a delicious breakfast, and sent us back by steam launch. Such a lovely sail of four hours. We went there by carriage across the island, and then sampan to Johore. During our drive we passed the spot where a tiger was taken a few days before. Everybody was talking about it, so I went to see the beast. He is a wild, roaring beauty. They had such a time getting him out of the pit. We dined with some English people yesterday. Of course, we finally got to talking about beasts and such like. And they told us of a dinner-party they had, when the punkah wallah, who was in the next room, saw a snake under the dining-table all through dinner. He thought it better not to alarm the ladies! So said nothing. After they had wiped their fingers and gone off, he spoke, and there was a lively scene! How commonplace are our dinner-parties after that. I took a leaf out of your book yesterday and spent the morning in the courts. It was interesting to see the witnesses take different oaths according to their religion. One prisoner was discharged, which was undoubtedly an unusual thing, for the guard was so taken aback that they didn't know which door to let him out of. Good-bye for this year, dear. Be a good girl for the next one, and be ever a friend to me, and may we have very many happy days together in the year that is before us. May it be a happy one to all yours. Please excuse my crumpled letter. Jack in one of his impatient moods has just snatched it out of my lap, so I shan't give him an opportunity to send you an affectionate message. . . .

January 2, 1884

We are off to-morrow via Malacca, Penang, Moulmain, and Rangoon. So at last this long ramble comes to an end. The sports yesterday were good fun. They were on the esplanade between us and the sea and *great fun.* In the morning the natives performed; in the afternoon the foreigners. And it was all such a brilliant scene; there were Malays, Chinamen, Javanese, Sikhs, Sepoys, Klings, Hindus, Mohammedans, even Japanese, all in their native garb and colour, well set off by the ridiculous garments of the Europeans. — My kindest remembrances to your mother, and ever so much love to you from

Affectionately yours

I. S. GARDNER

The dear little four-leafed clover I have stuck in my portfolio, where I can always see it.

This same evening they 'went to see Kellar, a *very* good magician, American.'

S.S. CHANDA, Monday, January 7, 1884

Of course it is a pleasant voyage, my dear, . . . or I should not be writing. At least it is so far — a soft, cool breeze, a still, calm sea. The ship is good, an entertaining, *un*English looking but very English Captain, and a few rather interesting passengers. We got away from Singapore last Thursday, where, by the way, I left a letter to be mailed for you. In less than twenty-four hours we had got to Malacca, which is an uncanny sort of a place, as if under a spell. The sea was pink and yellow and green and so shallow that we were anchored three miles out. A fringe of palms hung over the water and the houses had red roofs shining and bright. In the centre was a green hill with a ruined church on it. A Malay prahee took us ashore, and we wandered and drove about, and then climbed up the hill to the ruined church — Saint Francis Xavier's — and I wished I had had a taper, and I wished that it were all those years ago when the whole populace wound up the hill with tears and lights, as his body was brought back to rest for a while in his own church and town that he had loved so well. Mount Ophir (the Golden) was dreamy and misty in the distance, and everywhere were waving palms. It was all so still and quiet. No one was moving and the Malays leaned over the bridge, or slept on the pole of their bullock carts. I don't know where the enchanted princess was — but the prince surely had not come. And when we got back to our ship a mist had come down from Mount Ophir. It wrapped itself about Malacca and everything disappeared. Only ourselves left on the oily sea — so perhaps it was only a vision after all. The next day we got to Penang and had two glorious excursions. It is such a beautiful place. In the afternoon we went to the waterfall and came back late and our drive back through the palm forest

[80]

by moonlight was *one* of the things you should have seen. Off the road, in one place, was a beautiful little Siamese temple. So I got out of the gharry and walked through the trees to it. And there, all alone, was a yellow-robed priest chanting his evensong to his gilded Buddha. I crept up softly — no light but the moon and the service lamps and the burning incense, and I stood behind the priest, who never heard or noticed me. It was exquisite — but *very* sad. The next morning we went ashore by the light of the Southern Cross, drove to the foot of the hill and there found our chairs and carriers who swung us up to the top at a great pace. The road was through dense vegetation. On the top was a Government bungalow, where we breakfasted, with the people to whom we had letters. You would not know, from my speaking of the breakfast, that there was a view that is famed, worldwide. There *is* though, but I can't think of a word to say about it. Certainly it can't be described. In three days more we get to Moulmain. There is a young Burns on board, also writing. He and I are sole occupants of the saloon. After tiffin he said, 'She's awfully steady, better come and write.' So I came, and I can't help watching his face, he looks so delighted with the things he is putting into his letters.

January 11

We took on board our pilot an hour ago. And when the tide is a little higher we shall begin to steam up the great Salween River to Moulmain. And this must be dropped in the mail-bag. Kindest remembrances to your mother, and very best love for you.

Affectionately

I. S. G.

RANGOON, BURMAH, *January* 18, 1884

This is a pretty scene for your wonderful eyes, dear girl. And we are just leaving it after a week in these lands. We came on by our same steamer to Moulmain, and there I mailed you a letter, and please tell me did you get it, for every one told me of a different thing I must do with the stamps, because of the peculiarities of native officials. Moulmain was our first glimpse of Burmah, and a pretty one it was, with its Pagoda temples, its busy elephants, who do all the work in the timber yards. Then we came on to Rangoon a week ago, and have taken advantage of a long stop of the steamer to go up country. We have seen nothing at all like this part of the world, at least for brilliancy. In other Eastern countries dark blue predominates; here red and yellow take its place. A 'resident writer' calls it a stirabout of rainbows. Your more graceful mind would have thought of the 'windstirred bed of tulips.' And as for the Pagoda, it was even a *sensation* to Jack. Our first view of it was the night we arrived, by moonlight. We climbed up the steps, through the long, dark, covered galleries, not knowing at all what was before us, and suddenly stepped out on the paved plateau from which rose into the air the Pagoda, and all its many small ones in attendance — its gilding flashing and glittering in the light. We have met pleasant people here and last night dined at an æsthete's. Beautiful house, Venetian glass and Chinese porcelain, and such dainty things to eat and drink out of them. He is a brother of the Mr. Bryce who goes to Boston and gives Lowell Institute lectures. We came on board our steamer at 7 A.M. I am writing on deck, it is now 8.30 A.M., and we are just off. The stirabout of rainbows on the wharf is as vivid as ever and there is a flash of fire up to heaven from the Pagoda. I am so glad I had never heard very much about it all before. One little picture stands out — a woman with a long soft pink silk skirt tight about her trailing a foot at least; a light shimmery yellow scarf about her shoulders, and hanging down her back. She is holding, like Titian's woman, a large silver bowl curiously wrought in the barbaric Burmese fashion, and the bowl is filled with those long native cigarettes, the tobacco rolled up in green leaves. — Our sea life has begun again for four more days. A Parsee and his family are near me on the deck. I don't yet know how easily a Parsee is contaminated, or I would offer the children some of the bonbons they gave me in Rangoon. À propos *Rangún* is the way.

They reached Calcutta January 21st; after a week there, they made an excursion to Darjeeling, which Mrs. Gardner called a 'heavenly spot.' On their return to Calcutta, they were rejoined by de Baré and Fontmagne.

February 3d they arrived at Bombay, where they were met by Charles Lowell and 'a Mr. Slater.' In spite of their advice, Mr. and Mrs. Gardner started off for Hyderabad. When they arrived the next afternoon, they

were *boosted* by Colonel Lestrange into some Parsee's good graces, and were 'located' in tent No. 7, Public Gardens. Everything comfortable. Took a little drive about the place.

Tuesday, 5. Got invitations and went to the Installation. Met Agassiz. The Durbar pretty, the scenes in the streets wonderful. Only twenty-five European ladies at the Installation. *A grand sight.* After tiffin we saw that which pales everything before it. We went to the Durbar to see the native princes pay allegiance to Nizam. On the road princes and retainers, a vast mass.

Mrs. Gardner at Venice, 1894, by Anders Zorn, oil on canvas, 35¾ x 26 in.

Mrs. Gardner, 1888, by Sargent, detail

	NAME	RESIDENCE	ARRI
All I see in you is worthy love. *Shakspere.*	Joseph Lindon Smith	Palazzo Dario San Gregorio.	*Septem*
Studious of ease and fond of humble things. *A. Philips.*	Clayton Johns	Boston	*Sept*
Officious, innocent, sincere. *Samuel Johnson.*	George W. Proctor	Vienna	*Sep*
A heart to resolve, a head to contrive, and a hand to execute. *Gibbon.*		Venice	*Jone*
Sigh no more, ladies, sigh no more. *Shakspere.*	Saml W Whiteman	Boston	*Sep*
Kind as resolute, and good as brave. *Wordsworth.*	H.C. Mercer.	Philadelphia,	*Sep*

Now stir the fire, and close the shutters fast, let fall the curtains . . . so let us welcome peaceful ev'ning

Page from Mrs. Gardner's guest book from the Palazzo Barbaro, Sept. 5, 1894

John Lowell Gardner, 1895, by Antonio Mancini, detail

OING TO	EVENTS ✦ ADVENTURES ✦ REMARKS
– went off to Padova 19 ᵗʰ September	"Collenni" crossing the Grand Canal from his Palazzo Barbaro 16 Palazzo Barbaro ___ September 11ᵗᵉ 1894.
a.	C'aut go away without saying Something.
ll	"Venezia go la sola, Che me prea contentar O Venezia benedetta, No te vogio più lasar"
liaury.	beaucoup d Chotes.
della	
a	" Doch was alle Freundschaft bindet Ist das Geist mit Geist sich findet.

Thomas Howard, Earl of Arundel, ca. 1529/30,
by Rubens, oil on canvas, 54 x 45 in.

The Rape of Europa, ca. 1562, by Titian, oil on canvas, 70 x 80½ in.

THE ORIENT

In India they travelled north, south, east, and west, and the journal entries are of the briefest. By the end of March, Mrs. Gardner was beginning to feel the need of rest and was looking forward to Venice where she hoped 'to stop a beastly little cough I got a month or two ago. Wouldn't it be odd if the pleurisy I had two years ago were to be the beginning of my being obliged to take care of myself and go to warm places in the winters. But that can't be. As much as I adore travelling, I do love cold countries.' Although she had unlimited energy and vitality, her health was only apparently robust. The letters of her friends constantly express their regret that she is not well. March 27th she wrote from Ajmere:

Indeed it is a terrible loss to any country to lose such a man as Wendell Phillips. In the papers that came to us I found J[ohn] B[oyle] O'R[eilly]'s poem, and liked it much. But I have searched in vain for J. F. Clarke's sermon about him. I want to read it. If it is in some newspaper you have, can you mail it to me? How the great men are going!

Did I ever tell you of a day I had at Lucknow? Everything at the Residency there to-day just as it was at that terrible time — only beautiful flowers are growing over everything — fitting shrouds. I can't tell you how I felt it all and how every drop of my blood seemed then to be *undiluted* English. I may not mail this until Bombay, so do not close this very disjointed letter. . . .

As for poor, dear Tom Appleton — I loved him too — as every one did, I am sure, who ever came in contact with his kind heart, that was after all more noticeable than his eccentric and amusing, clever old head.

The following letter, written at Bombay, is dated April 3d:

We got back yesterday morning. And I found my letters — one from you, welcome as they always are — but, oh! oh! oh! I could cry and sob and break my heart. What do you tell me, that you think of coming abroad for *three* months this summer? So when shall I ever see you again. You do not say when your three months begin, whether you come alone, or with your mother, or with whom. Oh, if I only knew all these things! In fact, dear, I have been thinking of writing (before this) a scolding letter. And this is why. You write to me, and I *love* to get every word, even about the in-

[83]

different people, but I *crave* for details about yourself, and you literally give me none. I try to read between the lines, in vain — and now I can scarcely bear to think what my coming home will be without you. And the Lord only knows when, if ever, I shall see you again. You see I am a SELFISH BRUTE, but I am too wretched to be unnatural just now. We shall sail from Liverpool about the middle of July. If you come abroad, sailing in June, I might meet you *for a day* in London. I suppose we shall be there a week before sailing, and probably two weeks in Paris. Do, the very moment you get this, sit down and write to me every detail about yourself, the money for your book, your plans, etc., that you can think of. If I had only known sooner, perhaps we might have combined a fortnight in Paris. In the apparent utter darkness of the future it seems as if that might have been almost brilliant. Please write as fast as ever you can, and may the Post be kind! Oh, if I could only be unselfish I should say what I know, that you ought to have a change and a very good time (with Lords and Dukes at your feet) — and I *do* hope your book will bring in returns of money untold and fame and reputation of the very best kind. And, dear one, I feel it will. But we must meet somehow. Your little four-leafed clover is fastened in my portfolio and is my constant companion. You ask for a flower. Those of this country are generally fat and luscious and not for pressing. I have a dear little blue cornflower, though, that I picked in the Milayas — but I put it, at the time, in that precious book you gave me, 'The Imitation of Christ,' and I think I would rather leave it there. But flowers will come, and to you always.

We must meet. — Tired, but affectionately yours

I. S. G.

BOMBAY, *April* 7, 1884

DEAREST BACCHANTE

I sent off my last two or three days ago, with a wail at the end, because of the chance of your coming abroad and my missing you entirely, and I have not yet got over the horrid dread of it. But I cannot *know* for ever so long, although do write all details about it as soon as possible. So I shall try and not think horrid thoughts, until I must. If anything could blow them away, it would be this delicious sea breeze. It is heavenly on this verandah, only very difficult to write, everything is blowing about. Our life is a very lazy, deliciously lazy one, but we generally drive to the Fort (the business part of the town) some part of the day; perhaps lunch at the Bank, a gorgeous place that dear Charley Lowell is at the head of, often bringing up for afternoon tea at the Yacht Club — sometimes dining there. The other day we did and they sent me in a bunch of heavy-scented white flowers to wear, and I pressed one, and here it is — alas, no longer white.

THE ORIENT

To her sister-in-law, Mrs. J. Randolph Coolidge, she wrote
April 9th from Bombay:

You are so good, dear Julia — you write letters which are always delightful and you think of the very things I am wishing to hear about. Your February 26 letter was with the budget that awaited our return here, and in it the description of Nelly's[1] reception, something of Esther,[2] a little of Augustus, and all the new and queer things. How strange it will be to get home to such an altered family — altered in different ways, alas! For all the changes are not the bright and happy ones. We are *too* sorry not to get back for the weddings. May the sun shine on the happy brides! — What shall you all wear and will they eat after the service? But I know you will write all this, just as you do everything else.

It is more than a week since we got back from our thirty-six days of most interesting and successful journeying in India. We went to all the places we meant to, travelled at night for cool and comfort — and altogether consider that India is the easiest country to travel in and pays better on the whole than any other. There are so many different races of people and religion — the features, clothes, and architecture change from day to day, as the railways take us from Province to Province. And the Anglo-Indian life mixed up in it all is an odd thread to string Hindú and Mahommedan on.

Bombay we think the prettiest city we have seen, after Hong Kong. It has a little feeling of home to us now, for this is the third time that we are here. First we came en route for Hyderabad, then we had to come back to start for the northwestern tour, and at last here we are again getting ready to sail away forever, I fear, from this most interesting and wonderful country. This part of India is the hub of the Parsee. They seem interesting people, but Charley Lowell says they are more cunning and not so frank and honest as the Hindú. Dear Charley, I hardly think he would know 'Cunning' if he met it. He is so kind to us. Although I am living here in the house of three bachelors, I feel perfectly at home, and do exactly as I please. One of my performances would seem strange enough if I were staying with, say, Mrs. Brimmer at Beverly. When we got back from our journey, I was in rags. The swell dressmaker here had two dresses made for me, but such horrors and misfits as one sees in a nightmare. I was in despair — but the custom of the country came to my rescue. Here people have native seamstresses (males) who sit on the verandah and make all garments. They are

[1] Ellen Gardner, married Augustus Peabody Loring, June 3, 1884.
[2] Esther Burnett, married George Peabody Gardner (brother of Ellen Gardner), June 11, 1884.

[85]

called 'Verandah Tailors,' so they were sent for, and there three of them sat all day, on the verandah just out of my room; and after I had cut and basted, they sewed, and I now go about clothed and in my right mind.

We shall get to Venice (D.V.) about May 5, and there I hope for a long rest, for we have been rather unquiet for a year nearly, and one does get tired. So when we are there, 'whistling for want of thought,' isn't there a chance of Randolph's turning up? You say he thinks of going to Venice. If so, he must hunt us up. Our address will be Banca di Credito Veneto.

I have been arranging photographs in my albums all the morning; I hope some day you will care to see them. And now for siesta — then tea at five — then evening service at six at such a pretty little church on the hill (Malabar Hill) near here. It is Holy Week. I have known Easters at home with snow. Give our best love to all. We have had a very lazy day, neither of us going into the Fort, as they call the business part of the town, so Jack joins in messages.

Always affectionately yours

I. S. GARDNER

I am almost ashamed to say how sorry I am to leave India.

Several days were spent in Cairo on the way to Europe; Venice was reached May 14th. This was her first visit since her school-days, but henceforth every trip to Europe included a long sojourn in Venice. The first week was spent, as she foresaw from Bombay, in resting, floating idly up and down the Grand Canal, the little canals and rios in her gondola, delighting in all the charm of Venetian architecture, which, even in its exuberance, seemed quiet and homelike after the fantasies and elaborations of Eastern temples. Then began careful, thoughtful sight-seeing — not more than two churches or galleries a day. In the East, architecture and sculpture were the public arts which chiefly engaged the traveller's attention; in Venice, Mrs. Gardner seemed to have discovered for the first time the glory of painting. For the first time it is with photographs of paintings that she fills her album. The galleries of Vienna, Paris, and London had never so excited her. For the next five weeks she devoted herself to the masterpieces with which Venice is packed. As souvenirs of her visits to the Academy, she bought photographs of the works of Gentile and Giovanni Bellini, Bonifazio, Paris Bordone, Carpaccio, Cima da Conegliano, Mantegna, Palma Vecchio, Tiepolo, Tintoretto, Titian, and Paolo Veronese — of these and no others; almost every one of these men is now represented in her own collection at Fenway Court, Gentile by the exquisite drawing of 'A Turkish Artist,' Giovanni Bellini by a 'Madonna and Child,' Bonifazio by a 'Santa Conversazione,' Bordone by an appealing 'Child Jesus disputing in the Temple,' Carpaccio, less satisfactorily than the others, by two drawings, Cima by a Madonna (alas! now recognized as a copy), Mantegna by a small but precious 'Santa Conversazione,' Tiepolo by a brilliant sketch for his fresco, 'The Wedding of Barbarossa,' Tintoretto by two portraits, and Titian by the superb 'Europa.' There is also a handsome ceiling painting, 'The Coronation of Hebe,' now attributed to an assistant of Veronese.

At the close of this Venetian album she copied 'O Venezia benedetta, no le vogio più lasar.' As a souvenir she brought home a little sketch by P. Fragiacomo, to remain permanently among her other souvenirs.

From Venice to Paris and London, and then home. Before they arrived, Mr. Gardner's father had died.

The summer of 1884 was finished out at Beverly. To her old neighbor, Mrs. Gardner had brought a piece of embroidery for which she received the following letter of thanks:

ISABELLA STEWART GARDNER

MY DEAR MRS. GARDNER,

The embroidery is exquisite and the Dragon is a perfect love. A lamp-stand, indeed! Not while I have eyes to see its beauty. I don't believe the serpent that tempted our great-grandmother Eve was half so lovely.

It is a long way to carry my memory and bring it safely back — from Boston to Pekin and from Pekin to Boston. I cannot lose yours while I sit in the bower you had woven for me, and which — do you know it? — bursts into blossom on the 29th of August, just as the Glastonbury thorn is sure to bud at Christmas.

A thousand thanks for your charming gift, and all the best wishes of
Yours most truly
OLIVER WENDELL HOLMES

CHAPTER VI

UNDERSTANDING

THE liberalizing, tranquillizing effect upon Mrs. Gardner of her experiences in the East cannot be estimated. She was an ardent believer in the maintenance of native customs, native costumes, native ceremonies, and native religions. Oriental religious rites she found picturesque and fascinating; many of the elements of Oriental faiths, extolling peace, contemplation, the negation of desire, revealed to her ideals which her restless spirit had not previously conceived, and she had seen people whose lives, directed and controlled by these faiths, were beautiful. As she grew older, she regretted the gradual Europeanizing of Asia, the destruction of variety, the increase of uniformity and monotony, the passing of those things which were the outgrowth and the expression of natural environment and national character. When a distinguished Japanese came to Boston, she declined the honor of receiving him at Fenway Court because he wore European clothes; she liked to have her Japanese friends in her box at the opera, but they clearly understood that they would not be welcome unless they came in Japanese costume. The proprieties and conventions of a society where Puritan tradition still lingers had always been somewhat ostentatiously flouted by Mrs. Gardner; with maturity her own conduct became quieter, but she remained tolerant of any moral or perhaps immoral code, particularly if it was one followed by foreigners in accordance with their national habit.

Mrs. Gardner respected the great reality of death; the restrictions prescribed for mourning she observed punctiliously. Owing to the recent death of Mr. Gardner's parents, balls and frivolities were perforce temporarily given up, and even 'conversaziones,' the other form of evening party then in vogue, were for a time abandoned. To tell the truth, they had never been a complete success; Bostonians were not sufficiently fond of talking, the available lions who furnished the attraction of the evening were not sufficiently exciting; and although the men were ready to accept Mrs. Gardner's invitations, some of the cleverest women were still unfriendly. But one element of her parties was always a triumph — the supper, which was arranged under Mr. Gardner's personal supervision.

Mrs. Gardner's own temperament — or temper — was what is called, perhaps unfairly, 'artistic'; at any rate, she had the faculty of making artists feel that she understood them and their work. Besides finding her a 'life-enhancing' companion and a generous patron, they felt that she was a friend who comprehended their aspirations as well as their achievements. When Whistler gave her a copy of his 'Eden versus Whistler, the Baronet and the Butterfly,' he wrote in it:

> To Mrs. Gardner —
> whose appreciation of the work of Art is only
> equalled by her understanding of the Artist.

A newspaper said:

Boston society consists of fossilized conventions; Mrs. Gardner has not failed to spurn them. Boston society consists of antique genealogical distinctions and exclusive standards; Mrs. Gardner has not failed to break down social barriers and evidence her belief in society as a vehicle for the cultivation of art, music, and intellectuality and to create a social renaissance. Beyond her wealth and her social position, she has exercised a certain personal hypnotism in the ranks of swelldom.

UNDERSTANDING

Whether a social renaissance was created or not may be a question, but 'the Brimmer set, which represents the old Puritan aristocracy,' and 'the Apthorp set, which represents the new Bohemianism,' did 'meet in her house on a common ground.'

As the enjoyment of music is not forbidden to grief, Mrs. Gardner's new music-room was in constant use. In 1884, she made the acquaintance of Clayton Johns; that same year Wilhelm Gericke came to direct the Symphony Orchestra, in which Charles Martin Loeffler had been a first violin since 1881, sharing the first desk with the concertmaster, Franz Kneisel. Mrs. Gardner greatly admired Mr. Gericke, and he reciprocated; it was said that he would not begin a Symphony Concert until she was in her seat, but, as she invariably arrived early at any entertainment, there would have been no difficulty in carrying out such a resolution. Mr. Johns and Mr. Loeffler became two of Mrs. Gardner's most faithful friends. Together they gave a series of recitals at her house, playing the sonatas of Bach, Mozart, Beethoven, and Brahms, and she took her turn in lending her music-room for talks given by Mr. Johns on the music of the Symphony Concerts. These talks were illustrated by the performance of the music arranged as piano duets; to assist him, Mr. Johns engaged Mr. George Proctor, only a lad who had been a chorister at the Church of the Messiah, and who was now, at the age of fifteen, organist at the Church of the Redeemer in South Boston. Often Mrs. Gardner would ask a few people to come in the morning for music. When finally she gave a grand party with a programme by the Symphony Orchestra led by Mr. Gericke, many music-lovers forsook their previous hostile attitude and became obsequious admirers. They could afford to suspend a few puritanical prejudices when good music was offered them free. Mrs. Gardner said that at many a young musician's concert, she was the only person in the audience who had paid for a seat.

Scholarly men were also being added to her circle. General Walker, President of the Massachusetts Institute of Technology, wrote to her: 'What a power you have of understanding things! I never went with any one through our school who comprehended so quickly and so perfectly the significance of every part. It was a great pleasure to me, a great privilege. All I ask is: Don't see through ME; pray make this one exception.' In 1885, when Mrs. Gardner went to Washington to attend the inauguration of President Cleveland, General Walker wrote to her constantly; he was giving a course of Lowell Institute lectures, and after each one sent a report to Mrs. Gardner. After the sixth, when half the course had been given, he wrote that, if the next one could be postponed, he would leave Boston that night for Washington, taking advantage of an invitation to visit dear friends, in order to see the inauguration and have a cup of tea with her. His letters are full of clever, confidential comment on public men and public matters, the sort of inner-circle information Mrs. Gardner particularly enjoyed.

As William Crowninshield Endicott, a relative of Mr. Gardner, had been selected by Mr. Cleveland to be Secretary of War, and was in Washington with his family, he was able to provide Mrs. Gardner with tickets to all the official functions, and she made the most of the occasion. She was present February 22d when the Honorable John D. Long read the oration pre-

pared by Robert C. Winthrop for the exercises celebrating the
completion of the Washington Monument. In 1848, Mr. Winthrop had delivered the oration at the laying of the corner-
stone, but now illness prevented his delivering in person what
was perhaps the greatest oration he ever wrote. On March 13th,
he wrote to Mrs. Gardner:

MY DEAR BELLE,

I hear you are to be at home, *at last*, this evening. So I write a line, with a
still feeble hand, to greet you with my very best thanks for that most kind
and considerate telegram which you sent me from the Capitol. It gave me
the *first* tidings of the success of my *Oration* — coming, as it did, an hour
before I received any other information in regard to it. . . .

It was no mere chance that Mrs. Gardner's congratulations
were the first; she meant to be first, and she generally was. Her
promptness was amazing; every letter, every invitation was
answered as soon as read, and every gift acknowledged so
speedily that it often seemed as if the note of thanks were delivered before the gift could have been received.

One of the friends who most influenced and aided Mrs. Gardner's career was Professor Charles Eliot Norton. Courtly in
his courtesy, the gentlest and kindliest of men, and one of the
most courageous, devoted to the discouraging task of spreading
culture among his practical countrymen and of creating an
intelligent love of beauty and of honest, clearly perceived ideals,
he was happy to welcome a recruit so clever, so wealthy, and
in her own circle so influential as Mrs. Gardner. In the spring
of 1885, she attended his Dante readings which were held in his
study at 'Shady Hill,' and she also joined the Dante Society.
The President of the Society was James Russell Lowell; after
his death in 1891, he was succeeded in office by Professor Nor-

ton. Mrs. Gardner remained an enthusiastic member as long as she lived, and regularly attended the annual meeting. She took especial pleasure in the treasurer's report; the financial problems of the Society, which to her seemed Lilliputian, entertained her; she liked to hear such a group of scholars discuss anxiously the advisability of spending small sums of money. The cast of the so-called death-mask of Dante, sent by the Society in 1885 to each member, still remains in the case with her rare editions of the poet. In 1886, the Society was told that the Concordance of the 'Divina Commedia,' by Professor Edward Allen Fay, was nearing completion, and the Council must consider how the Society could aid and participate in the publication of it; within a year, a member of the Society had 'liberally undertaken to meet any deficit in the cost of printing left by the subscriptions.' In addition to this promise, Mrs. Gardner subscribed for four copies. When the Concordance was in the printer's hands, she suggested to Professor Norton that a copy be sent to the Queen of Italy. On July 20, 1888, Professor Norton wrote:

Your suggestion that a copy of the Concordance should be sent to the Queen of Italy is most excellent and shall be carried out. I have to-day been reading the proof of the Preface to the volume. The book will be published, I fancy, even before your return.

In his letter of June 2, 1885, acknowledging the receipt of Mrs. Gardner's dues as a member of the Dante Society, he said:

I shall send you to-day another Report of a work in which I am much more deeply interested, in which I am sure of your sympathy and wish I could gain your active interest and support. The work is the establishing of a School of Classical Studies at Athens. What the School proposes, and how it is constituted you will see in the smaller pamphlet I send you — and what I think of the need of the School, and what I desire for it, I venture to ask you to read in the Report of the Archæological Institute, on pp. 44–46.

UNDERSTANDING

If we (that is the Committee on the School) could now obtain three, four, or five thousand dollars, on condition that ten thousand more be secured within the year, the School would be established and we should have the satisfaction of having done something in honor of Athena.

Could I really interest you in this I should believe the work accomplished, and the honor paid.

I am Sincerely yours

C. E. NORTON

Mrs. Gardner immediately sent a cheque which Mr. Norton, with punctilious delicacy, acknowledged — and returned, saying:

With your gracious leave, I propose to put your name upon the list as a subscriber to the fund for the School, to the amount of four hundred dollars, payable in case the Committee succeed in raising an adequate sum for the building at Athens. Should we fail to do so, your subscription would lapse. I do not like to receive the money while success in our endeavor is still so doubtful. If you approve, I will therefore return your cheque, with the hope that I may ask for it again some months hence.

Thus Mrs. Gardner became associated with the beginnings of one of the finest and most productive coöperative enterprises of American scholarship.

At the death of Mr. Gardner's parents, their country place in Brookline, called 'Green Hill,' came into his possession. It was in charge of Charles Montague Atkinson, an old-fashioned English gardener with whom Mrs. Jack waged constant warfare. All her changes were opposed, but her purposes were never thwarted; she insisted on having large trees moved and others cut down so that she might secure the open spaces, the light and air and freedom she desired. Gradually she transformed the estate, steadily increasing its charm and beauty. Old Atkinson delighted her by telling her she reminded him of Beckford, the author of 'Vathek,' she was so determined to have her own way. 'Think of a gardener's knowing about Beck-ford!' When she decided to have a large garden of Japanese iris, her horticultural friends declared she could not make them grow, that she could not reproduce their native conditions; but she constructed a sunken garden, piped it, and the flowers were superb. If Atkinson disregarded her wishes, she had individual methods of discipline. At a dinner-party her friends found the table decorated with unfamiliar orchids; close inspection re-vealed that they were ticketed with little labels, adapted from Symphony Concert programmes: 'First time this orchid has bloomed in Boston'; 'First time this orchid has bloomed in the United States,' etc. But why, she was asked, had she squan-dered these rare flowers on a dinner-party, instead of taking a prize with them at the flower-show which was to open the next day. 'Because,' she said, 'I found that the gardener was giving all his attention to growing orchids for this show and neglect-ing the flowers I wanted.'

And yet, on December 17, 1893, Atkinson wrote as follows:

GREEN HILL, BROOKLINE, *December* 17, 1893

MRS. JOHN L. GARDNER

MADAME

When Jim brought the parcel I hied to my Den to unpack it for I guess^d its contents. The Frame is just the thing, simple and unobtrusive, another instance of your marvellous natural unique taste. What an elegant Xmas gift.

To-day I have placed you and Mr. Gardner on each side of the time-piece on the mantel. Nothing but time can efface the Love and gratitude I have felt and shall ever feel for all the kindness you have done me, and the few short years I have had the honour to serve you have been the happiest of a Chequered Life. When I die I want you to have them again for I want no Vulgar unappreciative eye to rest upon them.

I am Madame your ever indebted and faithful

Ser^t

C. M. ATKINSON

[96]

UNDERSTANDING

In these mournful days of restricted pleasure, Mrs. Gardner adopted the Boston habit of lecture-going. The following letter is in reply to a note about lectures; Mrs. Gardner's keenness and quickness of perception were a lecturer's delight:

SOUTHBOROUGH, MASSACHUSETTS, *October 23rd*, 1885

DEAR MRS. GARDNER,

Returning to my Cabbages after a week's absence, I find your note.

Thank heaven, I am not going to lecture, though the hope of seeing you again among my hearers might tempt me. But lecturing never did anybody good, and I have found it especially futile with Women — the more, the portlier they are!   Faithfully yours

J. R. LOWELL

Mrs. Gardner's mother died January 6, 1886; at the end of the month, Mrs. Gardner went with her father, the only surviving member of her immediate family, to St. Augustine, Florida. There they stayed, except for a week at Havana, till March 6th. The following year Mr. Stewart conveyed to his daughter the house which he had built for her in 1860, but which until now he had continued to hold in his name. He himself found a solitary life intolerable, and presently married Mrs. Henry D. Pick, the widow of a nephew. The marriage annoyed Mrs. Gardner.

With the aid of Professor Norton, an expert bibliophile, Mrs. Gardner was engaged in making a collection of rare books; as their bond was the Dante Society, he was especially interested to have her secure rare editions of Dante. Mr. and Mrs. Gardner sailed for England June 23, 1886; on Sunday, the 13th, Professor Norton had written:

DEAR MRS. GARDNER,

I have been away for the last three days, and must beg you to pardon me, therefore, for not sooner replying to your note.

And for a reply, I send you a Catalogue of the Library of an old acquaintance of mine, Mr. Edward Cheney, which is to be sold next week in London. Mr. Cheney was a great lover of Italy and of fine books, and among his books is a copy of the Aldine Dante of 1502. May I telegraph to Quaritch to buy it for you?

I send you the Catalogue because there are two other books in it which perhaps you might care for; one is No. 542, the Brescia Dante of 1487, with very curious interesting woodcuts. I once tried to get a copy of this edition which was priced at £30. — , but I did not obtain it. I dare say that this copy might sell for £40. or £50. The other book is No. 1441, one of the loveliest books ever printed. Could you come over on Wednesday or Thursday (or do you sail on Thursday?) I should be delighted to show you my copy of it. To-morrow and Tuesday I am engaged all the morning at examinations, and all the afternoons at other college work, but I will leave the book on my table where you could easily see it. It is so beautiful that I should like to have you have the 'finest copy known.'

With cordial good wishes for your voyage, and your return, I am,

Faithfully yours

C. E. NORTON

Number 1441 was 'Hypnerotomachia Poliphili vbi hvmana omnia non nisi Somnivm docet. Venetiis, Mense decembri. M. I. D. in ædibus Aldi Manutii, accuratissime.'

Mrs. Gardner must have deeply regretted that she could not have the excitement of attending the auction. As she could not reach London in time, the only thing to do was to accept Mr. Norton's suggestion of telegraphing to Quaritch. Upon her arrival she went to him at once for her books, only to find that he had not bought the Brescia Dante for her. As she told the story, she said:

'But you got my cable?'

'Yes, Madam.'

'Didn't it say buy the Brescia Dante?'

'Y-yes.'

'Don't you carry out the orders that you receive?'

A Lady and Gentleman in Black, 1633, by Rembrandt, oil on canvas, 51¾ x 42 in.

Christ Bearing The Cross, after Giovanni Bellini, oil on panel, 19½ x 15½ in. (formerly attributed to Giorgione)

The Annunciation, ca. 1481, by Antoniazzo Romano, tempera on panel, 39¾ x 45 in.

The Presentation of the Child Jesus in the Temple, by Giotto, tempera on panel, 17¼ x 16¾ in.

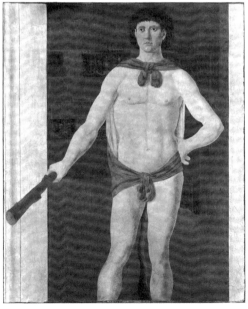

Hercules, ca. 1465, by Piero della Francesca, fresco, 59¼ x 49½ in.

Brahms and Strauss with autograph of Strauss to "Mrs. John L. Gardner zur freund-
lichen erinnerung (as a friendly remembrance) Johann Strauss Ischl 2 Sept. 94" and
the opening measure of *The Blue Danube*

'Yes, Madam, but it went for a very high price, a price that we considered exorbitant.'

'Did my cable put any limit on the amount you were to pay?'

'No, Madam.'

'Then why didn't you buy it?'

'Because, Madam, the price was very high, we didn't know you, we had never acted as your agent, and we did not feel justified in paying so much.'

Thinking that if Quaritch had not known her before, he might as well begin at once, Mrs. Gardner said: 'When I give an order, Mr. Quaritch, I expect it to be carried out; unless I set a limit on the price, there is no limit. If you can get the Brescia Dante for me from the person who bought it, very well; otherwise I shall never have any further dealings with you.' A few days later the coveted book was brought by Quaritch to Mrs. Gardner's hotel. At the sale a titled collector, an old customer of his, had bought it; when he heard of Quaritch's dilemma, he agreed to release the book if Quaritch would accept his offer for another rarity which he had long desired.

July 20th chanced to be the day that Mrs. Gardner went to Quaritch's to buy a birthday book. Just as she finished making her selection, Gladstone came in, was presented, and invited to write in the book. Against the date December 29th he wrote, 'W. Gladstone 1809,' and then said: 'This is the first time I have written my name since signing my resignation an hour ago.' 'Home Rule' had been the burning question in British politics throughout the spring; the election held in July indicated that there would be a majority against it, and on the 20th the Cabinet decided upon resignation. The pen with which Gladstone wrote was delivered to Mrs. Gardner with the birthday book.

Professor Norton continued steadily to aid Mrs. Gardner in her collecting; the following year he arranged for her the purchase of Meryon's etchings, 'Le Stryge' and 'Galerie de Notre Dame,' and from a Berlin bookseller the 'Rosario della gl'iosa v'gine Maria,' and a 'Book of Hours.' When the Earl of Crawford's library was sold, he advised the purchase of the Landino Dante with illustrations after designs by Botticelli printed in Florence in 1481, and the 'Livre d'Heures' of Mary, Queen of Scots, two of the most precious books at Fenway Court. From him, in 1902, she obtained the original manuscripts of Mrs. Hemans's 'The Landing of the Pilgrim Fathers,' Lowell's 'Mr. Hosea Biglow to Mr. James T. Fields,' which Mr. Norton considered the finest of the second series of 'The Biglow Papers,' and a holograph copy of Longfellow's 'Paul Revere's Ride'; in 1903, he sold her his collection of Venetian manuscripts, several of which had formerly belonged to Edward Cheney.

All her life Mrs. Gardner continued to collect rare books, manuscripts, and autographs. A catalogue of the books in her 'collection' was printed in 1906; before her death the collection was nearly doubled. In 1923, a catalogue of her illuminated manuscripts and of her fine bookbindings was printed. But after the eighties book-collecting was one of her minor pursuits.

In 1886, the Gardners went from London to Baireuth, where they were joined by their nephew Amory. Mr. and Mrs. Henry L. Higginson, of Boston, were also there with their niece Miss

UNDERSTANDING

Marian Shaw and her friend Miss Emma Eames. The occasion proved unusually interesting. There were three superb performances of 'Parsifal' and three of 'Tristan and Isolde'; Malten, Materna, and Reichmann were the chief singers. Materna was a friend of Mrs. Gardner, and early Sunday morning, August 1st, she was announced; there was just time to vacate the seat of honor, the sofa, before she was ushered in. With tears streaming down her cheeks she said, 'The master has gone.' Liszt had died late the night before. No one could be more responsively sympathetic than Mrs. Gardner, and she was Materna's companion and comforter during the sad days that followed. As wreaths were being sent by all the crowned heads of Europe, Mrs. Gardner ordered one with the inscription 'Hommage de l'Amérique.' This was placed beside the one sent by Queen Victoria. For the funeral, the town was draped in black, the street-lamps, lighted in the daytime, were shrouded in black; through the doleful streets the long procession of mourners passed, at the very head, Mrs. Gardner beside Materna, who accompanied Liszt's daughter, Frau Cosima Wagner. And Mrs. Gardner was among the first to whom the spade was passed to throw a shovel of earth upon the coffin.

From Baireuth, they went via Nuremberg and Munich to Vienna, where Mrs. Gardner visited the graves of Mozart, Haydn, Beethoven, and Schubert. But although books and music seemed to engross her attention during the eighties, she was studying paintings assiduously and choosing, perhaps unconsciously, the artists who were eventually to be represented in her great collection. In Munich, there were Dürers and Holbeins; in Vienna, Mantegna's 'Triumphal Entry of Julius

Cæsar'; in Venice, Titian above all; in Florence, Titian still, and Mantegna, Fra Angelico, Botticelli's 'La Calunnia' (which belongs to the period of her 'Death of Lucretia'), Pesellino, and Lorenzo di Credi. Each of these names appears in the catalogue of Fenway Court.

In Venice, Mrs. Gardner became the friend of the Patriarch, Cardinal Agostini, through whom she made gifts of clothing and money to the poor; four years later, he wrote that he wished she might remain forever in Venice to benefit it by her great charity.

At the end of October, Mr. and Mrs. Gardner returned to London for a fortnight before sailing. While there, as Mrs. Gardner told the story, she attended a dinner-party at which she was a complete stranger to the other guests; after dinner she was sitting rather alone while the other women gossiped, none of them paying much attention to her because, as she said, she was naturally retiring and inconspicuous; but when the men came in, one of them chanced to ask her if she took any interest in the international yacht races. 'Oh, yes!' she said, 'my husband was one of the owners of the Puritan.' Whereupon all the men formed a circle round her and talked to no one else for the rest of the evening. The Puritan had been built in 1884 for a Boston syndicate by Edward Burgess; as he was but little known at the time, she was referred to by members of the New York Yacht Club as the 'bean boat,' but she easily demonstrated her superiority over the Priscilla, the New York boat, and her contest with the renowned English Genesta, which was a glorious victory for the Puritan, was considered the most stirring and satisfactory cup-race up to that time.

UNDERSTANDING

During this London fortnight she saw much of Whistler, who did a miniature full-length portrait of her in pastel, which he called 'The Little Note in Yellow and Gold.' A pastel called 'The Violet Note,' representing Lyse Vazaeti, and an oil, 'The Note in Orange and Blue — Sweet Shop,' were bought at this time; another pastel, a nude, called 'Lapis-lazuli,' was purchased in 1895. Most precious of all, Whistler gave Mrs. Gardner several of the first little pen-and-ink sketches for the famous Peacock Room. On October 28th, Henry James took Mrs. Gardner to the studio of John Singer Sargent to see his portrait of Madame Gautreau, which had caused a stir both in Paris and in London.

She came home with a new interest, a new rôle — patroness of young painters. For the next few years, until his marriage in 1890, so soon followed by his death, Denis Bunker was constantly in her train. Original, but moody, he suffered from violent headaches and fits of depression; at such times he would lock himself in his room, go without food, and admit no one. Mrs. Gardner alone could persuade him to face the world again. T. Russell Sullivan, writing about him to Mrs. Gardner in 1889, said: '... put a little more of the arlecchino into him, if you can. It's the only rôle to play — except that of colombina — and those who play it best (whether it hurts, or not) get on best. I suppose that his dyspeptic fiend has fastened upon him again, and won't let him alone. Give him a grip from me, and tell him to stay with us. But don't read him my moral philosophy, or he will swear strange oaths, and the air will grow blue as the Apennines.' In 1888, he painted for her a brilliant picture of the chrysanthemums in her greenhouse, and in 1889, he did her portrait in the costume of a Venetian lady of the Renaissance. Through him she purchased, in 1888, Dewing's 'Lady in Yellow.'

Early in 1888, Sargent painted Mrs. Gardner's portrait; he was thirty-two at the time, she was forty-eight. One cannot help wondering if she had determined that her portrait should rival the one of Madame Gautreau; she was well aware of the fame of her figure, her neck, and her arms; she was proud of the length and flexibility of her hands; all these should be revealed in her picture, but unlike Madame Gautreau she would wear the jewels she loved, pearls and rubies, and she would look the world straight in the eye, with her head held high, dominant. Attitudes supposedly graceful were not for her, though grace was in her every movement; she always sat or stood perfectly straight and square. To accentuate the line of her figure, Sargent tied a black shawl tight around her hips, letting the ends hang down in front. The portrait was an ordeal for the young painter — Mrs. Gardner *would* look out of the window to see what was happening on the river, and more than once Sargent was for giving the whole thing up. A friend told him that was undoubtedly what Mrs. Gardner desired; a lady who found her portrait unsatisfactory, but did not wish to be responsible for breaking a contract, would endeavor to exasperate the artist to such a degree that he would quit. On the contrary, Mrs. Gardner was having such a good time that she sought to prolong the pleasure; but when the portrait had been done over eight times — so she used to say — she told Sargent that as nine was Dante's mystic number, they must make the ninth try a success, and they did. Once finished, Mrs. Gardner maintained it was the finest portrait Sargent ever painted, and often tried to make him commit himself to the same opinion. Her admiration of the painting equalled her affection for the painter. She imputed to him the statement that the portrait was so imbued with her personality that if it were cut up into pieces an inch square and these pieces were scattered on the Charles River, the finder of one piece would know it came from a portrait of her. For years her wardrobe contained a close-fitting, plain black dress, copied from the one in the picture.

The portrait was exhibited at the St. Botolph Club. 'Woman — an enigma' was suggested as a suitable title. One critic wrote, 'She is not a beautiful woman, but she has arms that are perfection — beggaring description'; another said the picture challenged speculation regarding the audacity of both sitter and artist — from a purely artistic point of view it was a wonderful piece of work, for all the strength, sweetness, subtlety, and contradictory variations of the woman's character were successfully presented. No old master had left a more puzzling personality upon canvas. For putting his ability thus to the proof in the midst of modern convention, the painter would, of course, be severely censured by people who could understand propriety better than they could art or the temptations of a good subject to a creative brush. And so forth. Mr. Gardner was so irritated by some of the comments that he said the picture should not be exhibited again as long as he lived; it may have been out of respect for his wishes that the room at Fenway Court in which the picture hangs was not opened to the public by Mrs. Gardner while she lived, although she directed that it should be after her death.

CHAPTER VII
EPISODES

THE objective of the brief European journey of 1888 was Spain, and the climax of the trip to Spain was Seville. Burgos and Madrid were visited on the way, and the Prado made its due impression, but in Seville she quoted 'Here one feels existence,' and she accepted the Spanish proverb —

> Quien no ha visto Sevilla
> No ha visto maravilla.

They arrived on Saturday, March 24th, the day before Palm Sunday, just in time for the mediæval pageantry of Holy Week. Seville has been called the Alma Mater of the bull-fighter. The season opens — or did open — Easter Sunday; crowds gather around the hotels to watch the heroes of the ring set out for the Plaza de Toros. There were few people Mrs. Gardner loved as she loved animals; she was a stanch anti-vivisectionist, and a liberal contributor to societies for the prevention of cruelty to animals; although she endured pain with unusual fortitude — once, when her hand was accidentally but badly bitten by one of her dogs, she had the wound treated and went as usual to the Symphony Concert — she could not bear the suffering of animals. But she could not sit still and watch life go by; she must be in the centre of the action, and on Easter Sunday afternoon she went to the Plaza de Toros where a bull was killed 'in her honor' by the great matador of the day, Luis Mazzantini. The Gardner party were in a box and, when anything particularly sickening seemed imminent, Mrs. Gardner crouched on the floor and covered her eyes. Then came the Fería with the horse-racing and the joyous festivity. Following the custom of the rich Sevillians, the Gardners hired a tent and entertained on the Fería grounds.

As a souvenir of Seville they bought a Madonna by Francisco Zurbaran, their first venture into the hazardous field of old masters. It proves that, in all the ceremonies and pageants of the Easter season, Mrs. Gardner had been conscious of more than the superficial show; much as she enjoyed that, she was herself so sincere that, if it had been only a show staged to attract travellers, she would have hated it. Even an elaborate procession can be conducted with a spirit of simplicity, expressing the pleasure and the inherited faith of the participants; only so could it interest her. Her own emotions were so deep and possessed her so completely that she quickly detected the shallowness of mere organization and saw only its defects. The realism of the Spanish images was an expression of simple honesty of belief, and with her whole heart, Mrs. Gardner believed. This Madonna was never to her merely a work of art — it was a religious picture, her altar-piece. In her Beacon Street house it hung in her bedroom; when Fenway Court was built, it was hung above the Chapel window; now it is the altar-piece of the little 'Spanish Chapel' near the entrance. At this altar masses were said while Mrs. Gardner's body lay waiting for the final funeral service; on the wall is a Spanish inscription,

Quien · a · esta · casa · da · luz · IESVS
Quien · la · llena · de · alegria · MARIA
Quien · la · abraza · en · la · fe · IOSE

and on another side the words, 'In Memoriam.' It is believed that Mrs. Gardner built the chapel in memory of little Jackie.

They were in Madrid for the festival of San Isidro, May 15th. At Toledo, a few days after, her interest centred in the church of San Juan de los Reyes with its beautiful cloister. Several years later, in 1895, she bought in Rome two handsome iron torchères of the sixteenth century with the arms of the Bishop of Toledo, and an iron escutcheon with an eagle mantling the arms of Isabella Catolica. The story has already been published of the American artist who had lived for years in Rome, and who was brought one day to see Mrs. Gardner in Boston. He told her of his own humble collecting and of his special desire to own a Spanish iron escutcheon whose beauty he described and whose historic significance he related. 'Oh! Mrs. Gardner, if you could see it!' Mrs. Gardner was responsive as ever, but, as ever, 'no one knew what was going on in the back of her head.' When the visitor took his leave, Mrs. Gardner followed him to the hall and, as she shook hands, she said, 'Look up.' — 'Oh, my God!' said the artist, for there, over the drawing-room door, was his escutcheon.

Naturally, the great Isabellas of history interested her. In Madrid she fell in love with Coello's portrait of the Infanta Isabella Clara Eugenia, daughter of Philip II; in her album she wrote under the photograph: 'Philip II always spoke of her as his "Mirror" and "the light of his soul."' In 1897, she purchased a later portrait of the Infanta by Pourbus. So were her purposes conceived and patiently borne until they could be accomplished.

In February, 1896, when Mr. Berenson urged the purchase of

a portrait which he attributed to Polidoro Lanzani, the 'best follower' of Titian, he wrote that it was in the highest degree valuable to her because it represented 'the greatest and most fascinating lady of the Renaissance — your worthy precursor and patron saint — Isabella d' Este, Marchioness of Mantua.' As Mrs. Gardner wrote after receiving a photograph that she did not like the hand, Mr. Berenson cabled that in the picture the hand was 'not at all offensive,' and added in a letter that solely as a picture he would not urge the purchase, but it would decorate a wall well and had 'potent attraction as the portrait of Isabella.'

June 3, 1888, they left Madrid, and after ten days in Barcelona, travelled slowly toward Venice. There the Daniel Curtis family was installed in the Palazzo Barbaro, which was regularly tenanted by the Gardners on their subsequent visits; its handsome rooms were among the chief aids to Mrs. Gardner's imagination in designing her own Venetian palace in Boston.

In Venice, she met Count Hans Coudenhove, a charming man in the service of the Austrian Government. Writing to her from Rome two years later, he said he was especially struck at that time (Venice, 1888) that Mr. Louis Dyer, a scientific man, University professor, was as loud in his praises as the worldlings who surrounded her. 'I remember,' he adds, 'you conquered the Cardinal [Agostini] in an inkling (twinkling?) and were presented with a souvenir by the Superior of the Armenians. These are very interesting particulars for a student of mankind, like me.' The souvenir was a little pamphlet of 'Proverbi popolari Turchi, scritti con lettere Armene e tradotti in Italiano,' printed at the Armenian Monastery. Coudenhove's studies of mankind led him to prefer the society of animals, and he finally established himself in Central Africa. There he was interned during the World War, and was at one moment unjustly in danger of execution. After the War he resumed a long-interrupted correspondence with Mrs. Gardner, and began writing for publication articles about the animals he knew and loved so well. When the first of these was accepted by the 'Atlantic Monthly,' he suggested to Mrs. Gardner that if she knew the editor, a word of commendation might be advantageous. Mrs. Gardner wrote at once to Mr. Ellery Sedgwick, who said he supposed that he had discovered an absolutely unknown man in the heart of darkest Africa, but that, as was to be expected, he turned out to be Mrs. Gardner's intimate friend.

The purchase of the Zurbaran had kindled the desire to collect works of art, but assurance had not yet come. In a Venetian antiquary's shop she saw a bas-relief which she wanted, but she allowed herself to be persuaded to pass it by. It must have stiffened her resolution to be told by Professor Dyer a few months later that the relief had been acquired by the Louvre. He wrote: 'This certainly shows that you can trust your eye to pick out a good thing and leave a bad one, and it proves that you do not need to lean upon the advice of other people in the purchase of antiquities.'

After Venice, there was a week at Baireuth and then from July 29th to August 22d they were in London. Here she had her own way and unwisely purchased a marble relief of the Madonna and Child erroneously attributed to Rossellino. In it her love of beauty and her devotion to religion were united; was set over the fireplace of her entrance hall, with a vigil light always burning before it. From now on Mrs. Gardner worshipped both the Madonna and Art. Her album is filled with photographs of the paintings by the great Italians in the National Gallery, but as always she found plenty of time for play; there were days on the river with London friends, and gay breakfasts with Whistler, who had married Beatrix Godwin on August 11th. Three weeks in Paris, where the paintings in the Louvre were diligently studied, brought to a close this brief but significant journey, with her career as an art-collector well started.

The little house at Beverly Farms which she occupied in summer was called 'The Alhambra'; with its decoration of brilliant flowers, it was as gay as the courtyards of Seville. A newspaper writer described the house as conspicuous

for its fanciful design, which is a queer compound of the ancient and modern, as well as for the exquisite taste displayed in its surroundings. . . . The trimmings are of a peculiar shade of dark green. A veranda shades the front and one end of the house, between the pillars of which are suspended rustic baskets filled with gay flowers. Brackets covered with ferns and velvet begonias hang on either side of the old-fashioned doorway, and a row of scarlet geraniums forms a bright border round the low lattice work of the piazza meeting the climbing vines of scarlet nasturtiums. A low stone wall that bounds the lawn is one luxuriant mass of these brilliant blossoms, while a granite rock in the centre of the lawn is radiant in its green and scarlet mantle. Even the little pump at the side has its crown of bright beans and pale green leaves.

These exquisite decorations no longer distinguish the summer villas of the rich; they are within the reach of all, and have generally been discarded, but then they were an exciting innovation. When the Gardners occupied a larger house and 'The Alhambra' was rented, Mrs. Gardner stipulated that the tenant maintain the tradition of the garden.

The most important friendship in the history of Fenway Court, if not in the story of Mrs. Gardner, began at this period — her friendship with Bernhard Berenson. She made his acquaintance while he was a student at Harvard — he graduated in 1887 — and to his solemn academic well-wishers it seemed unfortunate that such a brilliant young fellow who had his way to make should waste so much time in Mrs. Gardner's sparkling, frivolous circle. But her friendship was always practical; after his graduation she helped to make it possible for him to go to Europe to see life, widen his horizon, and gather material for the literary work to which he expected to devote his evident abilities. He was soon absorbed in the study of old masters and the correction of attributions; early in the nineties he had become a confident expert, and after 1894 was Mrs. Gardner's constant adviser. Although his affiliations with art dealers affected his reputation to some extent, Mrs. Gardner's allegiance never wavered. As a mark of her appreciation for him and for his wife, she gave Mrs. Berenson one of her most precious rubies.

Her developing interest in works of art did not lessen her interest in music; she was constantly adding to her enthusiasms, never subtracting, and she had extraordinary facility in 'focussing and unfocussing' her mind, or shutting up one compartment and opening another. At her house, on January 19, 1888, the Manuscript Club gave its first concert. The Club had been organized to secure for local composers an intelligent and sympathetic hearing of their compositions. The first programme was as follows:

EPISODES

Sonata Dramatico in D minor, op. 25,
for Violin and Piano.....................Clara Kathleen Rogers
The Composer and Mr. Loeffler

a. 'Were I a Prince Egyptian'
b. 'No Lotus on Ganges Floating' } .... Clayton Johns
c. 'Deep in a Rose's Glowing Heart'
Mr. William Winch, accompanied by the Composer

'Come to Me in My Dreams' .... Owen Wister
Mr. William Winch, accompanied by the Composer

Petite Suite for Piano and Violin (unfinished)...........Clayton Johns
Berceuse — Intermezzo — Romanze — Scherzino.
The Composer and Mr. Loeffler

'O, Römerin'
'Ghosts'
'Lebe Wohl' } .... Margaret Ruthven Lang
'Songs in the Twilight'
'Der Sommer'
Mr. William Winch, accompanied by Mr. B. J. Lang

Suite in E major, op. 12............................... Arthur Foote
Allegro comodo — Andante con moto — Gavotte — Allegro deciso.

On Mrs. Gardner's programme are the autographs of all the composers. This was her way of humanizing records and of giving her friends the pleasure of knowing that she believed their achievements would one day make them famous. The following year, on February 28th, the Club gave another concert at 152 Beacon Street, with this programme:

Prelude and Fugue in G minor........................Edwin A. Jones
The Kneisel Quartette

a. 'When the Earliest Roses Come'
b. 'Why When, My Love, I Pass with You' } .... Clayton Johns
c. 'Happy Brook, Why on Thy Way'
Mr. George F. Parker, accompanied by the Composer

[113]

ISABELLA STEWART GARDNER

Sonata in D major, for Pianoforte and Violin............J. Phippen
Allegro piacevole — Largo — Scherzo allegro — Allegro moderato.
Mr. Franz Kneisel and the Composer

a. 'Oh, What Comes Over the Sea' ⎫
b. 'Ojalà!'   ⎬ ....Margaret Ruthven Lang
c. 'To Night'   ⎭
Mr. George F. Parker, accompanied by the Composer

Romanze in E minor, Op. 35, for 'Cello and Piano-forte..E. A. MacDowell
Mr. Fritz Giese and the Composer

a. 'Menie,' Op. 34, 1,   ⎫
b. 'My Jean,' Op. 34, 11, ⎬ ....E. A. MacDowell
Mr. George F. Parker, accompanied by the Composer

Quartette in F major.............................H. W. Parker
Allegro moderato — Andante lento — Scherzo — Allegro molto.
The Kneisel Quartette

Again Mrs. Gardner secured the autograph of each composer with the opening bars of one of his compositions. A few other concerts were given in other places, but unfortunately the Club had only a brief existence.

In November, 1888, Mrs. Gardner gave an entertainment surpassing anything previously given in Boston. The invitation said 'Music.' The programme which follows, copied from Mr. Gericke's manuscript, was given by the Symphony Orchestra directed by him:

> Mozart. Haffner Serenade
> Allegro, Andante, Menuett.
> Bach. Pastorale (from Christmas Oratorio).
> Berlioz. Danse des Sylphes
> (from Damnation of Faust).
> Schubert. Balletmusik (Rosamunde).
> Wagner. Siegfried Idylle.
> Mendelssohn. Scherzo.
> Brahms. Hungarian Dances.
> Herbeck. Tanz momente.

EPISODES

This ended the outward hostility of society to Mrs. Gardner; thereafter it seemed unwise to decline her invitations — it was impossible to foresee what one might be missing.

On March 20, 1889, Mr. Gericke sent her the programme he proposed for 'the next court-concert at Beacon Street.' He said the rehearsal would take place on the 25th at ten o'clock and he hoped it would not be too early for her or too noisy for Mr. Gardner. The programme, as he wrote it, was:

BEETHOVEN — 3 Movements from the Symphonie N^{ro} 8
    Allegro vivace e con brio.
    Allegretto scherzando.
    Allegro vivace.
GLUCK. Reigen sel'ger Geister, from Orpheus.
GERICKE. Romanza (composed 1866)
               (Arranged for Orchestra by request)
BERLIOZ. 'Queen Mab' from the Symphonie 'Romeo and Juliet.'
WAGNER. Introduction and Selection from the 3d Act Meistersinger.
BRAHMS. Waltzes (arranged for the Orchestra).

Mr. Robert C. Winthrop called the musicale a 'most brilliant and delightful entertainment, surpassing even that of last year, and altogether unique.' Gericke gave Mrs. Gardner the autograph manuscript of the score of the Brahms Waltzes on which he wrote 'Orchestrated by request for a privat concert in Beacon Street 152 (by Wilhelm Gericke). To Mrs. Gardner in kind remembrance of the privat Concert in March, 1889.' He also gave her the score of his 'Romanza for Violin and Piano Accompaniment,' orchestrated for this concert. At the end of that season, Mr. Gericke gave up the leadership of the Orchestra; the only one of his successors who satisfied Mrs. Gardner was Dr. Karl Muck, but, before his advent, Mr. Gericke had served a second term, from 1898 to 1906.

One of the most interesting Americans living in Venice at this time was Mrs. Arthur Bronson (Katherine de Kay). She had a genius for friendship and it was said that a letter of introduction to her was more useful than one to an ambassador. To her Browning dedicated his last book of poems 'Asolando,' which appeared on the day of his death. Mrs. Gardner asked her to get for her, if she could, an 'autograph' of the poet, and in November, 1889, she enclosed in a letter, which begins 'My dear Charmer,' Pippa's song, 'The Year's at the Spring,' written out by Browning.

December 14th, Mrs. Bronson wrote: 'The autograph I sent you was the last he ever wrote.' The letter gives a detailed account of his last hours: 'He asked — "Have you news from my publisher?" — "Yes," they answered, "he says the first edition is already exhausted and we have the second in press." — "That is very gratifying," he said with a smile. After that he spoke to his son: — "Pen, my dear old boy — my dear Pen" — and those were his last words.' In January, 1890, Mrs. Bronson sent Mrs. Gardner a tiny lock of Browning's hair; she had cut it at Asolo, and, although he had urged her to take all she wanted, she was too nervous to take much because it occurred to her that he was thinking it was the last time any one would ask for his hair, and so it proved. The terms of Mrs. Gardner's letter of thanks were such as to satisfy Mrs. Bronson, who wrote February 8, 1890: 'I felt *sure* that you of all women would gladly possess so precious a relic — but I like to know it through your own words.' These few hairs are preserved at

EPISODES

Fenway Court in a moonstone locket, which rests on Pippa's verses.

During the spring of 1890, Carmencita was New York's chief diversion. She had come over with Kiralfy in the summer of 1889, but her first appearances had little success; a tour through Western cities had been no better. When she returned to New York, however, where she danced at Koster & Bial's in Twenty-Third Street, she created a sensation; nearly every night she was engaged for a private soirée after the theatre. As Sargent was painting the dancer's portrait, Mrs. Gardner asked him to arrange for a performance in the studio. The following letters from Mr. Sargent give the details of the arrangements:

MY DEAR MRS. GARDNER,

You are up to the mark as is your wont! Only day before yesterday I was sending you a message through Dixey to tell you that by hook or by crook, here or in Boston, you *must* see the Carmencita. I will be delighted to make the arrangements for you and there will be no difficulty excepting the place. I should have asked you to come and see her in my studio long before this if there were any means of lighting it at night and if the floor were tolerable, but it is not. Could you have her at your house in Fifth Avenue? If so, might I go and see whether the floor or carpet would be good, and whether there is a chandelier against which she would have to break her head. It would have to be about twelve o'clock at night after her performance.

Just a line to say whether it can be at your house or whether you had rather it were somewhere else.

Yours sincerely

JOHN S. SARGENT

Wednesday

MY DEAR MRS. GARDNER,

It is all right for Tuesday April 1st (eleven-thirty or twelve o'clock at night) at Chase's studio 10th Street, a capital big place. I will contribute wine and supper, and the Carmencita with two guitars will cost you $120, which is her price en ville.

May Chase and I ask a few people? Chase says he only cares to invite two or three, and I dare say you and I would think of the same people, the

[117]

Chapmans, Miss Dunham, Miss Lockwood — I should like besides to ask Mrs. Derby, Mrs. Cleveland, the Laffans, Millets, Mansons, Wister.

Please let me know about how many people you think of asking, from the point of view of sandwiches.

There was no having it in my studio, the gas man could not arrange any more light.

Yours sincerely
JOHN S. SARGENT

DEAR MRS. GARDNER,

I accept with pleasure for Delmonico's and have forwarded your notes. I will ask *very few people* and must keep extremely dark about it, as hundreds would want to come. You must come to the Studio on Tuesday at any time, and see the figure I am doing of the bewilderingly superb creature.

In haste.

Yours sincerely
JOHN S. SARGENT

The success of the party may be imagined.

A month later, on May 3d, the Gardners sailed for England. It was the year of the Passion Play; in addition to seeing that, there were many special purposes to be accomplished, but not too many to interfere with a good time. They landed in Liverpool, and after three days in London went on to Paris, but in a fortnight they were back in London for the Derby. Mr. and Mrs. Gardner were members of a merry party that went down to the races on a coach, Mrs. Jack resplendent in fresh Paris frills, particularly a wide-brimmed, much-plumed hat. As they rode, it began to rain, and Mr. Gardner begged his wife to put up her umbrella to protect her expensive hat, which had never been worn before; he was lavish in his expenditures, but he was practical and hated waste. Mrs. Gardner flatly refused. 'Whoever heard,' she said, 'of any one's carrying an umbrella on the way to the Derby?' — and the brim drooped more and more and the feathers got wetter and wetter till the hat was a total loss. This, however, was more than offset by a characteristic contribution by Mrs. Gardner to the success of the party. Her attention was attracted by a field of grain, and she asked if any one could tell her what it was. 'Sainfoin.' — 'Sainfoin? Sainfoin? Where have I heard of Sainfoin? Isn't there a horse called Sainfoin entered for the race to-day? Put all your money on him. God can't have made me see Sainfoin for the first time to-day, without some reason.' Although Sainfoin was a horse with no reputation, it was impossible to resist Mrs. Gardner, and, after arriving at the course, each member of the party put a small bet on Sainfoin, getting heavy odds. It detracted a little from their interest in the race to feel that they were backing a sure loser, but they were roused by the sudden excitement of the rest of the crowd when it became evident that the favorite was beaten and that an unknown horse was winning. An exceedingly hilarious, though damp, party drove back to London to celebrate Sainfoin's victory by a dinner at Morel's in Piccadilly. At the Henley races, for which the Gardners took a house-boat, they were persuaded by a charming undergraduate to cheer for the Oxford boat, and Oxford won.

After returning to Paris, they went to Mont-Saint-Michel for a day, and made a little excursion through Belgium and Holland to study the works of the Dutch and Flemish painters. Then on to Munich and Oberammergau. The Passion Play was to her significant and impressive, but she could stay in the little town only twenty-four hours, as she was chaperoning two young girls, sisters, who had been left behind in Munich, as one of them was ill — but not ill enough to prevent Mrs. Gardner's carrying out her own purpose. From Munich they went directly to Verona, where Mrs. Gardner gave an exhibition of her indefatigable energy as a sight-seer. In part of a day they visited all the important churches, the Amphitheatre, the Giusti Garden, Juliet's tomb, and came away with photographs of them all — the Mantegnas in San Zeno having made the deepest impression. Except for a swift excursion to Siena to see the Palio, the month of August was spent in Venice at the Palazzo Barbaro. The friend who made the arrangements for Mrs. Gardner's stay in Siena wrote afterward: 'Dear little Mary Chigi was strongly impressed with your walk and pretty little feet and *carina* way you held your gown when she saw you in the Duomo that Sunday morning.' Another friend who had travelled with Mrs. Gardner said that her daintily shod little feet and coyly displayed ankles must have fluttered many an old sacristan.

Early in October they sailed for home.

It was on the following Easter, March 29, 1891, that the reredos which Mrs. Gardner gave to the Church of the Advent was first seen by the public.

In June, she gave a trophy cup to be competed for by the Lowell Cricket Club and the cricketers of the Boston Athletic Association. The secretary in his note of thanks said he hoped the cup would grace the trophy case of the B.A.A. and that Mrs. Gardner would continue to grace their matches with her presence. She shared the belief of others that she was a mascot. When the Red Sox of Boston played the Giants of New York in the World's Championship Series of 1912, she happened to invite a very unintelligent friend to the opening game; as it was won by the local team, she insisted that the same friend must go with her to every game, in order not to change the luck. The Red Sox won the series.

On July 17th, Mrs. Gardner's father died, and she inherited about $2,750,000; it would be called a small fortune to-day, but it proved to be enough for her.

That autumn one of the prettiest compliments was paid her that she ever received: — Mr. Guy Waring, a classmate of the younger Joseph Gardner, named the highest peak in the vicinity of Winthrop, Okanogan County, Washington, Mount Gardner, and a beautiful range of mountains extending generally north-northwest of Winthrop he named the 'Isabella Range.' The name 'Mount Gardner' has been officially recognized, but the 'Isabellas' have never been officially surveyed and the name, even locally, is used only by a few.

Mr. Waring's tribute may have prompted the similar, but very different, tribute paid Mrs. Gardner the following year by Dr. William Sturgis Bigelow. Early in March he wrote:

Now I come to a very delicate matter to communicate — so much so that I hardly know how to approach it — I have taken a great step — a great liberty — there is a lady involved — you are directly concerned — I tried to act for the best — the fact is she was *so* beautiful and *so* intelligent and had *such* grey eyes and *such* perfect ears and *such* a disposition that I have ventured to christen her Mrs. John L. Gardner and to call her Belle for short, as I could not really use the whole name and then whistle.

She is a Chesapeake puppy.

Mugs are in order.

Yours sincerely

W. S. B.

P. S. She is *very* attractive.

In August, Mrs. Gardner received the following announcement:

MMES. Rose et Minnie, et MM. Grover Cleveland, Rough, et Marengo II (dit Ring) ont l'honneur de vous faire part de la perte douloureuse qu'ils viennent de subir dans la mort de

Mrs. John L. Gardner II
(dite La Belle)

leur sœur, belle-sœur, nièce, cousine, et fiancée, décedée à la suite d'une convulsion de dentition, dans le 5me mois de son age, le 14me Aout, 1893.

Priez pour elle!

In January, 1892, a friend in Paris wrote: 'I have just received a clipping from a newspaper describing you, your charms, your court, your adorers, and it is with awe that I take up the pen to write to such a person. You certainly deserve this praise and Boston owes you a debt of gratitude for living. Please do not die or move to some other place.'

The advent of Paderewski was the sensation of that season. Not only did Mrs. Gardner engage him to play for her friends, but she first engaged him to play for herself alone. His programme as written in pencil on a sheet of note-paper, was:

Sonata appassionata . . . . BEETHOVEN

Deux romances sans paroles:
    en Fa majeur, en la maj. . . . . MENDELSSOHN

Fantaisie, op. 17 . . . . SCHUMANN

Chant du voyageur
Nocturne . . . . I. J. PADEREWSKI
Thème varié

Impromptu Fa♯
Sonata Si bemol . . . . CHOPIN

EPISODES

She was the only auditor in the room, but at least one musical friend — perhaps two or three — was secreted 'behind the arras.' Finally, Mrs. Gardner engaged Paderewski to give a concert in Bumstead Hall in the old Music Hall building, and sent all the tickets to the musicians of Boston. Paderewski himself gave a recital at the New England Conservatory of Music at which he was host to the Conservatory students; in return for this courtesy, the Conservatory invited him to a recital given by the students at which the programme consisted entirely of his compositions. At this concert, young Mr. Proctor, in whom Mrs. Gardner had never lost interest since Mr. Johns first brought him to her house, played the first movement of Paderewski's Concerto in A minor, which the composer himself had introduced to Boston at a Symphony Concert. Mrs. Gardner asked Paderewski's opinion of the young man's ability and, acting on his advice, decided to make it possible for him to go to Vienna to study under Leschetizky. In the autumn he went forth with a letter of introduction from Paderewski.

When Jean and Edouard de Reszke, who had just joined the New York Opera Company, came to Boston, they were persuaded by Mrs. Gardner to break their rule not to sing at private musicales. She particularly enjoyed the company of Jean, with whom she studied the scores of Wagner's Ring. He often stayed for luncheon, but always on condition that there should be apple pie. Writing up a performance at which the de Reszkes sang, a newspaper man, after speaking with pleasure of the fact that only a few of the ladies in the audience wore hats, said:

ISABELLA STEWART GARDNER

Had the hatted women only known what Mrs. J. L. Gardner was going to wear, they would doubtless have gone and done likewise and so have won the everlasting gratitude of the multitude back of them. That ever ingenious and original lady dressed her hair close to the back of her head, then swathing her face in an exquisite white veil of finest mesh, with edge of black and white lace, brought it up and tied it in wing-like effect. Long pins with turquoise heads were thrust through the wings giving them form. It was a simple and most becoming head-dress, and it is devoutly wished that the women of the country will follow suit. The green turquoise in the veil ornaments was matched in the Frenchy bodice of greenish and silver glace silk which fitted her like the immaculate white gloves which were partially hidden by the long sleeves. Her skirt was black.

CHAPTER VIII
THE TURNING-POINT

TILL now Mrs. Gardner's life had been a series of miscellaneous adventures, all of them amusing to herself, many of them entertaining to her friends. No experience had been profitless; her naturally quick perceptions had been quickened, she had acquired a perfectly clear understanding of the qualities she valued in people and things, and her decisions to like or dislike, to possess or reject, were instantaneous — and rarely altered. Her ability to recognize essential beauty amounted to genius. Provided with the funds received from her father's estate, Mrs. Gardner now settled down definitely to the business of collecting works of art. The idea that her collection would be important enough to be considered a museum was not yet born, but she had found the absorbing purpose for which she had been groping the past twenty-five years. In the next eight years her collection had attained a size and distinction to justify building Fenway Court; before the end of 1896, she and Mr. Gardner knew that the Beacon Street house was no longer adequate.

On April 2, 1892, Mr. and Mrs. Gardner sailed for Europe. The day she sailed, Mr. Ralph W. Curtis, acting as her agent, bought for her at the sale of the Borghese collection seven gilded and painted arm-chairs [1] which it was claimed had been presented by the Doge of Venice to Pope Paul V (1605–21). They were sent to Venice to await her arrival. In Paris Mrs. Gardner met the painter Albert Besnard and purchased from

[1] These chairs are XVIII century.

him a pastel portrait of a woman. She also purchased her first piece of Gothic carving, a panel representing Saint George, and her first fine tapestry, described as a 'Tapisserie gothique du XVe siècle'; it hangs beside the Sargent portrait of her in the Gothic Room at Fenway Court.

In the middle of May, they went over to London, attracted by the approaching sale of the F. R. Leyland collection. Mrs. Gardner bought two pictures, 'Love's Greeting,' by Rossetti, the only Pre-Raphaelite painting in her collection, and a Madonna and Child at that time attributed to Filippo Lippi, but now given by Hendy to Pesellino. In connection with this purchase, Mrs. Gardner studied the paintings by Lippi in the National Gallery, and purchased photographs of them, not with any intention of arrogantly assuming to be able to prove the authorship of her intended acquisition, but to create a mental background for it. That the attribution to Lippi was afterward discredited did not disturb her; the picture still possessed the quality for which she chose it. She professed not to value most expert opinion — she certainly had no use for pedantry; but she was in her own way a student, very well-read and very well-informed.

While she was in London she arranged for the purchase of the ruby that became her favorite jewel. She used to say that, having received a legacy from her brother, she wished to put the money into some one thing which should be a souvenir of him, and she decided upon a ruby. Her procedure in this matter, as she narrated it, was not at all in accordance with her usual methods and not at all what would be expected from such a shrewd buyer. She went to Tiffany's and asked to see what rubies they had for the price she wished to pay; she expected a tray of them would be produced for her to make a selection — instead she was told they had none. When she got to Paris, she went to Boucheron, from whom she had bought most of her pearls, and asked him to show her such a ruby as she wanted; to her astonishment, he had none. While she was in London, word was brought to her at her hotel that three gentlemen had come to see her. They turned out to be M. Boucheron, the representative of an Indian Prince who had sent a ruby to London to be sold, and a representative of the Bank of England where the ruby was kept. With much formality the gem was produced, Mrs. Gardner examined it, and then with equal formality it was wrapped up, sealed, and the three men departed. The price was more than the amount of the legacy. On May 21, 1892, M. Boucheron wrote:

I am returning to-day to Paris. I have made the day before yesterday, the offer of —— for the ruby. But the negociations will require some days, as it is necessary to wire to Calcutta and from there to the interior of India. I do not expect one answer before Wednesday or Thursday of the next week, when I shall be back in London to see you.

A week later Boucheron wrote again:

I am sorry to say that as far as the present hour 3 o.c. P.M. I have had no answer for the Ruby. The Banker says that if there is no answer on Monday after 3 o.c. I must consider the offer as refused. But I hope to see you in Paris, and give better news.

The next day the Gardners left London and did not hear again from Boucheron till after they reached Venice. There they received word that, after many long negotiations, Mrs. Gardner's offer had been accepted. Boucheron added: 'This magnificent ruby is one of the finest I have ever seen, and I do not think there is a better one.' Later in the year she purchased her last string of pearls.

Except for a week at Baireuth and a month in Paris, the summer and autumn were spent in Venice. They occupied the Palazzo Barbaro, where Mrs. Gardner soon had 'her court established.' In July, Henry James and Joseph Lindon Smith were her guests. Mr. James was at work on a novel; Mr. Smith, a young painter with an enchanting personality, had come to Venice with his parents and his brother, and was painting Saint Theodore on top of his column. Alfred Q. Collins, 'robust but restrained,' as James described him, and his wife were also guests. Writing to Theodore F. Dwight on July 5th, Mr. Gardner said:

> Mrs. Gardner celebrated the glorious fourth with a surprise. After dinner we all went over to the garden and were enjoying the moonlight from the second story when Guillermo and his music boat arrived and gave us a delightful serenade. We all five then got into the gondola and floated along the outside, the music accompanying us and the moon sinking into the lagoon, when just before the moon disappeared we got to San Giorgio and they bid us good-night. It was nearly one o'clock when we got home and of course I growled about keeping the servants working all day and all night. Still it was a success. I wish you could have been there. I believe Tirindelli is coming to fiddle this evening.

It was characteristic of Mr. Gardner to think of the other fellow, to realize how his own pleasure might be another's pain. Mrs. Gardner, on the contrary, might have joined the gouty gentleman in the musical comedy who sang 'I want what I want when I want it' — and nobody's inconvenience mattered. This did not prevent her being, when circumstances were propitious, exceedingly kind and considerate. Mr. Gardner was so clear-sighted, so practical and honest, that he often could not refrain from exasperating his wife by speaking the simple true word that brought to earth her soaring imagination, reducing to prose her poetic romancing.

On August 2d, Mr. T. Jefferson Coolidge, who had recently been appointed United States Ambassador to France, wrote to Mrs. Gardner from Paris:

I received your charming note from Palazzo Barbaro and notice that you have got a new fad — a certain Mr. Tirindelli. Amuse yourself, squeeze him and throw him overboard, when you like, provided you don't forget your old loves. . . . The Foreign Minister has gone out of town and I almost wish you were where I could run down for a vacation of ten days. In reading the life of the Duke de Nivernais I came across some verses of his to Madame de Rochefort, and they apply so well to a certain lady of my acquaintance that I can't help sending them to her. Try to translate them into English

> Elle a plus d'esprit toute seule
> Que n'en ont tous les beaux esprits,
> Et ne fait jamais la béguele
> Comme on fait souvent à Paris.
> > Indulgente,
> > Complaisante,
> Elle sait pardonner aux sots;
> > Sans malice,
> > Sans caprice,
> Elle anime tous les propos.
>
> .   .   .   .
>
> Je voudrais sans cesse autour d'elle
> Voir les femmes se rassembler,
> Et la prendre pour leur modèle
> Dans l'espoir de lui ressembler. . . .
> > Sage école
> > Où la folle
> Perdrait son air éventé,
> > Douce étude
> > Où la prude
> Perdrait son air affecté. . . .
>
> > C'est sans peine
> > Et sans gêne
> Qu'elle charme à tout moment.

Every day and every evening were full; with Tirindelli, Amherst Webber, and many others to make music; with James for escort on a 'little evening journey, so romantic, so Italian,' to see Mrs. Bronson at Asolo; with 'Zozo' Smith to make sketches of the Redentore fireworks and drawings of himself and his fellow guests; with Don Carlos for intriguing, exiled royalty; and with Ludwig Passini painting portraits of both Mr. and Mrs. Gardner. Although she liked the painter, these portraits never gave her pleasure.

While Tirindelli's opera 'Atenaïde' was being prepared for its first production, Mrs. Gardner went regularly to the rehearsals, 'the only listener in the dark, dingy theatre'; besides supporting the composer with her sympathetic interest, she tried to secure for him the best possible press endorsement, and asked William James Stillman, who was then in Rome, to assist at the première and report it to his paper, the London 'Times.' As political events prevented his leaving Rome, Mrs. Gardner telegraphed him an account of the performance. Acknowledging it, he wrote:

Please accept my best thanks (I have but one quality, however) for your kindness in telegraphing me the opera report. I hope the telegraphic receipt is on its way to me, but if you have not thought to take one, that you will let me know the cost of the telegram — besides which (if the telegram is not crowded out in our always overflowing Monday's paper) I shall have the sum of 10/s to transmit you for the honorarium — don't laugh, but it is not everybody who earns 10/s out of the Times, and if you like I will send it in a half sovereign which you might make a breloque of.

In due time the half sovereign was received, and found its place, with similar souvenirs, on Mrs. Gardner's 'chain of thought.' It was the only money she ever earned.

Tirindelli had been professor of violin at the Liceo Benedetto Marcello since 1884; in 1894, he was appointed director; he made his American début with the Boston Symphony Orchestra December 16, 1895, and the following year joined the faculty of the Conservatory at Cincinnati. His was one of the many careers Mrs. Gardner assisted, and among her manuscripts are twenty-four of his songs.

The Borghese chairs had been sent to the shop of Antonio Carrer to be repaired; when Mrs. Gardner went to see them, she found a picture which interested her — an Adam and Eve, by Cranach. It was owned by a friend of Prince Fritz Hohenlohe, but the unhappy man was so poor that Mrs. Gardner said it was years since he had been to the Piazza for his evening coffee. That the rich Americans had admired his picture was enough to raise his hopes of temporary alleviation of his distress and to start him pulling what wires he could. He got the Prince to write to Mrs. Bronson begging her to use her influence to persuade her friends to buy the picture, assuring her that authorities in matters of art considered it 'one of the best of that rare maestro,' adding that as the owner is 'presently very hard up' the asking price would probably eventually be reduced. Mrs. Bronson admitted that she considered the picture a treasure — 'the nude can be and so often is repulsive, but that enchanting Eve is a model for modern painters, the thing of beauty which is a joy forever.' For a month the destitute owner was tantalized by uncertainty, but after the price had been reduced a third, Mrs. Gardner took it.

After Fenway Court was completed, the Thursday Evening Club was invited by Mrs. Gardner to meet there on the 19th of February, 1903. At this meeting, William Everett read a poem entitled 'Man and Monarch,' the greater part of which is a dialogue between the Adam created by Cranach and Charles I as portrayed on a white charger by Van Dyck. Aware that he is the father of all men, Adam resents the contemptuous look of the King, who in turn refuses to admit that Stewarts can have any kinship with one so uncouth as Adam; but Adam insists that the royal flesh is but clay, clay like his own, no more, no less divine, and 'the gardener' chides the King for treating common men like beasts and thinking they would bend like slaves to kingly grace.

> They ceased — the monarch and the man —
> Nature's hot force; art's crafty plan.
> On the dark Stewart's forehead still
> Throbbed the full veins of lordly will,
> Assured that o'er the ignoble throng
> To higher souls should power belong.
> And still on Adam's ruder mien
> The blood of all mankind was seen,
> To claim the share of breath divine
> Instinct in all of Eden's line.
> Who shall the endless strife appease?
> Nature and art who set at ease?
> How shall the kings of mind bear sway
> O'er men as truly kings as they,
> And art her deep-wrought craft reveal
> For soul of simplest man to feel?
> Here only, where a royal heart
> Flings wide for all the doors of art.
> Adam and Charles are dead and gone —
> Stewart and Gardner reign in one.

A portrait of a young man, then identified as the Duke of Monmouth, by Suttermans, was also purchased in Venice in 1892. Mrs. Gardner had told the dealer in September that she would take it, but would not pay for it till she returned from

Paris in November. While she was away, the Empress Frederick saw the picture and coveted it, but the dealer held to his bargain with Mrs. Gardner. Many messages were sent to ask her if she would part with the picture, and after her return to Boston she received a letter from Mr. Ralph Curtis saying he had heard that the Empress wanted the picture because it was a family portrait! Mrs. Gardner answered that on that very ground it more properly belonged to her, for she and Monmouth were both Stewarts uncontaminated by German blood. Two years later, she sent word from Vienna to her friend Passini the painter that she was coming to Berlin and that she hoped she could hear Joachim's quartette. Passini replied that it was great luck to have her come, although he did not believe the city would please her, the weather was so dull and the streets so monotonous. Still, there would be sights enough to fill three days, and perhaps she would like to go to the opera — 'the auditorium is not too ugly, but the performances leave much to be desired.' He was not sure when the next Joachim quartette concert came, but thought it was on Saturday, November 24th. The concert that Mrs. Gardner attended was on the 29th; after it Passini gave a dinner and Joachim presented her with an autographed photograph. When she arrived in Berlin, Passini met her at the station and told her the Empress had sent word that she had heard he was giving a dinner for Mrs. Gardner of Boston, and wished particularly that he would invite her friend Count Seckendorf. Mrs. Gardner at once understood. After dinner the Count asked her if any of the pictures she had bought were still in Europe. 'Oh, yes,' she said, and mentioned several she had recently acquired. At length he was forced to say that the one he was interested in was a portrait of the Duke of Monmouth. Then Mrs. Gardner answered: 'But I bought that two years ago, and as I am an American, all my pictures are naturally in America.' 'Is there no chance that any of them will ever be brought back to Europe again?' he asked. 'None whatever.' And the Count said 'Good-night.'

To continue with the year 1892, Mr. and Mrs. Gardner returned to Paris December 3d, just in time for the sale, at the Hôtel Drouot on the 5th, of the Vermeers in the Thoré-Bürger collection. On the 4th, Mrs. Gardner went with Mr. Ralph Curtis to the exposition of the collection, and chose for herself Number 31, 'Le Concert.' Telling Mr. Curtis that they must not arouse the interest of others by looking at it too long themselves, she left the gallery and went to place her order with her agent, M. Fernand Robert. Robert asked how high he might bid; as Mrs. Gardner was unwilling to set a limit, she told him to get her a reserved seat for the sale, and to keep bidding as long as she held her handkerchief to her face. The next day she went to a luncheon which lasted rather long — but no one imagined she had any important business on her mind — and when she arrived at the Hôtel Drouot, Number 31 was one of the three pictures on the auctioneer's platform; it was not actually being sold, but was to be sold next. Mrs. Gardner took her seat, not seeing Robert, but trusting he could see her, and when the bidding on Number 31 started, she took out her handkerchief and held it to her face. As soon as she heard Robert's first bid, she knew her plan was working successfully. The bidding went to twenty-five thousand francs, the last thousands coming a little slowly; then, following Mrs. Gardner's instructions,

Robert bid twenty-nine thousand — and got the picture. She said she was told afterward that both the Louvre and the National Gallery wanted it, but thought it was not etiquette to continue bidding against each other; each imagined the other had secured the picture and was dismayed to find it had gone to an outsider. A few years later, Mr. Curtis wrote from The Hague: 'He [Hofstede de Groot] says your Concert (which cost thirty-three thousand francs) is now worth *easily* between one hundred and fifty and two hundred thousand! Tell G——HE can't make investments like that in State Street!'

At Whistler's studio — he was then living in Paris — Mrs. Gardner saw a picture upon which she set her heart — 'Harmony in Blue and Silver: Courbet on the Beach at Trouville.' Whistler agreed that she should have it, but characteristically could not bear to part with it. As Mrs. Gardner herself could not take it away, she asked Will Rothenstein, the painter, to go with her to the studio, making him promise at her command to carry off the picture. They had a delightful visit, admired everything, and, when they came to this particular 'Harmony,' Mrs. Gardner said: 'This is my picture; you've told me many times that I might have it, Mr. Whistler, and now I'm going to take it. Mr. Rothenstein, please take this picture down to the carriage.' Off Mr. Rothenstein started, down the steep stairs, followed by Mrs. Gardner keeping Whistler safely in the rear; he protested all the way down that the picture wasn't finished, he hadn't signed it. Mrs. Gardner invited him to come to her hotel to luncheon, come as often as possible — every day if he would — and sign the picture there. Whistler did turn up the next day, and begged to take the picture back to the studio, but

Mrs. Gardner was firm, and eventually a butterfly fluttered behind Courbet's back. At one of her last parties before leaving Paris the guests were Mr. and Mrs. Whistler, John S. Sargent, Etta Reubell, Ethel B. Philip, and Howard G. Cushing.

CHAPTER IX

FRIENDSHIPS

THE year 1893 was marked by the beginnings of two notable friendships, with Mr. and Mrs. Anders Zorn and with Monsieur and Madame Paul Bourget. At the World's Columbian Exposition in Chicago, Mrs. Gardner's picture of Saint Denis Cathedral, by Paul Helleu, was hung in the loan collection of the United States section of the Department of Fine Arts, and she and Mr. Gardner accepted the invitation of the managers to visit the Exposition before it was opened to the public. While she was walking through the galleries of paintings, her eye was arrested by a very skilful portrayal of a group of people in an omnibus; finding a solitary man in a gallery near by, she asked him if he could tell her anything about a painting of an omnibus, which was signed, as nearly as she could make out, 'Zorn.' He replied that he could tell her all about it, because he was the man who painted it. It took only a few minutes for each to discover the distinction of the other, and before they parted, not only had Mrs. Gardner purchased the picture, but the foundations of an enduring friendship had been laid. No one ever surpassed her in the quality of her friendship; besides never failing to say the pleasant word of deserved appreciation, she never failed to do the practical, helpful, kindly, gracious things that proved the genuineness of her ardent affection. Invariably her acts spoke louder than her words. Zorn was unknown in the United States, but with customary energy Mrs. Gardner undertook to make her new friend a success. At her suggestion, the Museum of Fine Arts in Boston held an exhibition of his work, including a number of paintings that had been shown in Chicago, three members of the Gardner family ordered portraits, and Mrs. Gardner herself sat for an etching.

When the Zorns sailed for Europe in February, 1894, the etching had not been delivered; it was so completely unsuccessful that Mrs. Gardner meant to retain the whole edition. Zorn sent her forty-five proofs and kept six; when she learned some time later that a proof had been offered for sale, she wrote to him in great displeasure. He replied that he was equally displeased and that 'none of those prints have been offered for sale, only, as far as my memory goes, on some occasions been added to complete public collections.' Nevertheless, a very few copies did get into private collections.

In August, Paul Bourget and his wife arrived with letters of introduction from Henry James and Paul Deschanel. After a stormy passage, they went first to Newport; writing from there, August 26th, Bourget said, in his letter thanking her for an invitation to come to Beverly Farms: 'Mon cher Henry James m'avait trop dit votre grâce et votre bonté pour que je ne m'attendisse pas à un bien charmant accueil. Aussi vos lettres ne m'ont-elles pas surpris. Elles n'en ont été que davantage les bienvenues.' In his next letter he said he had a story to write for 'Scribner's' and if he should find the necessary quiet under her roof, it would be a pleasure. Friends brought the Bourgets up from Newport on a yacht and, according to the inevitable story, they regaled the strangers with tales of Mrs. Gardner's disastrous flirtations. Presently one of the party noticed Madame Bourget had disappeared; she was found in the cabin, weeping bitterly. She was but twenty-five, Bourget was forty-one, and they had been married only three years. She said that in Paris she had no fears for her husband, but she was overcome by the thought of what might happen when he encountered such a siren as Mrs. Jack. What did happen was that all three became devoted friends, and the visit to 'Beach Hill,' a larger house than 'The Alhambra,' but on the same estate, was exceedingly happy and delightful. Monsieur Thiébaut, who was then the French Consul at Boston, said that Mrs. Gardner's hospitality gave even her guests of a day the impression that they belonged to the family. As Bourget expressed a special desire to make the acquaintance of Oliver Wendell Holmes, who was then eighty-four years old, Mrs. Gardner gave a little luncheon September 10th; the only other guest was Mrs. Henry Whitman. The young man and the old man charmed each other. Dr. Holmes recited his own 'Last Leaf' and 'The Chambered Nautilus,' and wrote in Mrs. Gardner's guest-book, 'The public destroys the author as of old the monsters destroyed the virgins.' At Beach Hill the Bourgets read Richard Harding Davis's story 'Gallegher,' which, as the result of negotiations conducted with the author by Mrs. Gardner, Madame Bourget translated into French.

As contrast is one of the best means of deepening an impression, the Bourgets went from Beach Hill to Chicago, where they visited not only the Fair, but also the abattoirs, and went to see 'the perfect man,' Sandow, who supported three horses standing on a plank balanced on his chest. Mrs. Gardner scandalized Boston because, not content with being a spectator of Sandow's exploits, she actually felt of his muscles. In November the Bourgets again visited the Gardners, this time at 'Green Hill' in Brookline. There they had the pleasure of meeting Mrs. James T. Fields, Sarah Orne Jewett, Mr. and Mrs. Thomas Bailey Aldrich, Alexander Agassiz, Mr. and Mrs. Ernest Fenollosa, Mr. and Mrs. William James, and Edith Wharton. When Monsieur and Madame Bourget sailed for home the following April, he wrote:

Adieu, chère Madame et Amie, si je dois pas vous revoir sur cette terre des elevators, des fast trains, des hands up, des smash up, et des pet gators (C'est une inscription que j'ai vue en Floride sur un petit étang: Don't shoot: pet gators!) que ce soit prochainement dans l'autre pays, celui des diligences, des fiacres à l'heure, des gendarmes, des employés et des canons Krupp — avant que les dynamiteurs n'aient fait sauter ce qui reste de ce vieux monde vermoulu.

Among his souvenirs of the United States, Monsieur Bourget carried home a certain number of shares in the Chicago, Burlington & Quincy Railroad, one of the chief sources of the Gardner income. The following June (1894), when Mrs. Gardner arrived in Paris, it was not possible for Monsieur Bourget to be there, but to greet her he sent a charming letter with a copy of 'Cosmopolis,' 'spécialement tiré pour Madame John L. Gardner.' Thereafter he sent her a copy of each of his books as soon as published.

On Thanksgiving Day the Gardner family regularly dined with Mr. and Mrs. Jack at Green Hill. This dinner marked the close of the country season.

In January, 1894, Ferruccio Busoni and Charles Martin Loeffler were the artists at a musicale given by Mrs. Gardner; they played Sonatas by Fauré and Bach, and Busoni also played four compositions by Liszt. Busoni's charge was two hundred dollars. Again, on February 18th, Mrs. Gardner engaged Busoni to play. This was the thirty-fourth birthday of Anders Zorn, who was her guest, and the musicale was a birthday party. Zorn gave his hostess a tiny pencil drawing of Busoni at the piano, and a very interesting pen-and-ink sketch of Loeffler holding his violin. The programme as Busoni, confusing the activities of the saints, wrote it out was:

Beethoven Sonata Op. 106 (fuer das Hammerklavier) —
      Rondo Op. 129 (la rage pour un sou perdu) —
      Ecossaises.
Liszt — Legendes. (St. François de Paule la Predication aux oiseaux. St. François d'Assisi marchant sur les flots.)
Liszt–Beethoven — Ruines d'Athènes.

Mrs. Julia Ward Howe, who was present, thought Busoni pounded frightfully. Although the pianist was already famous, his funds were low; in October, he asked Mrs. Gardner to lend him a thousand dollars; she sent it immediately. In 1896, he wrote that he was dedicating to her a 'petit morceau de piano.' Not many years later he owned a beautiful house in Berlin, with a fine library of rare books, first editions and fine bindings.

After Zorn's return to Paris, he wrote to Mrs. Gardner that he hoped he might soon see her and Mr. Gardner there, and told her Grieg was giving concerts with success; 'I mention this,' he writes, 'because I know the key to your heart is music.' A month later, he wrote: 'Your letters make me love life.'

Much as Mrs. Gardner loved music, she loved fun even more; she and Julia Ward Howe were the leading spirits in a lunch club named 'It,' of which Mrs. Barrett Wendell, Margaret Deland, Sarah Orne Jewett, Mrs. J. Montgomery Sears, Mrs.

J. Templeman Coolidge, and Miss Martha Silsbee were also members. The ladies of Boston had definitely accepted Mrs. Gardner.

At the end of February, Mr. William C. Whitney, of New York, begged Mrs. Gardner to take an interest in a new singer, Madame Nellie Melba. He had such faith in Mrs. Gardner that he had asked her the previous year to recommend a bright, attractive young woman as a companion for his daughter, telling her she was one of the few persons whose judgment could be trusted in such a matter. Now, February 27th, after telling of Melba's success in New York in spite of the jealousy of another singer in the company, he wrote: 'She has been told the same thing by every one — "Mrs. Gardner" — "Mrs. Gardner" — "Mrs. Gardner." She is the one who takes talents by the hand and marshals them to the front — so they all say. Well, I have had my say, except to say that George Haven and I have made a point of helping Melba to demonstrate herself here, and we want you to be kind to her there — she is to be at The Vendome after Wednesday.'

On April 1st, the 'Boston Sunday Globe' printed what it claimed was the first photograph ever published of Mrs. Gardner, stating that the cut was a 'careful and successful reproduction of a snap-shot by The Globe's lightning photographer'; it was made as Mrs. Gardner was entering her carriage and would have added little to a stranger's knowledge of her appearance. About this time a newspaper gave the following account of her:

No woman in Boston has been so much discussed, both privately and publicly, as Mrs. John L. Gardner; indeed, here is a case of a woman's reputation having been made entirely by the papers. Mrs. Gardner is now always before the eyes of the public. All her movements are heralded in the press, and she is treated almost as England treats royalty. . . . Mrs. Gardner really does more for the entertainment of Boston society than anyone else, for she not only entertains her friends, but her vagaries entertain the world at large. Few women in Boston have done so much for young men as has Mrs. Gardner; to know her, indeed, is a liberal education. Mr. F. Marion Crawford developed into a novelist under her eye, and the lamented Dennis Bunker gave evidence of real talent while he was acting as Mrs. Gardner's escort.

How well she entertained her friends, Dr. William Sturgis Bigelow bears witness in the following letter.

60 BEACON STREET

MY DEAR MRS. GARDNER

I am thinking of having a little medal made for you, as the 'Champion All-Round Samaritan.' As a gloom-dispeller, corpse-reviver, and general chirker-up, you are as unrivalled in the fragrance of your flowers as in the sunshine of your presence.

I am very grateful for both, even to that form of gratitude which is called a lively expectation of favors to be received — that is to say, I wish you would stop in again when you have a minute to spare, and exhilarate me some more. I did not have to take any champagne the last day you came.

With many thanks, and some hopes

Very sincerely

W. S. B.

This exhilarating visit may have been the conclusion of one of those little vagaries which exasperated the victims and entertained the rest of the community. There had been a heavy snowfall, and the snow from the sidewalks was piled in a high bank along the curb; Mrs. Gardner had been to the Friday afternoon concert of the Symphony Orchestra; something had annoyed her; to recover her composure, some self-indulgence which should prove her above the law was needed; she decided to pay a visit to Dr. Bigelow; the coachman, driving a booby-sleigh, stopped in front of the door, but between Mrs. Gardner

[143]

and the sidewalk was a mountain of snow. 'It's impossible for me to get out here,' she said irritably, 'drive up on the sidewalk.' When her order had been carried out, and the sleigh had made a barricade completely blocking the passage of the hundreds of pedestrians who were taking the air after the storm, Mrs. Gardner descended in a perfectly happy frame of mind.

During the annual races at The Country Club in Brookline, Mrs. Gardner invited Mr. Harry K. Vingut to lunch. In an expansive moment he said: 'If ever you have a racing stable, let me take charge of it.' She replied: 'Don't speak too lightly, I may take you up.' Then and there they selected a motto for the 'stable' — 'Win as though you were used to it and lose as if you liked it' — and the racing colors would be green and yellow. June 9th, Mrs. Gardner paid Mr. Vingut thirty-six hundred dollars for Halton, and the horse, she said, justified all the frills by winning enough money to pay his expenses. Her interest in racing never waned; in 1923, for preservation in her memorabilia, she cut out of the newspapers the pictures of the first international race at Belmont Park, Long Island, in which Zev, ridden by Earl Sande, defeated Papyrus, winner of that year's Derby.

June 23d, Mr. and Mrs. Gardner sailed for Europe. As Mrs. Gardner was in poor health, they planned to be away nearly a year. The summer and autumn were devoted to recreation, with only an occasional indulgence in the exciting game of collecting; but treasures of one sort or another were constantly drifting in on the tides of friendship, either gifts or opportunities, and every one was accepted with due appreciation. With his note wishing her 'bon voyage and safe return,' Ethelbert

Nevin sent her the autograph score of his setting for 'Eternal Father! Strong to save.' No such gift was ever mislaid.

Having arrived in Paris just in time to witness the state funeral of President Carnot — whenever they went to Europe, some one's funeral provided a magnificent spectacle — they went almost immediately to London, where they spent the month of July. There Sargent wrote to ask if Mrs. Gardner would like 'to see or buy a magnificent Persian rug of the finest design and period, worth all the pictures ever painted? It belongs to a little Turk whose shop is too small to unroll it, and who is going to send it to my studio to show one of my sitters on Tuesday the 17th at five o'clock. He wants between three and four hundred pounds for it and it is worth the money. O that I were not so practical and full of forethought — I would buy it myself.' On the 23d, Sargent sent her the Turk's receipt for three hundred and fifty pounds, the price paid for a sixteenth-century Ispahan rug that has few equals. How many times that it is worth to-day! Sargent asked permission to use it in a picture; he tried it in the portrait he was painting of Ada Rehan, but found it would not do, for Miss Rehan 'became a mere understudy and the carpet played the principal part.' Finally in October he wrote: 'The picture of the carpet never came off. Whenever I put my model on it, she covered up something infinitely more beautiful than herself, so I gave it up and merely did a sort of map of the carpet for a pattern.'

The greater part of August was spent in taking a cure at Langen Schwalbach; from there Mr. and Mrs. Gardner went to Ischl, especially to see Mr. Proctor, who had come from Vienna for his summer holiday. His teacher, Leschetizky, who regularly went to Ischl for his vacation, and Mr. Johns were also there. A Boston friend, Mrs. Wirt Dexter, and her daughter, who had been with Mr. and Mrs. Gardner at Langen Schwalbach, had preceded them to Ischl, and as soon as the Gardners arrived Mrs. Dexter went to see her friend. She found Mrs. Gardner full of excitement over the presence of Brahms in the town, and anxious to know if Mrs. Dexter had seen him. It chanced that as she was walking on the 'plage' she had, and Mrs. Gardner said that somehow she must meet him. She was to be in Ischl only four days, and on the second, as Mrs. Dexter was taking her promenade, she saw Mrs. Gardner and Brahms having tea together like old friends. He gave her an autographed photograph, and Johann Strauss, who was also in Ischl, gave her a photograph of Brahms and himself on which he wrote his name and a few measures of 'The Blue Danube.'

September 5th, Mr. and Mrs. Gardner reached Venice. Joseph Lindon Smith and Tirindelli were both there; Johns and Proctor came the next day, and, following them, distinguished visitors, European and American, constantly turned up for longer or shorter stays at the Barbaro. Mr. Smith went with Mrs. Gardner to Asolo to see her friend Mrs. Bronson, and in her 'sweet little out-of-door room' made a water-color sketch of the two ladies. Soon after, he left Venice, and before the end of October was back in Boston. December 4th he wrote:

MY DEAR MRS. GARDNER:
Everybody misses you here in Boston, U.S.A. We all wish you were home, at 152, which looks so very deserted and unlike itself. . . .

My exhibition is now on at the Botolph, and many people go to it. . . .

A splendid Belgian violinist, Isaye, has been here, and he was pleased to go wild about my things and in his madness bought three pictures. . . .

FRIENDSHIPS

Things don't seem to happen here now as they do when you are here. Distinguished people come and go, and we sleep on forever. Day before yesterday, when this Belgian was here, and woke up Music Hall as it hasn't been waked for years, he was allowed to depart as quiet as you please. We know how different it would be if 152 had its mistress within its walls. . . .

Early in October, Zorn and his wife arrived; they were photographed so often in gondolas with Mr. and Mrs. Gardner that at first one would imagine all their time was spent on the water, but Zorn's artistic nature could not rest and Fenway Court is the richer for this Venetian visit. As the etched portrait had been a failure, he was anxious to try again; he kept making little drawings and throwing them away, to be rescued by his hostess, and then one evening he found what he was seeking: Mrs. Gardner had stepped out into the balcony to see what was happening on the canal, and as she came back into the drawing-room, pushing the French window wide open with her extended arms, Zorn exclaimed: 'Stay just as you are! That is the way I want to paint you.' He went instantly for his materials, and then and there the portrait was begun. When it was exhibited in Paris the following spring, it was called 'one of the most striking pictures in the two salons.' A newspaper man wrote: 'The drawing is faultless, and if Mrs. Gardner's arms have made her famous in Rome, as is the report, surely the painted ones will make her famous at Paris. . . . The figure is so graceful, so full of life, girlishness' — Mrs. Gardner was fifty-five at the time — 'strength and beauty, the arrangement is so dashing and so original . . . that it is sure to make a sensation.'

The next time that Zorn planned a journey to the United States, he wrote to tell Mrs. Gardner that if she would like to see him again, off he would go to Boston as soon as he landed, if only for a day. 'My first visit,' he wrote, 'is yours, as my first everything that you wish.'

On the 26th of October, Mrs. Gardner gave a musicale, at which the artists were Tirindelli, Luigi Agostini (a nephew of the Cardinal), and F. Trombini. Among the guests were Don Jaime de Borbon and his sisters Doña Elvira and Doña Alicia. Mrs. Gardner believed that music deserved to be heard. As she knew Venetians were poor listeners, and that Don Jaime was sure to be the worst offender, she asked him to see that every one kept quiet; this caused him to keep his finger to his lips most of the time, and, because his blood was royal, no one in the company disregarded his admonitions — at the moment.

Early in November, the Gardners went to Vienna for a fort-night. Mr. Proctor was back at his work with Leschetizky and Mrs. Gardner was anxious to see both maestro and pupil. On her way from Vienna to Paris, she stopped in Berlin and had the encounter with Count Seckendorf which has already been re-lated. In Paris she met Massenet, who played his new opera 'La Navarraise' to her and gave her an autographed photograph.

The collecting urge had seized her again — or new dividends had come in — and with soaring ambition she desired to possess a Botticelli, a Titian, and a Holbein. The Botticelli was secured first; this was the first picture obtained for her by Mr. Bernhard Berenson, and the most expensive work of art she had purchased. She had seen Berenson in London in July, and as a result he had written, August 1st, to ask her how much she wanted a Botticelli. If a handsome offer were made, Lord Ashburnham might be willing to part with 'The Tragedy of Lucretia.' With a faithful and grateful memory for the assistance she had given him seven years previously, Berenson wrote that he could probably help her to get the best terms if she cared to buy the picture and that it would be a pleasure in some sort to repay her for her kindness at a time when he needed help. December 19th, she sent him thirty-four hundred pounds to pay for the picture. Hereafter most of Mrs. Gardner's important paintings were purchased with Mr. Berenson's advice; sometimes she asked him to get a specified picture, sometimes she asked for an example of the work of a certain master, more often he proposed paintings which he knew were for sale. In 1895, on his recommendation, she purchased 'The Riva degli Schiavoni, Venice,' by Guardi, a portrait of Anna van Bergen, Marquise of Veere, by Mabuse (called at one time 'Margaret of Austria' by Scorel), 'Santa Conversazione' by Bonifazio, and 'Delivery of Keys to Saint Peter' by Catena (these two from the collection of J. P. Richter in London).

In January, 1895, with a fresh wardrobe from Worth, Mrs. Gardner descended upon Rome to storm the citadels of both the Blacks and the Whites. Her desire for a private interview with Leo XIII was fulfilled with the aid of Cardinal Schönberg, the Pope's Chamberlain; eleven o'clock in the morning of January 20th was the day and hour. At the suggestion of Cardinal Rampolla, she had worn her pearls in one long string, and, as she knelt at the feet of His Holiness, he took the pearls in his hands and seemed to find pleasure in them. These two people were worthy of each other, and although such an interview could not but be confined to elementary question and answer, so astute a man as Leo XIII must have discerned the superiority of Mrs. Gardner's intelligence and the force of her character, and she from that day experienced a growing affection for the Roman Church. When he asked her if she wished to request any favor, she replied that she would like the privilege of attending a mass celebrated by him in his private chapel. This was arranged for the following Sunday; the intimacy and sincerity of the service deeply impressed her.

January 28th, she was presented at Court, and a week later she went to a Court ball. On the King's birthday, March 14th, she sent him a bunch of yellow roses; for a lady to send flowers to the King was so contrary to the formality of Court etiquette that the King was puzzled to know what her intentions or desires might be. That evening, while Mr. and Mrs. Gardner were waiting in the hotel drawing-room with a number of other guests for a large dinner-party to begin, an equerry came to ask an elucidation; instead of being allowed to speak directly to the lady, he was referred to the husband, which created an awkward situation for both. When Mr. Gardner had finished the interview, he could not resist reproving his wife for the pretty mess she had made, but she said she had a great admiration for the King and she had all her life sent flowers to gentlemen she liked and admired, and she could not see why Umberto's being a king made any difference. However, Mr. Gardner felt obliged to ask Mr. Wayne MacVeagh, then United States Minister to Italy, to call on the King's secretary, and explain that Mrs. Gardner really was a lady and that her motives were innocent.

Two days later, she bought her famous halberd, one of six that belonged to the Borghese Pope, Paul V, the previous owner of the gilded chairs she had purchased in 1892. Two of the halberds had been purchased by Umberto, two by Kaiser Wilhelm II, and the last was still owned by the Borghese family. The association of her possessions with those of royalty gave her pleasure.

Among the Roman aristocracy, Mr. and Mrs. Gardner rapidly made friends; menus with their autographs are among her souvenirs; to their pet charities she gave judiciously. She attended hunt meets and was escorted on various excursions by the young swells of the city.

But neither royalty nor aristocracy could absorb completely Mrs. Gardner's attention. Creative genius and achievement she cared for more. In Rome she found Mancini, struggling to make a living, and Lanciani illuminating history by his excavations. Mancini's methods had not found favor; fads were not then so readily accepted as they have since become. In April, Mrs. Gardner bought a pastel, 'The Little Groom,' for four hundred lire, and it was arranged that Mancini should follow them to Venice to paint Mr. Gardner's portrait. For this excellent portrait and excellent work of art, only fifteen hundred lire were paid. There is no record of the date when she purchased Mancini's plaintive picture of a Roman peasant boy called 'The Standard Bearer,' of which the artist wrote: 'While bearing the standard of the shrine, the oil for the lamp, the natural sadness of his face is lessened by his joy at his newly bought red waistcoat and the piece of satin destined to make a jacket for his sister. All which serves even for luxury is first offered to the Madonna. The subject would have been superb, had I been able to treat it outdoors, not in my cold, dirty studio, where I was obliged to curtail the grandiose surroundings of endless plains of wheat representing immense space of peasant happiness.'

With Lanciani she visited the Forum, the palaces of the Cæsars, the villas of Frascati, and the ruins at Ostia. He gave her not only photographs of the early frescoes in the 'House of SS. John and Paul' under their church, but also one of his own water-colors.

And then there were dealers, most delightful among them the Spaniard Villegas, from whom Mrs. Gardner bought two superb fifteenth century green velvet copes, the iron eagle mantling the arms of Isabella Catolica, a pair of iron torchères with the arms of the Bishop of Toledo, and numerous other items. Being in Rome, she should have purchased antiquities, but she acquired none of special interest unless it be the Egyptian stone hawk that reigns with such dignity over the court of Fenway Court; even he was bought more or less by chance at a shop where she found two pictures that attracted her — one supposed to illustrate incidents in the life of Caterina Cornaro, Queen of Cyprus, and 'The Story of David and Bathsheba' by Herri Met de Bles. On April 1st, she purchased a grandiose red velvet baldacchino, which had belonged to Francesco Cenci, father of the celebrated Beatrice. His initials are repeated throughout the appliqué design, initials which are interpreted by many a visitor to Mrs. Gardner's museum as standing for Fenway Court.

This Roman sojourn, filled with such varied pleasures, was broken by an excursion to Naples, with a stop on the way to see the frescoes at Monte Cassino. From Naples Mrs. Gardner, escorted by Mr. Ralph W. Curtis, made the regulation tourist visit to Sorrento, Amalfi, Ravello, and Paestum. At last, on the 16th of April, she and Mr. Gardner said farewell to the Eternal City and returned for a final month to Venice. There Mounteney-Jephson, who had been with Stanley in Africa, succumbed to her charm; the poisoned arrows which he gave her now keep in place the autographs of the Presidents of the United States. Mancini immediately began Mr. Gardner's portrait; Berenson came April 26th for a day which he described as the 'most quintessential, halo-fitting day I ever spent in Venice'; there were special festivities for the King and Queen of Italy, who arrived on the 29th, including a gala performance at the Fenice; and altogether the days were packed as full of pleasure as possible.

May 16th, Mr. and Mrs. Gardner turned their faces homeward, but loitered on the way. June was spent in Paris, where Mrs. Gardner bought from Whistler a 'Nocturne: Blue and Silver — Battersea Reach,' as well as the pastel mentioned in a previous chapter. Through her agent, Monsieur Robert, she purchased a Madonna and Child attributed to Lucas van Leyden, and she instructed him to secure for her if possible an enamel which she had seen and coveted. Robert's first duty was to discover the owner; not till August 7th, when Mrs. Gardner was once more established at Beverly Farms, did he send her word that the enamel was owned by the Comtesse de Reculot, daughter of the Marquis de Caux, to whose family it had always belonged. The Comtesse stated that it had recently been examined by experts who considered it of great value and attributed it to Pénicaud; as Robert thought the price demanded was high, it was two months before the negotiations for its purchase were concluded.

The first visitors at Beverly Farms were members of the Gardner family; then for the rest of the summer old and new friends came and went — Russell Sullivan, Theodore F. Dwight, Librarian of the Boston Public Library, which had opened its new building February 1st; Joe Smith, Alfred Collins, Lena Little, Loeffler, Mr. and Mrs. John Jay Chapman, B. J. Lang, and various neighbors and relatives. August 22d, Tirindelli arrived, coming to try his luck under Mrs. Gardner's auspices, and finding the tide which led to fortune. While she was at Beverly Mrs. Gardner received a letter addressed to

> Mrs. Gardner, Esq.
> well known lady in high life
> Boston
> Mass.

The post-office clerk had added, 'Try Mrs. Jack.' As long as she lived, she enjoyed that tribute to her fame.

In September, through the agency of Berenson, a portrait of an Italian nobleman by Moroni was acquired.

That autumn Mrs. Gardner created the Italian garden at Green Hill, a garden surpassed by many in elaboration and sumptuous architectural effect, but, like every product of Mrs. Gardner's genius, unequalled in charm. It was laid out according to a design found in an old book of Italian gardens; a baroque lead statue of Neptune, purchased in England the previous October, rose flamboyantly from the central pool, pergolas shaded its broad walks, statues marked the end of its vistas, and from the moment one entered it one knew that it was created by a lover of beauty and a lover of flowers, their color and their fragrance. The following summer a friend, writing

[154]

about the garden, speaks of an effect Mrs. Gardner was always able to produce: 'the real miracle is the way in which you have made a past for it, the very earth is rich with tradition before the first year's rose petals have given themselves to it.' Another friend, to whom she gave photographs of this garden in 1924, only two months before her death, wrote: 'I marvel more and more as they bring back to me more and more clearly what you did. How could anybody do it? How in little new Brookline create such a vast ancient Paradise?'

CHAPTER X
MASTERPIECES

IN Mrs. Gardner's career as a collector, the year 1896 was memorable, for the purchases made then, relatively few in number because she did not go to Europe, were of such significance that she at last realized that her collection of works of art was likely to become famous, and that her house was quite inadequate for its proper installation. Already friends were calling it the 'Musée Gardner.' In January, Berenson recommended a portrait of a Venetian Senator [1] by Tintoretto; it was a modest purchase, and even Rembrandt's portrait of himself at the age of twenty-two was not so expensive as to seem rash, but Berenson described it as 'one of the most precious pictures in existence' and said that if it were not sold by February 18th it would go to the National Gallery in London. Mrs. Gardner cabled just in time to secure it. It had been in the collection of the Dukes of Buckingham and Chandos; for years it hung at Stowe House, and was disposed of during the famous Stowe House sale in September, 1848. The day it arrived, Mrs. Gardner invited only three dear friends to dine and to share her excitement. Although she kept her purposes absolutely secret until they were accomplished, she took the greatest pride and pleasure in showing a new treasure to her friends, a very few at a time, and regularly made them promise not to tell, so that each new surprise might astonish as many as possible.

This Rembrandt may be called the corner-stone of Fenway Court, for it was the first picture — so Mrs. Gardner said —

[1] Since identified as Zacharias Vendramin, a Procurator of St. Mark.

that she bought with the intention of developing a real museum collection. From now on, it was her determination that her acquisitions should be masterpieces; no difficulties daunted her, no desire seemed to her extravagant; she pursued her game with a zeal, a courage, a determination, and a wisdom hitherto unsuspected — except by Mr. Gardner, who was always aware of her abilities — and her joy in her successes was the elation of a spirit that never outgrew enthusiasm. No longer, she said, could she afford to buy second-rate things, because all her money was needed for the first-rate ones. Yet she knew that the first-rate ones must have background and congenial environment.

Her next venture was a test even of her unrivalled nerve. In May, Berenson asked her if she would like to buy Titian's 'Rape of Europa,' painted for Philip II of Spain and reported to have been called by Rubens, when he made the copy of it that now hangs in the Prado, the greatest picture in the world. The picture was given to Charles I when he went to Madrid to negotiate for the hand of Philip III's daughter; but, as the negotiations failed and Charles left in a hurry, the picture remained behind, carefully packed. In the eighteenth century it was a chief ornament of the Orleans collection, and finally it came into the possession of Lord Darnley and was hung at Cobham. The price asked was high, several times as much as Mrs. Gardner had yet paid for any work of art, and Berenson might have hesitated to propose the purchase if he had not known that she was prepared to pay even more for Gainsborough's 'Blue Boy,' which he had tried in vain to get for her. But she had seen the 'Blue Boy' and she had never seen the 'Europa.' Moreover, Berenson, expecting the 'Blue Boy' to exhaust her funds, had offered the picture tentatively to another Boston collector, and Mrs. Gardner had forbidden him to bring her into any competition with her neighbors. Nevertheless, as he wrote, 'it would be poetic justice that a picture once intended for a Stewart should at last rest in the hand of a Stewart.' In order that her decision might actually reach him before the other person's, he begged for a cable reply, and he got it. It was said that Dr. Wilhelm Bode fully intended to buy the picture for the Berlin Museum, but to pay the asking price was contrary to all precedent. He expected a leisurely haggle over it, and when he found that an American, and worse still a woman, had recklessly cabled that she would take the picture without argument, he was furious. June 7th, Berenson wrote: 'Why can't I be with you when Europa is unpacked! America is a land of wonders, but this sort of miracle it has not witnessed'; and on August 2d: 'I hope you have received her and had your first honeymoon with her. What a beauty! Titian at his grandest, Rubens at his strongest, you have both matchless artists' dominant notes singularly combined in this one picture. . . . How I wish I might see you in your first raptures over her!'

According to Mrs. Gardner, the purchase of the Titian was considered by the Museum of Fine Arts in Boston, but was given up as too much of a risk. This crystallized Mrs. Gardner's opposition to the purchase of works of art by a committee; she herself could only work single-handed, and never served on committees; she was so sure of herself and her judgments that she would not waste her time trying to coöperate with a number of people who could outvote her. She said that if a museum must make its purchases through a committee, the following would be the best method: Suppose the committee has ten members and the museum has a million dollars; give one member of the committee authority to spend a hundred thousand dollars for whatever he pleases, but preferably for one or two things, and allow him one year to do it; at the end of the year, give a second member of the committee a hundred thousand dollars under the same terms, but with the privilege of destroying his predecessor's purchases; continue in this way till each member of the committee has had his turn, the tenth being allowed, if he chooses, to destroy whatever has survived the other nine. Thus, at the end of the tenth year, the museum will at least possess one work of art that one person likes, whereas, if purchases are made by a committee, the museum is liable to own nothing that anybody likes.

The Titian was only a goad to further effort. In September, Mrs. Gardner wrote Berenson that she wanted 'Christ Bearing the Cross' by Giorgione, in Casa Loschi, Vicenza. The complicated negotiations for this purchase lasted till January, 1898. This picture also was considered by the Boston Museum, but was rejected, and Berenson told Mrs. Gardner it was not the kind of picture he thought of for her. This had no influence whatever upon her determination. The following March, Berenson wrote that he thought the picture had already been sold, although he could not discover to whom; a letter two days later reported an entirely different situation, with good prospects of getting it, but stipulated that it must go to Cavenaghi in Milan to be cleaned and restored. As soon as Mrs. Gardner received this letter, she cabled absolutely forbidding him to send it to Cavenaghi; she would not have its appearance so changed that any one could deny it was the Casa Loschi picture. Finally, in June, 1897, after Berenson had been to Vicenza to interview the family, he reported to Mrs. Gardner that she could have the picture the following November. One of the conditions was that a copy of it should be furnished to hang in Casa Loschi. When November came, however, there were further obstacles, but on January 11, 1898, the picture was safely delivered in Paris; the copy was made by Mr. Robert D. Gauley, and was sent to Vicenza the following November.

To return to Boston and 1896, the current of life flowed on for Mrs. Gardner as gaily as usual. Tirindelli had been much in evidence, and a new protégé had made his appearance, a young painter of Swedish descent, Andreas Andersen, who seemed to his contemporaries, and especially to Mrs. Gardner, exceptionally gifted. A portrait of George Proctor and a landscape by him are included in the Fenway Court collection; a portrait of Julia Ward Howe, painted by him, was given by Mrs. Gardner to the New England Women's Club in 1899. A constant stream of visitors filled the guest-book at Brookline and Beverly. In the middle of the summer, Mr. Proctor came home from Vienna; immediately he was invited for a week-end at 'Beach Hill,' and for the rest of her life Mrs. Gardner took the keenest interest in his career and in his happiness.

Her love of animals made her a frequent visitor at the Zoo, which had been established by Bostwick in the building on Boylston Street opposite the Common, formerly occupied by the Public Library. In November, 1896, a lioness presented the Zoo with two cubs. When they were six weeks old, Mrs. Gardner persuaded the manager to allow her to take them in her carriage to spend the afternoon at her house. Before returning them, she tied a red ribbon on the one she liked best, which was immediately named Mrs. Jack, and continued to wear the distinguishing ribbon 'to let the world know that it was a society lion.' The following April, a particularly fierce lioness became the mother of three cubs. Mrs. Gardner was notified of the event and soon arrived to see the babies. She insisted on taking one of them to fondle, an act which infuriated the mother, whom the keeper with his iron pole had difficulty in preventing from seizing Mrs. Gardner's hands. The lioness was not quieted till the cub had been put back in the cage and Mrs. Gardner had disappeared from sight. The cub was at once named Mrs. Jack II. Another day she took a fine young lion, 'Rex' by name, for a stroll through the main hall. She led him about by his mane, and he seemed to enjoy her company. The manager knew that Rex was thoroughly tamed and fully to be trusted; nevertheless, there was a panic among the visitors.

Although such trifles filled in the time, they did not distract Mrs. Gardner from her great purpose. In November, Berenson proposed that she buy the portrait of Philip IV in the Kingston Lacy collection. He had been trying, he said, for a whole year to get a Velazquez, and, although this one would cost a large sum, he considered it cheap. As usual, he asked for an immediate reply by cable. A later letter from Berenson implies that when Mrs. Gardner received the picture she was somewhat disappointed in it. Indeed, of recent years, its genuineness was doubted, but in the autumn of 1924 the thick yellow varnish was removed by Mr. H. E. Thompson, who then attended to the preservation of Mrs. Gardner's collection, and the handiwork of the master was unmistakably revealed. The picture is now considered one of the great prizes of the collection.

A Rembrandt, a Titian, and a Velazquez in 1896. How could a suitable installation for these great works and for the others that would surely come be provided? Mr. and Mrs. Gardner's first idea, finally abandoned, was to replace the Beacon Street house with one that would fill the entire lot, and, if necessary, to purchase the adjoining house on each side. Mr. Willard T. Sears, who had carried out certain alterations to the house at 'Green Hill,' was engaged to submit plans; the drawings were made by Mr. Edward Nichols, but the design was entirely Mrs. Gardner's. Mr. Gardner's interest in this important project was quite equal to his wife's, and it was definitely agreed between them that, if either one died, the other would carry it out.

In January, 1897, Berenson, writing from Paris, proposed a Van Dyck portrait of a lady, from the collection of the Duke of Osuña; this he said the National Gallery and private collectors wanted, and, if Mrs. Gardner wished to get it, she must cable. He said the lady deserved to be called Van Dyck's 'Mona Lisa,' she was so magnificent and so refined. Three weeks later, he received Mrs. Gardner's answer that she would take the picture. In March, Mrs. Gardner bought in New York the portrait by Pourbus of the Infanta Isabella Clara Eugenia, daughter of Philip II of Spain; in May, on Berenson's recommendation, she bought 'a severe little Madonna' by Cima da Conegliano, which Berenson wrote was the first picture of any importance by that master he had seen for sale; in June, Berenson finally secured the portrait of Juana of Austria and her niece, a daughter of Maximilian II. In February, 1896, Mrs. Gardner had asked him to investigate the picture, and at that time Berenson said positively it was not what Mrs. Gardner had been informed, a work by Titian, and therefore was only worth a modest sum. By April his opinion, based on a photograph, and his estimate of the value had begun to rise, and a fortnight later, having seen the picture, he was entirely in favor of the purchase. It was not, however, until a year had passed and he had seen the 'ravishing' picture again, that he asked Mrs. Gardner if she would take it at ten times his first estimate of its value. It was actually bought for a little less; the picture is now attributed, with some hesitation, to Coello. To Mrs. Gardner what she paid was a minor consideration; she bought what she wanted and forgot what it cost — the 'Europa' was the only picture of which she could remember the price. A year or two before she died, she said she had never regretted any of her purchases.

At the sale of the famous Gavet collection, which took place at the end of May and lasted into June, Mrs. Gardner's agent, Monsieur Robert, secured several important items for her; among them a Madonna and Child by Jacopo della Quercia, a terra-cotta relief by Andrea della Robbia, a magnificent carved chest, a fine Gothic credence, and a Bavarian fifteenth-century altar-piece, 'Die Heilige Sippe.' This relief, according to Professor Ernst von Dobschütz, illustrates a mediæval legend interpreting certain New Testament passages. As given in an old translation of 'The Golden Legend,'

Anne had thre husbondes, Joachym, Cleophe, and Salome, and of the fyrste she had a daughter named Marye, the moder of God, the whiche was gyven to Joseph in maryage, and she childed our Lord Jhesu Crist. And whanne Joachym was deed she took Cleophas the broder of Joseph, and had by hym another daughter named Marye also, and she was maryed to Alphee. And Alphee her husbond had by her four sones, that was James the lesse, Joseph the Juste otherwyse named Barsabee, Symon and Jude. Thenne the second husbond beyng deed Anne maryed the thyrdde named Salome, and had by hym another daughter whiche yet also was called Marye and she was maryed to Zebedee. And this Marye had of Zebedee two sones, that is to wyte James the more & Johan the evanngelyst.

The summer and autumn were spent by Mr. and Mrs. Gardner in Europe collecting materials for the proposed new building, but first there were a few weeks of absolute holiday during which they visited Sicily. As Mr. Gardner's health was not tip-top, and he wanted to save himself, and as he feared there might be difficulty in finding accommodations out of season, he decided to engage a courier. Mrs. Gardner disapproved; she thought a courier would be a nuisance and would increase rather than lessen responsibilities. But Mr. Gardner was firm. It must be admitted that Mrs. Gardner had a temper; no character approaching hers in strength ever lacked one, and the thought of the courier exasperated her. When they took the train in Paris for Marseilles, the station was unusually crowded, a prelate was leaving for Rome, a general was going — somewhere, and their friends and subordinates were seeing them off; an extraordinary number of unexplained spectators had assembled. The first spark was struck when Mrs. Gardner discovered that the courier had not reserved a whole car, but only part of one; then, when she ascended to her compartment, she found it filled with pillows — white pillows — of every size and shape. Indignantly she asked the courier where they had come from; he had procured them hoping to increase her comfort. 'Never do anything you are not ordered to' — and with that she began throwing the pillows out, with no thought of where they might land. There was an avalanche of pillows, one knocking off an officer's eyeglass, another hitting a Monsignor, and others astonishing lesser dignities. Mr. Gardner could not quiet her, and the poor courier was in despair, for it happened that he was president of the couriers' club in Paris, and he knew that the large crowd was made up of club members who had come to see him off. They had come because their money was at stake. The president had retired from active service, but when, tempted by Mr. Gardner's generosity, he had been persuaded to take on this Sicilian trip, he could not help boasting at the club that he was not yet altogether on the shelf. When his mates heard who had engaged him, they began to banter him and laid their bets that he could not stand Mrs. Gardner's vagaries for a week, or that he could not finish his contract, or whatever, and when the train reached Marseilles, the poor man received telegrams from all his friends doubling their bets. But they all lost. For the rest of the journey, Mrs. Gardner was most appreciative of all he did, and ten years later she engaged him to take her through Spain.

Another anecdote of her travels which Mrs. Gardner herself loved to tell, and which she said must surely be included if her biography was ever written, has its setting in Venice, where she came to be almost as conspicuous a figure as she was in Boston. A Venetian girl came upon a girl friend at the railroad station and asked why she was there.

'I'm waiting for the train.'

'Why are you waiting for the train?'

'Because Mrs. Jack Gardner of Boston is coming on it, and I want to see her.'

'Why do *you* want to see *her?*'

'Because she's so wicked.'

'How wicked is she?'

(With awe) 'More wicked than Cleopatra.'

Mr. and Mrs. Gardner reached Venice August 12th; on the 15th, they were in Munich, and the following afternoon they went to Nuremberg. In Munich, Mrs. Gardner bought a series of little figures of saints, wood-carvings in low relief with flat backs, and a collection of Gothic ecclesiastical utensils. In one shop where she made extensive purchases, she discovered a statuette which the dealer was unwilling to sell; it was something he kept for himself, and no amount of wheedling could persuade him to name a price for it. Mrs. Gardner was quite put out. On the way back to the hotel, Mr. Gardner had a chance to ask Mr. Gericke, who was with them, to return to the shop and make another attempt; he said Mrs. Gardner had set her heart on having the thing and he didn't like to have her disappointed. On the way the friend met the dealer, who said he was going to tell the lady she might have his treasure, because, he said, 'she knows a good thing, she really understands, and I am glad to have this little figure which I love owned by some one who can appreciate it.'

After their return to Venice on the 18th, their days were spent in shops, buying columns, capitals, reliefs, frescoes, glass, mirrors, cassoni, chairs, fountains, balconies, and 'facciate di palazzo.' Most of the Venetian architectural details of Fenway

Court were bought that summer, and sketches for the façades of the interior court were drawn.

In spite of the time spent in the arduous pleasure of buying antiques, there was plenty of leisure for lighter entertainment. On the 30th of August, when Clayton Johns and Theodore Byard were her guests, Mrs. Gardner hired a barca, had a piano put on board, and, with Johns to play and Byard to sing, had her own music on the canal. Mr. Johns had arrived on the 28th, and had been met at the railroad station by Mrs. Gardner, although, as she told him, she was suffering severely from a heart attack; the next day the pain was so great that she could not stand erect, but, as it was the Festa of the Madonna of San Stefano, she insisted on going to see the celebration. When the statue of the Madonna was carried by, Mrs. Gardner suddenly felt entirely well; her maid explained that she had prayed the Madonna to cure her.

On September 14th, 'Il Sindaco e la Giunta municipale di Venezia' gave a reception in honor of the English squadron. The newspaper report said:

Fra le straniere furono rimarcate Mrs. Jack Gardner, che portava una straordinaria collana di perle di una magnificenza, di una bellezza, di una perfezione impareggiabili, e il diadema di brillanti che le fulgeva sui capelli era altretanto splendido, e poi Mrs. Nelson, Mrs. Bethune, miss Elliot Lockhart, miss Wolff.

The jewels of the other ladies were not described.

The following day Joe Smith arrived, to remain till the Gardners left a fortnight later, and for the final week Berenson was a guest. This was a week of most extensive purchasing, almost an orgy of wholesale buying, in the midst of which Berenson chanced to discover a drawing which he attributed to Rubens of three heads from Mantegna's 'Triumph of Cæsar.'

Just before saying farewell to Venice, Mrs. Gardner made another little visit to Asolo. Berenson returned to his home at Fiesole, and Mr. and Mrs. Gardner spent part of the first week in October at Florence. There the marble doorway with a re-lief representing Saint George, which forms the main entrance to Fenway Court, was bought — the lions that flank it came from Venice — and there Mrs. Gardner found her enchanting little Lippo Memmi Madonna. Then in Rome more columns were bought, more reliefs, and the beautiful mosaic pavement from the Villa Livia which occupies the centre of the court at Fenway Court, one of the finest examples in the United States. In Naples, in addition to things of less note, a fresco of musicians by Brusasorci and a tapestry representing the Tower of Babel were secured. In November, Mr. Richard Norton, then Director of the American Academy in Rome, bought for her an old painted ceiling, the small panels filled with flowers, the beams decorated with mythological scenes — Hero and Leander, Mars and Venus, the Judgment of Paris, Leda, Hercules, etc. Mr. Norton tried to secure the 'Ludovisi Throne,' but the Italian Government exercised its right and the throne is now in the Museo delle Terme. In December, Mr. Norton did buy for Mrs. Gardner her great sarcophagus with figures in high relief representing the 'Procession of Bacchus'; and during the next few years several masterpieces came into her possession through his agency.

In November, Berenson asked her to buy a picture which he said he preferred to every Titian, every Holbein, every Giorgione, 'a gorgeous thing . . . decorative as no other picture whatsoever . . . it is a Saint George and the Dragon, by Crivelli. You never in your life have seen anything so beautiful for colour, and in line it is drawn as if by lightning.' Moreover, the picture was really cheap. As he said he must have an answer by wire at once, it was only five days later that he was thanking Mrs. Gardner for taking it. He said other pictures in her collection might be greater, but this was the one he loved the most; it had formerly been in the Leyland collection. A few days later, Mrs. Gardner notified him that she would take two cassone panels by Pesellino, 'the Giorgione of Florence,' which he had recommended in August.

December was spent in Paris, where, to crown the year, Mrs. Gardner bought a large number of fine Gothic pieces from the Emile Peyre collection. Her best tapestry, 'The Amazon Queens,' came from this source, and two other splendid tapestries, 'Jezebel' and 'Esther before Ahasuerus,' were bought at this time. She returned to Boston with her hands full and her pockets empty.

Although she did not go abroad in 1898, the masterpieces added to her collection that year form a group rarely, if ever, equalled in the annual report of the greatest museums; that year she finally got possession of the Giorgione, and she bought the portrait of Tommaso Inghirami by Raphael, the portrait of the Earl of Arundel by Rubens, the bust of Bindo Altoviti by Benvenuto Cellini, the portrait of 'A Gentleman and his Wife in Black' by Rembrandt, and 'The Storm on the Sea of Galilee' by Rembrandt. All these great works of art were secured for her by Mr. Berenson; in addition he secured for her a portrait attributed to Masaccio, a self-portrait by Baccio Bandinelli, an interior by Terborch, and a portrait by Bronzino. The Bandinelli portrait was recommended by Berenson as a portrait of Michelangelo by Sebastiano del Piombo, the only absolutely authentic one in existence; for years it had been accepted as such, although the final proof that it was not seems strangely simple. From the first, Charles Eliot Norton doubted, and apparently Mrs. Gardner more than once asked Mr. Berenson for further evidence to substantiate the claim that it was of Michelangelo; in 1900 and again in 1902, he sent references to authorities, but still Professor Norton, to whom this evidence was submitted, refused to be convinced. In August, 1902, he wrote to Mrs. Gardner:

I cannot be persuaded that it is a portrait of Michelangelo. It bears no resemblance to the authentic contemporary likeness of him, and the nose shows no mark of Torrigiano's blow. Would it not be worth while to have a good photograph taken of it and copies sent to the leading connoisseurs in London, Paris, and Berlin? With enquiry if they can tell of whom it is the portrait. This might answer for one number of the 'Fenway Court Papers,' which I want to see issued.

Finally, by good luck, the panel needed the attention of a restorer, and when the picture was removed from the frame a paper was found which stated that the portrait was of Bandinelli. Then Professor Norton discovered that the drawing which the sitter is displaying is of Bandinelli's group of Hercules and Cacus, made by the sculptor in the hope of demonstrating his superiority over Michelangelo. Writing with scholarly caution, he said:

In your corrected catalogue it seems to me that you would be safe in entering 'Portrait of Bandinelli by S. del Piombo'; to which it might be well to add a note to the effect that 'this seems to be the portrait concerning which Vasari gives an entertaining narrative in his 'Life' of Bandinelli; he refers to it also in his 'Life' of Sebastiano del Piombo. The drawing in the hand of Bandinelli represents his famous group of Hercules and Cacus, which has long stood at one side of the doorway to the Palazzo Vecchio in Florence.

I am not absolutely sure that Vasari refers to this portrait in his 'Life' of Sebastiano — but this is easily ascertained. Nor am I sure that Bandinelli's group still stands where it used to stand opposite to Michelangelo's David on the other side of the doorway. The David has been moved, I believe, since I was in Florence, and whether the Hercules and Cacus was also moved, I do not *know*, but I think not.

February 7th, Mrs. Gardner had the misfortune to break her leg; as she was descending the stairs in a friend's house, she looked back when near the bottom to speak to her hostess, and made a false step; after she reached home she put through a luncheon-party before yielding to the pain and summoning a doctor. In a day or two, after the manner of Madame de Rambouillet, she was holding receptions in her bedroom. Before she was able to walk again, Kellar, the magician whom she had seen fourteen years before in India, came to the Boston Theatre; to Dr. George H. Monks, who had married Mr. Gardner's niece in 1897, Mrs. Gardner was forever grateful because he arranged that she should be taken to the theatre on a stretcher and carried in at a special door, to occupy a box during Kellar's act.

Enforced leisure gave her time to consider the problems of her new building. Although Mr. Gardner had already become convinced that the middle of a residential block on Beacon Street was not the place for it, she was with difficulty persuaded that the obstacles were insurmountable. She did finally agree that a location which would give open space around the building and allow windows on four sides, instead of only in the two ends, would be preferable. As the Fenway land, which was then quite on the outskirts of the town, was purchased only a few weeks after Mr. Gardner died, it seems safe to infer that he approved of the site.

At her birthday party that year, there was a performance by a burlesque orchestra, conducted by Otto Roth. The Symphony Orchestra season was just ending, Nikisch had resigned the conductorship, and this party was a celebration of the prospective return in the autumn of Mrs. Gardner's friend, Wilhelm Gericke. The members of the Orchestra and their instruments, as written by themselves, were:

Franz Kneisel (Ocarina)
Alwin Schroeder (Triangle)
Wallace Goodrich (Piano)
Max Zach (Xylophone)
T. Adamowski (Tromba)
Louis Svečenski (Violino II)
Ch. M. Loeffler (Autoharp)
A. Rotoli (Castagnette and Tamburrin)
Alex Blaess (Cello)
Daniel Kuntz (Primo Violino and Concert-meister)

When the Gardners returned to 'Green Hill' in October, after their summer at Beverly, the Gerickes were their first guests; not long after, Theodore Byard came over from London, and it was arranged that he and Mr. Proctor should give a concert in Cambridge on December 8th.

The family Thanksgiving dinner was not held at 'Green Hill' that year. Mr. Gardner's health was unsatisfactory; he was so apprehensive that he asked Mr. William C. Endicott to go over the bills and the invoices for the purchases Mrs. Gardner had made in Europe the previous year, and to familiarize himself with her affairs as a collector, so that if she should need assistance he could give it.

December 8th, Mrs. Gardner went to the concert in Cambridge; the next day she moved to town; on the 10th, Mr. Gardner was stricken with apoplexy at the Exchange Club. He was taken home at once, and was attended by Dr. Paul Thorndike and Dr. George C. Shattuck, but he died that evening. What Mrs. Gardner felt, no one can say; what this loss meant, she herself could only realize slowly. Mr. Gardner had shielded and protected her, had done everything to make life go smoothly for her and to provide the setting and background for her fascinating personality. He was delighted to see her surrounded by brilliant men, artists, and musicians, and to have his house the centre of a coterie unrivalled in Boston. In the business world he held a high place; he was a member of the Board of Overseers of Harvard College and treasurer of the Museum of Fine Arts. His business associates loved him and all who knew him deeply admired his splendid qualities.

With his steadiness and his wisdom to maintain the balance, Mrs. Gardner had been able to indulge every whim, knowing that he could and would always set things straight. In all the delight and excitement of collecting he had shared, and he had preserved methodically all the memoranda of objects examined at shops and the bills for purchases. Never was his superb confidence in his wife more magnanimously shown than in his last will and testament; although he provided that the bulk of his property should be held in trust and the income paid to her, he authorized her at any time to demand the payment to herself of any part of the principal she might wish. There were plenty of critics to say that this was folly, that Mrs. Gardner was so recklessly extravagant by nature that she would soon run through the entire estate and be left penniless; but Mr. Gardner knew that she had a level head and a great purpose, and so far as he could prevent it he did not wish her to be handicapped by lack of funds.

Letters of consolation and tributes to Mr. Gardner poured in; all of them she kept till her last illness; the one that follows, written evidently by the shaky hand of an old lady, she never destroyed:

To

Mrs. J. L. GARDNER

152 Beacon Street.

In these sharp extremities of Fortune, the blessings which the weak and poor can scatter have their fit season.

In your sharp extremity of this late fortune permit me to offer my humble blessing. The frequent passers by your house are very grateful for the very beautiful exhibition of flowers which you have so long and so generously displayed for us in your bay window. I find nothing equal to it in Boston, and you do not permit your great sorrow to interrupt it.

Thanks!

INCOGNITA

It is said that many a poor person who never saw the inside of a house like Mrs. Gardner's made a weekly pilgrimage to see the display of flowers in the window over her front door.

On January 31, 1899, Mrs. Gardner purchased a parcel of land at the corner of the Fenway and Worthington Street, the lot on which Fenway Court actually stands; several adjacent parcels, making possible the 'Monks' Garden,' were acquired at later dates. At that time the Fenway, which has been made beautiful by Mr. Olmsted and has become a centre of art, education, and medicine, was a bleak, barren waste. As soon as the Fenway land was acquired, the architect was set to work to revise the plans originally made for the new house on Beacon

Street. These so well embodied Mrs. Gardner's general scheme that they needed only to be altered in detail to fit the new conditions; the interior court and the exhibition rooms remained much as before, but it was now possible to have windows on four sides, and to add a large music-room.

The Beacon Street house was not sold till June, 1904. The house built by Mr. Stewart was deeded to his daughter in 1887; the second house, purchased by Mr. Gardner, was made over to Mrs. Gardner in 1897; before selling, Mrs. Gardner removed the interior woodwork which had been specially carved for her, the fireplaces, and whatever else she could, reproducing as nearly as possible in her private apartment at Fenway Court the rooms she had so long occupied. Not only had Mr. Eben S. Draper, who purchased the house, agreed to tear it down and build a new one, but also to give up the number 152 and use the other number 150, to which the frontage was entitled. Thus Mrs. Gardner, who craved continuity and the perpetuation of her personality, transported to the new location whatever intimate association she could and obliterated what must be left behind.

One little incident made her realize the expense of the luxurious life she had hitherto accepted so lightly. To maintain the smart appearance of her coachman and footman, new furs were needed; a friend of Mr. Gardner, whom she consulted, asked if he might get for her such furs as he bought for his own people. When Mrs. Gardner saw the bill, she resolved that those were the last furs she would buy for such a purpose and that was the last time she would blindly trust herself in the hands of a friend. As the years went by, she gradually reduced her establishment and her scale of living. There were times when her friends thought she did not have enough food, and indeed her table was for years almost entirely supplied from her Brookline estate, but besides fresh vegetables, fresh butter, fresh eggs and poultry, that provided also hothouse grapes and nectarines. It cannot be said that such economy was irksome to Mrs. Gardner, for whatever she did, she made a pleasure; but the reason for it was her determination that nothing should interfere with the fulfilment of the purpose which was now the centre of her life.

Mrs. Gardner had, however, no thought of curtailing her expenditures for works of art. In December, 1898, Monsieur Robert undertook to buy for her the ceiling painting then attributed to Paolo Veronese representing 'The Coronation of Hebe.' It was made for the Palazzo Turriano at Udine and remained there till 1692; at that time, the attempt of Conte Sigismondo de la Torre to sell the picture led to long litigation. In 1770, it was bought by the Marchese Manfrin and placed in his gallery at Venice. January 19, 1899, Robert cabled that he had bought it and it had been delivered to him. On the advice of Mr. Ralph W. Curtis, the picture was cleaned by Brissan Frères, whom he called 'the best picture doctors in the world'; he suggested that when Mrs. Gardner knew the dimensions of the room it was to go in, she have a design for the surrounding panelling made by Cajrati in Milan.

At the same time, Berenson was persuading her to buy the portraits by Holbein of Sir William Butts and Lady Butts. Of these he could not even send photographs, but their exceptional interest as a pair of portraits by Holbein was evident. As if this important purchase — and an expensive one, also — were not enough for the moment, he was also urging the purchase of Fra Angelico's 'Death and Assumption of the Virgin.' Not even in Florence can one find a lovelier example of this precious master — or one in better condition. Mr. R. Langton Douglas, writing to Mrs. Gardner on May 15, 1924, said: 'I would like, too, a photograph of your Fra Angelico. I covet that picture more than any work by Fra Angelico that is in private hands, and more than any Fra Angelico in any American gallery, private or public.'

In Rome, Mr. Norton bought for her a large Pietà by Giovanni della Robbia. In March, Berenson called her attention to a polyptych by Simone Martini, five panels, which had been exhibited for many years in the Museum at Orvieto; these were absurdly cheap, and are, in the opinion of at least one scholar, the chief glory of Fenway Court. On May 23d, she sent Berenson a cable asking his advice about the Chigi Botticelli, perhaps the most famous of her pictures; both this picture and a Francia were bought in June. In November, 1901, the Botticelli was exhibited by Colnaghi in London for the benefit of the Prince of Wales Hospital Fund.

For three days in March, 1899, her Beacon Street house was open to the public, the proceeds being given to charity.

On a day in June, in Mrs. Gardner's presence, the pile-driving for the foundation of Fenway Court actually began. When she arrived on this momentous occasion, she saw at her feet as she got out of her carriage a four-leaf clover, the only one she ever found; it is forever preserved in a crystal locket in the museum. Sometimes she was not quite sure which crystal held the clover leaf and which held a relic of Santa Chiara, but both are there.

Aug 16

PALAZZO BARBARO,
VENEZIA.

Dear Mr. Sears
    I write to
acknowledge
Your letter. The
places will arrive
soon I hope —
Please let me
know about the
Street & where

finished —.
It is most
interesting &
delightful, looking
up materials
here —

Yours
Isabella S. Gardner.

As pile-driving was entirely a practical matter and could safely be left to the architect and the contractor, James Smith, Mrs. Gardner sailed for Europe early in July in search of such additional architectural material as she needed. Just before she sailed, Mr. Loeffler sent her the score of his 'Divertimento,' dedicated to her, which he had played January 4 and 5, 1895, at the concerts of the Boston Symphony Orchestra, and suggested that she show it to two publishers in Paris and ask them if they would like to publish it.

At the end of July, she was established at the Palazzo Barbaro. Her first guests were Miss Lena Little and Mr. George Proctor. Theodore Byard and her old painter friends, Ludwig Passini and Ettore Tito, were all in Venice; but, although there was time for picnics on the Island of Poveglia, excursions to the Lido, and the constant entertainment of friends, the business of these two months was the purchase of columns, capitals, ironwork, and furniture. In her mind's eye, Mrs. Gardner had so clear an image of the house she was to build that she said she knew exactly where each thing she bought was to go.

August 16th, she received a letter from her architect, Mr. Sears, stating that a complete set of plans was being sent to her. In reply she said:

DEAR MR. SEARS,

I write to acknowledge your letter. The plans will arrive soon, I hope. Please let me know about the street, and when the piles will be driven. I hope to find all the underpinnings finished by my return, the end of November probably. But I do not want anything else done, as I want to be present. I shall order here all *pilasters* and *arches*, and probably the *staircase*, so do nothing about them, at least until I see you. Is the Street finished? It is most interesting and delightful, looking up materials here.

Sincerely yours

ISABELLA S. GARDNER

MASTERPIECES

The order for the staircase was given to Dorigo; much other material was purchased from him, including four beautiful 'Fior di Persica' columns. From Venice she went to Florence, where Bardini not only sold her a lovely terra-cotta relief of the Madonna and Child by Benedetto da Maiano and her best piece of ironwork, a convent grille, but gave her the recipe for the 'Bardini blue' which she used on her corridor walls. The effect of these water-colored walls was delightful, but they were so delicate that they had to be done over constantly, and Mrs. Gardner finally persuaded herself to have the walls painted in oil.

The purchase of masterpieces continued; October 31st, Mr. Norton wrote that the Mantegna from the collection of Prince del Drago was hers, and on November 4th, Mr. Berenson wrote that he had secured for her a Schongauer Madonna (now considered a copy) which he had offered her a month before. Mrs. Gardner was now in Paris, making additional purchases and worrying Monsieur Robert by insisting that he send from the secure custody of his storerooms some of her most valuable paintings, to adorn her hotel apartment.

On her way to London, she spent one night, November 29th, as the guest of Henry James at Lamb House, Rye. It had taken many letters and telegrams to arrange for this visit, which she proposed while she was in Brussels, before her final days in Paris. James wrote: 'How mysterious and complicated you are! You need, really, a few hours' contact with my rustic simplicity. I long greatly for your Bourget news.' As he sensed that she was alarmed by his careful directions for getting from her Channel steamer to Rye, he sent her on November 27th the following type-written letter:

ISABELLA STEWART GARDNER

Dear wild and wandering friend,

Here is an intensely legible statement of your needful proceeding at Dover on the arrival, at the nominal 2.30 of your boat from Calais. It will consist simply of your looking out for me, as hard as possible — if not as soft! — from the deck of the vessel. I shall be on the dock to meet you, penetrating with eagle eye the densest crowd: so that, after all, *your* looks won't so much matter. I shall try to have mine of the best. I shall await you, in other words — reach out the friendliest of hands to you as you step, de votre pied léger, from the plank. The rest is silence. You will have nothing whatever more to do but what I mildly but firmly bid you. If you only mind what I tell you, all will still be well. We shall combine convenient promptitude with convenient deliberation and reach Rye in time for tea and tartines. Be therefore at peace — and keep your powder dry. I wish you as smooth and swift and simple a business of it, all through, as may be possible to so complex an organism. The weather here is lovely now and the Channel a summer sea — which I trust we shall still profit by. *Thursday* then, I repeat, on the Dover pier at 2.30.

Yours more than ever impatiently

HENRY JAMES

A month later he wrote: 'I think of you as a figure on a wondrous cinque-cento tapestry.'

The recommendations of Mr. Berenson were not confined to paintings; in November, he advised the acquisition of a pair of choir-stalls, which Mrs. Gardner finally purchased in January, and some of her most important pieces of scuplture were acquired as the result of his enthusiasm. In 1900, he bought for her a little panel by Giotto, 'The Presentation of the Child Jesus in the Temple,' a little Pietà by Raphael painted in 1505 to form part of the predella for the altar-piece of San Antonio, Perugia; an Annunciation then attributed to Fiorenzo di Lorenzo; and a landscape by Rembrandt. To Mr. Norton belongs the credit for a portrait by Bartolommeo Veneto, and for another very precious object, a superb chalice. The Annunciation was painted by a man who revelled in his mastery of perspective; a loggia and corridor paved in colored marbles leads to an open doorway in the background, through which, in the words of Professor Charles Eliot Norton, 'one sees the whole of Italy.' Mr. Hendy attributes the panel to Antoniazzo Romano, and Lionello Venturi attributes it to Melozzo da Forlì. Almost immediately after the panel was brought to Boston, the climate affected it and the paint became loosened; Mr. John Briggs Potter treated the picture and saved it; for the next ten years he supervised the care and preservation of Mrs. Gardner's collection.

After 1900, masterpieces were added one by one, but the record of the previous four years was never equalled.

CHAPTER XI

C'EST MON PLAISIR

WHEN Mrs. Gardner returned to Boston in December, 1899, a newspaper announced that she had bought an Italian palace and would ship it to Boston and set it up as an art memorial to her husband; it was a Florentine palace, built during the Renaissance when Florentine architecture was at its height, and those who knew the Pitti Palace would have a good idea of the one Mrs. Gardner had bought. This was called 'the latest whim of America's most fascinating widow.' During the next few years the newspapers in Boston, New York, and Philadelphia reflected the widespread interest in Mrs. Gardner's mysterious construction by publishing full-page articles about it, illustrating them with almost any photograph of a Venetian or Florentine building. Even the 'Kansas City Times' gave Fenway Court half a page in September, 1901. A friend in Florida wrote that she must be the person referred to in a local paper which said: 'The Boston woman who is getting columns upon columns of free advertisements out of her love of privacy is a genius in her way.' Such of these articles as were sent to Mrs. Gardner she kept, and found reading them over in later years intensely amusing.

As the hundreds of cases arrived from Europe, they were sent to a storage warehouse, where Mrs. Gardner and Mr. William C. Endicott with his carefully prepared lists supervised the unpacking. The cases were stacked high, but the unpacking did not begin at one point and proceed methodically round the room; in each instance Mrs. Gardner decided what case should be opened next; if it was at the bottom of a pile those on top must be lifted — they contained marble columns — and placed at one side to await her pleasure. As each column, capital, and base was unpacked, she indicated the place in the storeroom where it should be put; when the labor was over, they were all arranged as she wanted them to stand in the colonnade at Fenway Court. Meanwhile, near the new building, two long sheds had been erected, to which this material was gradually moved. Among the employees of the contractor was an Italian, Teobaldo Travi, who showed such interest in these materials that had come from his native land and handled them with such affectionate care that Mrs. Gardner gave him official supervision over them. Each load was selected at the storehouse by Mrs. Gardner and Mr. Nichols; each load was accompanied in transit by Teobaldo Travi, who was soon known to every one as Bolgi, and who still exercises the same affectionate supervision over Fenway Court. Many a workman was saved from losing his job by Bolgi's explanation that the column was broken when it arrived.

True to her word, she was present every day to watch each operation; like the workmen, she brought her luncheon and took her noon hour; like them, she contributed her ten cents for oatmeal to be put into the drinking-water. Even in the foundations her personality expressed itself; for the regulation course of dressed stone which the architect had planned to have show above the ground as underpinning, she substituted a course of undressed blocks of varying height, so that the brick building does not appear to rest upon a layer of stone, but to be knit into it. With the artificiality of steel construction she had no patience; it was not 'real,' and certainly it was not Venetian. She wanted obvious support for her building and insisted that the architect give up the steel frame indicated in his original plans. Even in the middle of some of the galleries, he had shown steel columns but these did not survive the first glance of Mrs. Gardner's determined eye.

Her insistence that marble columns could support a palace in Boston as well as in Venice created a prolonged conflict with the building inspector, who perhaps was not as familiar with Venice as she was. A certain indefiniteness as to the future use of the building complicated the situation. Was it to be a public museum or a private residence? If a public building, the plans must be submitted to a building inspector, but Mrs. Gardner's plans had not been filed at the City Hall and it was understood that they would not be until she saw fit. The following report appeared in a local paper:

Mrs. Gardner and her representatives found that the law did not specifically state when the plans should be given over, before the commencement of the work, during the construction, or after completion. Acting on this technical construction of the ordinances, she has kept the plans and will continue to do so, it is said, until such time as she chooses to supply the city with the requisite information.

An inspector is allowed admittance to the museum, passes upon the construction, and says whether the law is being lived up to, but he never knows what is to be done next and waits upon the pleasure of the society leader.

One of Mrs. Gardner's favorite stories was an account of an interview with the inspector. She said to him: 'I am well aware that you can stop my building, but in view of what that would mean to Boston, I think it would be folly for you to do so; if, however, Fenway Court is to be built at all' (this was said slowly and impressively), 'it will be built as *I* wish and not as *you* wish.' Calling her attention to a neighboring building which he said was being properly constructed, he asked why she didn't build her house like that. While they were looking at it, the building collapsed. As she herself would have said, 'Se non è vero, è ben trovato.'

Mrs. Gardner had taken as a motto some verses by Thomas Bailey Aldrich:

> Build as thou wilt, unspoiled by praise or blame,
> Build as thou wilt, and as thy light is given;
> Then, if at last the airy structure fall,
> Dissolve and vanish — take thyself no shame.
> They fail, and they alone, who have not striven.

To Mrs. Gardner's great annoyance, the inspector did insist that at least a piece of one of the columns be sent to the Watertown Arsenal to be tested for crushing strength; she could not bear to sacrifice any part of a column, but did finally send the smallest possible amount. The inspector's wisdom is proved by the fact that two columns had subsequently to be removed from the colonnade, and one or two others have been reënforced.

With due ceremony a corner-stone was laid; after three copper boxes had been submitted to Mrs. Gardner and rejected, she arrived one morning with a box she had obtained herself and had filled and sealed. Under Bolgi's direction, the stone was put in place, and she applied the mortar; to make sure that no curious person should try to investigate the sealed box, she stood by and watched until the brick wall had risen several feet. Because he was so tactful and because he played the cornet, Bolgi became Mrs. Gardner's personal attendant about the works. As the building progressed, she would clamber over it with Bolgi at her side, cornet in hand, to summon the master-workmen as wanted — one toot for the mason, two for the steam-fitter, three for the plumber, four for the carpenter, five for the plasterer, six for the painter.

Rest and relaxation she found in music and in the company of her friends and her dogs. At 'Green Hill' on May 10, 1900, Miss Julia Heinrich and Messrs. Loeffler, Proctor, and Blaess gave a concert; on the 17th, the artists were Miss Heinrich and Messrs. Proctor and Gebhard. Several times Lawrence Smith Butler came to sing.

On May 10th, Major Henry L. Higginson invited her to go with him to see the new Symphony Hall; in his letter he wrote:

As the Music Hall nears completion, you may like to see it — and showing you what may be seen would be a great pleasure to me.

It is very dirty just now and lime is flying about, and also the great staging fills the hall. But I'll go at your pleasure, if you wish me — when you like — after three or four o'clock suits me best.

I was very glad to see you on the last evening of the old hall's life — for your own sake and for Jack's — and tho' it was little enough, still we all went up together — for the last time. And I meant every word and more of deep gratitude to numberless friends and to the great public for kind, courteous, steady support throughout my experiments. They've said 'Whatever you do, is right' — and more cannot be said to any one — and without I should have failed.

'Tis well in this world that no success is won by one alone.

Thank you and the dear old fellow for many, many kind words and kinder deeds.

Yours truly

H. L. HIGGINSON

C'EST MON PLAISIR

For the last time, she spent the summer at 'Beach Hill.' A few days after her arrival there she had the pleasure of attending the christening of her first godchild, Sybil Appleton; wishing to be as magnificent as possible, she got out her big barouche with C springs, dressed her coachman and footman in their smartest liveries, and drove a spike-team of beautiful black horses. Interest in the ceremony and in the baby was entirely dissipated by the arrival of Mrs. Jack in her equipage. It was a way she had. In January, 1902, while she was visiting in Chicago, she was invited to a farewell supper given for Mrs. Patrick Campbell. The papers said: 'Mrs. Gardner is a favorite with Chicago society, and the women at the reception for Mrs. Campbell seemed to be as much interested in the woman from Boston as in the actress.' Even at the wedding of a President's daughter, Mrs. Gardner received her full measure of attention. The air at a wedding is full of romance, and the report that Mrs. Gardner was engaged to the Honorable W. Bourke Cochran originated at the wedding of Miss Alice Roosevelt to Mr. Nicholas Longworth. Mrs. Gardner found no one more diverting than the 'silver-tongued orator' whose gallantry in shielding her by his coat from impertinent photographers, and whose constant attendance upon her set all tongues wagging, although no one — probably not even the reporters — took it seriously. In 1904, after she had been his guest over a week-end at 'The Cedars,' Sands Point, Long Island, he wrote that 'no one who has ever descended on Long Island effected a conquest so quickly and so completely.'

On December 1, 1900, John Chipman Gray, Henry Walton Swift, Harold Jefferson Coolidge, Willard T. Sears, William

ISABELLA STEWART GARDNER

Amory Gardner, Charles L. Peirson, and Isabella Stewart Gardner subscribed to an agreement to associate themselves with the intention to constitute a corporation; on the 15th, these subscribers met 'for the purpose of organizing said corporation by the adoption of bylaws and election of officers and the transaction of such other business as may properly come before the meeting.' December 19th, a charter was issued to the new corporation, describing it as 'formed for the purpose of art education, especially by the public exhibition of works of art.' The capital stock was placed at fifty thousand dollars in shares of ten dollars each. Mr. Gray, Mr. Swift, and Mr. Coolidge were elected directors. Of the three, Mr. Coolidge, who is now President of the Trustees of the Museum, alone survived Mrs. Gardner. For the information of the corporation, he made a preliminary inventory of the collection.

On the seal which Mrs. Gardner designed for the Museum, there is a shield bearing a phœnix, emblem of immortality, and the motto, 'C'est mon plaisir' — it is my pleasure — the reason and, in her opinion, the justification for her every action.

As the exterior walls of the 'palace of mystery' were now three stories high, the newspapers were able to reproduce actual photographs of it. Over the main entrance had been placed a tablet inscribed 'The Isabella Stewart Gardner Museum in the Fenway MDCCCC.' Although this was soon covered with a marble slab, which remained over it until Mrs. Gardner's death, it had not escaped the eye of the ever-watchful reporters, and the truth was told, if not believed, that the building was to be both a dwelling-place and a museum.

C'EST MON PLAISIR

April 10, 1901, the 'Boston Herald' published an entertaining account of the actual state of the 'huge structure' that was 'going up before the astonished gaze of residents of the Back Bay district'; one stranger had asked if it was to be a warehouse, another had said, 'Begorra, it 'ud make a foine brewery,' but it was generally referred to in the neighborhood as 'Missus Gardyner's Eyetalian palace.' The extraordinary secrecy maintained by the architects and the contractors had stimulated curiosity; Italian workmen had been imported who did not know English enough to explain to reporters what they were doing; Mrs. Gardner herself was a sphinx. The roof had recently been put on, adding greatly to the beauty of the house. To many the severity of the exterior was disappointing. By the middle of June the simple brick garden wall had been begun; this was called 'the weirdest wall ever conceived by whim of woman.' It shut the house in as if it were a convent and allowed the spectator to wonder what could be done with the space it enclosed — 'it seems doubtful if this area can be made strikingly beautiful.' It is now the 'Monks' Garden.'

In July her man of business sent her, at her request, a statement of her expenditures for living expenses including all the expenditures for the Brookline estate and the Beacon Street house: they amounted to $21,500 per annum, which he said he thought was not extravagant.

No delay by workmen or contractors was tolerated. The architect intended that the wood floors should be of oak, but, because the contractor did not deliver his material on the appointed date, the order was cancelled and floors of hard pine were laid. (They have since been replaced by floors of oak and teak.) Mrs. Gardner kept a sharp watch on all the artisans and discharged any man whose work she disapproved; one day she telephoned to the architect's office that she had discharged a plumber and that the plumbing firm must have another man on the job in an hour or she would employ another firm.

She herself not only enjoyed working with her hands, but particularly enjoyed showing skilled workmen how she wanted them to work. When the walls of the court were ready to be painted and her explanations to the painters of the effect she wanted failed to produce the desired result, she ordered a pail of white paint and one of pink to be brought, then climbed upon the staging, and with a sponge dipped first in one pail and then in the other began smearing the wall. The method produced a charming variation in color which makes many people think the wall is pink marble. The ceiling of the Gothic Room is supported on huge beams; as she wanted these to be hewn by hand, the architect secured from a shipbuilding firm in East Boston their most skilful workman, whose hewing was so perfectly done that the beam looked as if it had been planed. With this effect Mrs. Gardner was not at all pleased, and, taking the broadaxe, she hewed one face of a beam while the workman hovered over her begging her not to cut herself; the rest of his work was an imitation of hers.

Early in August, Mrs. Gardner took Mr. Nichols to New York to see, measure, and sketch certain decorations in Mendelssohn Hall which had suggested a possible treatment for the walls of her Music-Room. At the hall they did not find the official for whom she had been told to enquire, but they went in and under her direction Mr. Nichols set to work. Presently a man appeared who said that, much to his regret, as he had received no instructions to permit what they were doing, they would have to stop. Mrs. Gardner argued and explained; while she talked Mr. Nichols worked, and the argument did not end in a victory for Mrs. Gardner's antagonist until Mr. Nichols put up his notebook with his measurements and sketches completed. Then Mrs. Gardner took him to see a mansion just built for one of her friends by Stanford White; it was very handsome, palatial, filled with beautiful things. 'But what a pity,' said Mrs. Gardner, 'that Mr. —— didn't have the fun of doing it himself.' That points to one of the chief elements in the charm of Fenway Court; every detail of it is personal, every detail speaks of the fun Mrs. Gardner had in doing it, and the visitor in a sense experiences her creating pleasure. Yet one is aware that it was not an easy task; one is conscious of the effort and the labor, but always of the joy in work and the exhilaration of success.

The Music-Room walls were achieved with difficulty; these were to be white, but not flat; in the plaster on the lower half an effect of drapery was to be produced. The first man who tried it was discharged. The second man was selected for his name's sake; he came from Venice and was known as Joe Venetia. Surely Mrs. Gardner would approve his work — but she did not. Finally a big sheet was draped against the wall, and with that as a model the third plasterer, a Scotch-Irishman, got the desired result. Yet she knew even then that the Music-Room would not be permanent; it must be perfect, though temporary.

Before Christmas the actual construction of the house was finished, many of the sculptures were in place and plants were growing in the Court; the mosaic from the Villa Livia in the centre, which has now sunk nearly five feet, was then level with the Cloister. The Chapel was entirely in order, and there, on Christmas Eve 1901, Father Frisbie, Rector of the Church of the Advent, celebrated the first midnight mass. Besides Mrs. Gardner, six other members of the Gardner family were present. On Christmas Day, Miss Lena Little, Mr. Archibald C. Coolidge, and Mr. Proctor lunched with Mrs. Gardner in the new house. The next day the house was shown to Mr. Joseph H. Choate, Miss Mabel Choate, and Mr. and Mrs. J. Montgomery Sears; as Mr. Sears provided the picnic refreshments, Mrs. Gardner called it 'Mr. Sears's coffee party.' On October 7, 1904, Mr. Sears gave another party at Fenway Court, this time in honor of the Archbishop of Canterbury.

Among her Christmas letters was one from Mr. Henry L. Higginson in which he said:

I ask leave to speak my respect and admiration for the manner in which you have carried out your plans, which dear Jack so highly approved. It is well to leave one stone on the great heap of human work, isn't it? and you have surely done it.

... I've also wished to send some little thing to your house, worthy of it. May I? Would a bit of good lacquer please you? or a rugged bronze — from Japan — It can hardly help you, but it might fill some gap (?) and please me.

A large lacquer box was his gift.

The year 1902 was devoted to the careful installation of the collection, but the galleries were already sufficiently in order for Mrs. Gardner to permit a few very specially privileged friends to see them.

After such a visit Mr. T. Jefferson Coolidge wrote on January 10th:

C'EST MON PLAISIR

My dear Mrs. Gardner
    You are a
        Genius
but that I knew before; I had also found out in an acquaintance of many
years that your taste was unexcelled. What surprised me most in looking at
your beautiful building and its wonderful contents was the enormous labor
you must have given to it for years. You must have a double, one devoted
to society, music, admiration, and pearls, and the other sterner sister given
to labor and duty. A kind of Aphrodite with a lining of Athene.
    May I subscribe myself their devoted servant
                        Sincerely yours
                                T. Jefferson Coolidge

The existence of the Museum Corporation had just been discovered by the newspapers; it suggested many lines of speculation, in particular concerning the attitude of the United States
Government. Would works of art for the museum be admitted
free of duty? The attitude of public and press was generally
friendly and appreciative. On January 2d the 'Boston Post'
said:

> The consensus of opinion on the part of the public appears to be a wish
> that the career of the 'palace' will be free from bitterness and controversy.
> The Government, however, has often been found to be without sentimen-
> tal scruples when a question of the revenue laws being infringed upon arises,
> and it is this possibility, as explained in yesterday's 'Post,' that causes
> general concern.

The laws had not been infringed upon; Mr. Lyman, Collector
of the Port, was quoted as saying that 'all the dealings of the
Museum with the Government had been conducted with the
most scrupulous care to obey the requirements of the law.'
There was, nevertheless, a disagreement between Mrs. Gardner
and the Government. She had paid duty on her recent impor-
tations under protest and was trying to recover the amount; it

[193]

would enable her to enrich the community with additional masterpieces.

Views of the interior of Fenway Court were published in the 'New York World' for Sunday, January 5, 1902; in the accompanying text, which gave the first intelligent account of the building that had been published, are these sentences:

> The dream of Mrs. Gardner is almost realized, for she has raised in an ideal spot a wonderful building, which is destined to be regarded by the public at large as an important treasure of the city like the Public Library, the Art Museum, Trinity Church, or the State House. . . .
>
> It is manifest to any thoughtful observer that Mrs. Gardner has not built for self alone, and that this vast structure is designed for pleasure and instruction beyond the limits of any private circle. In short, the conclusion is irresistible that Mrs. Gardner's generous planning is for the ultimate benefit of the entire community.

The 'Boston Post' of February 2d said:

> She is the only woman alive who has been able to do things which no other woman would have dreamed of doing, without having offered the world the slightest opportunity to attack her. The word 'unique' can describe everything she has done which has caught the attention of the people. The word 'daring' can be applied to many of her performances. The word 'risky' might have been used by some careful mothers as they told their daughters of Mrs. Jack's latest fad.

When her faithful friend, Professor Charles Eliot Norton, was going through the house with her in February, he saw that she needed something to put between the windows of the Veronese Room, and he presented to her for that place the splendid portrait of Alessandro Contarini, a Venetian Senator, by Longhi.

Only enough Bostonians were admitted to the palace to disseminate a stimulating report of its beauty; others were kept waiting for the official opening which Mrs. Gardner was planning. But to distinguished foreigners she was more lenient; to Henry Irving and Ellen Terry she exhibited her new house early in March, and on the 19th to Madame Milka Ternina. The court already looked centuries old and the palms seemed to have been born there. There was a long summer in Brookline, from May 1st till after the middle of November. Among her guests was an Englishman, Matthew Stewart Prichard, whose name appears with steadily increasing frequency in the record of her hospitality. He had been assisting in the acquisition of the examples of Greek art which distinguish the Boston Museum of Fine Arts, and had now joined the staff of the Museum. A brilliant thinker, with an indomitable will and endless energy, he lifted minds out of the ruts of thought and led them far along untrodden paths in search of truth. In July, he moved into the little apartment on the first floor of Fenway Court, which he occupied throughout the summer and autumn. October 28th, he speaks of 'banqueting in the Sala degli Ambasciatori at Fenway Court: first banquet given there.' The banquet was a tea given for Lady Henry Somerset in the Dutch Room.

The Trustees of the local Museum of Fine Arts were working on the problem of a new building; in August, their president, Mr. Samuel Dennis Warren, wrote to Mrs. Gardner that he was happy to learn from Mr. Prichard that the Museum Building Committee might have the benefit of her opinions. He assured her that any suggestion from her would receive careful consideration. No one foresaw that out of this desire for the best possible museum building would develop a controversy so bitter that lifelong friendships would be broken. The subject which divided Boston into two hostile camps was ostensibly the æsthetic value of plaster casts. Mrs. Gardner, Mr. Warren, Mr. Prichard, and Mr. Benjamin Ives Gilman, secretary of the Museum, led the progressives; a treatise entitled 'Aims and Principles,' prepared by Mr. Gilman and Mr. Prichard, endeavored to make clear the difference between the enjoyment of beauty and the study of art history. Personalities became involved and good old Bostonians rallied to the defence of the plaster casts which they had helped to buy and which had served to illustrate for them mythology, history, and biography. Although the Museum finally deprived itself of Mr. Prichard's services, the leading art institutions in the country are now directed in accordance with his theories. For several years he pursued his studies in Europe. Shortly after the outbreak of the World War, he was arrested at Freiburg and interned at Ruhleben; he became the centre of the intellectual life of the camp, and in the school which he helped to organize he gave lessons in Italian and philosophy. Since the armistice, he has been employed by the British Government. In loyalty to his friends he is Mrs. Gardner's equal; during her last five years of illness, hardly a week passed without a refreshing letter from him.

Mrs. Gardner closed her Brookline house earlier than usual in November, 1902; she wished to get thoroughly settled in her new apartment at Fenway Court before the formal opening which she planned for New Year's Night, 1903. When everything else had been attended to, and she was satisfied with the effect of the court and of all the galleries, there remained one unknown quantity — the acoustics of the Music-Room. They needed to be tested with an audience, but she did not want the room seen before the opening. The Perkins Institution for the Blind was invited to send the children in its care to hear some music at Fenway Court. One unfortunate incident seriously marred the afternoon, but established a precedent that continued for many years. As there was deep snow on the ground, the children had all worn rubbers; when they entered the house, their teachers carefully placed the rubbers of their respective charges where they could find them; when the music was over, it was discovered that a servant had gathered together all those wet rubbers which seemed to him unnecessarily disorderly in his beautiful new palace, and had dumped them on a piece of canvas which he had spread over his clean tile floor. To the teachers and the blind children that pile of rubbers was staggering. On days when Fenway Court was open to the public, Mrs. Gardner occasionally cut short a flow of compliment from a well-intentioned stranger with the abrupt question 'Have you got your rubbers?' The public never realized what a nervous strain those open days were to her.

The most important works of art acquired during 1901 and 1902 are the tondo attributed to a contemporary of Botticelli, a Madonna by Botticini, a relief portrait by Mino da Fiesole, the splendid portrait of Mary Tudor by Antonio Moro, 'The Child Jesus Disputing in the Temple' by Paris Bordone, a Madonna by Pintoricchio, Portrait of a Man by Dürer, and a terra-cotta group, Madonna and Child, by Matteo Civitali. The last is one of the many lovely things discovered and secured for Mrs. Gardner by Mr. Joseph Lindon Smith. From

Rome, November 15, 1902, he mailed her a little photograph of the group, and wrote:

It seems to me one of the most beautiful as it is unusual of the many terra cottas of this subject. . . . When I first saw the group, it had only just come and the heads and hands and body of the Child still had the common, pink flesh-color paint which in modern times had been applied; since then, the three coatings of paint have been removed, excepting on portions of the Child's body, which is now being worked upon, and I saw the group to-day for the fourth time and am more and more impressed with its beauty and importance. . . .

We are enjoying Rome immensely . . . my interest is, however, tremendously active in home affairs, and I mean Fenway Court. I learn daily how remarkable your work there is, and what priceless things you have gathered together, and it is my happiest wish to fill in a chink here and there in your splendid edifice.

CHAPTER XII

TRIUMPHS

THE evening so long awaited by Boston society finally came. The guests all agog entered Fenway Court by the door now used to admit the public and found themselves in a small lobby; at the right was a dressing-room for the ladies, a room hung with light blue brocades which served as a background for a few interesting modern pictures, not sufficiently arresting to hold a lady's attention on this eventful evening; in the small coat-room for men at the left, hung with yellow brocades, there were drawings and etchings which did little to gratify eager curiosity. These rooms seemed to merit no special enthusiasm, and for the moment the other picture galleries were inaccessible. One thing at a time was Mrs. Gardner's rule. From the lobby the guests entered the rather narrow, rather high, pure white Music-Room with Donatello's dancing boys across the front of the stage and a horseshoe staircase leading up to the balcony at the rear. On the landing at the top of the horseshoe stood Mrs. Gardner, dressed in black, her diamond antennae waving above her head; up the stairs the representatives of Boston's proudest families climbed to greet their hostess, and then — except the chosen few, perhaps possessing less family pride, whom she invited to sit in the balcony — they climbed down the other side, some of them inwardly fuming, but most of them amused at the homage Mrs. Gardner had exacted of them. The reception over, she herself sat alone in a high Italian chair on the landing while fifty members of the Symphony

ISABELLA STEWART GARDNER

Orchestra, conducted by Mr. Gericke, and nine singers from the Cecilia Society performed the following

PROGRAMME

I BACH

CHORALE

II MOZART

OVERTURE TO
THE MAGIC FLUTE

III CHAUSSON

VIVIANE SYMPHONIC POEM

IV SCHUMANN

OVERTURE
SCHERZO
AND FINALE

FENWAY COURT
JANUARY THE FIRST
MDCCCCIII

When the music, which sounded so beautifully in this 'perfect hall' that Mr. William F. Apthorp called it 'a concert of rare enjoyment,' was over, a great mirror in one corner of the hall was rolled back and the guests were admitted to the court. No one was in the least prepared for the fairy beauty that greeted his eyes; even those who had been privileged to see the court before had never seen it like this, and for those to whom it was entirely new it was overwhelming. Here, in the very midst of winter, was 'a gorgeous vista of blossoming summer gardens ... with the odor of flowers stealing toward one as though wafted on a southern breeze. There was intense silence for a moment broken only by the water trickling in the fountains; then came a growing murmur of delight, and one by one the guests pressed forward to make sure it was not all a dream.'

From the eight balconies that once graced the Ca' d' Oro hung round flame-colored lanterns, brilliant and yet soft globes of light in the lofty court, and through windows and arches came the flickering gleam of myriad candles. The whole scene was indescribably beautiful, and as the rooms gradually filled with people it seemed as if the Venetian Renaissance had been re-incarnated in twentieth-century Boston. The thrill of it was beyond words. The next day Professor Norton wrote: 'The combination of the arts for a beautiful and impressive effect in the festival of last night was unexampled I believe in the experience of everyone who had the honor of being present at it'; and Professor William James, 'May I add, dear Madam, that the æsthetic perfection of all things (of which I will not speak, for you must be tired to death of praise thereof) seemed to have a peculiar effect on the company, making them quiet and docile and self-forgetful and kind, as if they had become as children (though children are just the reverse!). It was a very extra-ordinary and wonderful moral influence — expected by nobody, not designed, I am sure, by you, but felt, I am confident, by everyone to-day. Quite in the line of a Gospel miracle!'

Even on these festive occasions, when guests were allowed to wander at will through the galleries, they were barred from the Chapel and the Gothic Room, but to Sargent, who spent much of that winter in Boston, Mrs. Gardner offered the Gothic Room for a studio, and there he painted several portraits, among them one of Mrs. Fiske Warren and her daughter. When he went to Washington in February to paint the President, Theodore Roosevelt, he stopped in New York, and at Mrs. Gardner's request went to see a portrait of a lady by Tintoretto from the collection of Prince Chigi, which a dealer had offered Mrs. Gardner. Sargent recommended the purchase and, like Mr. Smith, wrote that he would be happy to think he had had a hand in swelling her wonderful collection. Among the examples of his own work which he gave her are an oil portrait of Mr. Loeffler, a marvellous pencil sketch of Jascha Heifetz, and a water-color portrait of herself.

It was her desire that her house should be used; she wanted to be surrounded by life and activity. Besides providing Mr. Sargent with a studio, she put her Music-Room at the disposal of Mr. Loeffler for the rehearsal of his 'Pagan Poem' which he had recently finished, but he was obliged to choose a place nearer the residences of the musicians.

Fenway Court was first opened to the public on Wednesday, February 23, 1903. The price of admission was one dollar; the number of tickets was limited to two hundred, and they were sold at Herrick's Ticket Office. For several weeks the house continued to be open regularly, and gradually the public and the press began to comprehend what an amazing thing Mrs. Gardner had created. The 'New York Sun' on February 24th said:

> This creation is no slavish copy, but a noble, deeply felt reproduction on American soil of the picturesque beauty which charms one in the Old World. The resolution, the enthusiasm, the untiring and patient energy, the true artistic feeling of a woman who could silently conceive and steadily carry out such a design as this are beyond praise.

What the public enjoyed most on those opening days, and has continued to enjoy most, was Mrs. Gardner's own creative work, the charm and beauty of the house as a whole. Here at last was a museum where works of art of great individual beauty were arranged with such harmonious background and suitable environment that the whole effect was beauty. The pleasure in the beauty of the single object was not destroyed, as so often happens in public galleries, by the dreariness of the setting; instead of being wearied or bored, which is the usual museum experience, visitors were stimulated and refreshed. Every room was inviting; every room welcomed the visitor and made him feel it would be a pleasure to stay. Because it expressed one individuality, it possessed unity and harmony; because in everything Mrs. Gardner had followed her motto, 'C'est mon plaisir,' the result gave others pleasure.

Letters of appreciation poured in; all the happiness that superlative praise can give Mrs. Gardner enjoyed.

From Florence, Mr. Smith wrote:

We have kept run of the great 'Spring opening' in Antiquities at Fenway Court — we thought of you, all through that first great day, and now letters and newspapers begin to come, bearing the news, and showing clearly that, tho inadequate and commonplace, the things written are enthusiastic and appreciative of you, at least, and of your noble and remarkable work, if the grand things under your roof fail to get a half even of the praise and appreciation they deserve. In justice to the public and the newspaper men and women, we must remember that an avalanche of Art can hardly be described by a witness, and such it must have seemed to your first visitors — and only repeated visits will bring about more knowledge of the quantity as well as the quality of your treasures.

And in April, Mr. James Loeb:

Sometimes I fear I share the so easily adopted view that life has become sordid and ugly in this new century of ours, but when I saw, as I did yesterday, that there still live those, who like you, need but to stretch out their hand and say

Quod erat, erit,
Quod fuit, sit!

I awoke to the cheering knowledge that it is as true to-day as it ever was that 'he who seeks shall find' beauty.

ISABELLA STEWART GARDNER

Perhaps the most subtle appreciation of her achievement was expressed by Mr. Henry Adams in the following letter written nearly three years later, after his first visit to Fenway Court:

KNICKERBOCKER CLUB, 9 *Feby:* 1906

MY DEAR MRS. GARDNER,

You have given me a great pleasure and greater astonishment. You will not feel it strange that I should write to thank you for it. Not that I know what to say that could be new to you, but that you can have no objection to hearing the same things said and re-said.

As long as such a work can be done, I will not despair of our age, though I do not think any one else could have done it. You stand quite alone. Only I must admit that no one has ever done it before you, though many have tried. If I were obliged to treat it like the scientific gentlemen of our world who preach Evolution, I should have to say that your work must be classed as a *tour-de-force* — no Evolution at all — but pure Special Creation in an adverse environment. You are a creator, and stand alone.

Creators are so rare as to have no atmosphere to live in, but must create it all. You would have been almost equally alone two thousand years ago. America is a terribly pathetic picture to any one who wants something else, but it is hardly worse off than Germany or Sweden or Russia or England have nearly always been; only the reasons are different. We are not quite so stupid and impenetrable as some. We can, in a certain proportion — say one or two in a hundred — feel what you do and have done.

All the same, this living with one or two in a hundred — or a thousand — is living in rarefied air. The effect of an hour with you is that of the Absolute — vertigo — loss of relation — absence in space, time and thought. It is peace, repose or dream, rather like opium; but the return to air and dust is painful. It hurts me. I feel as though you must need something — not exactly help or flattery or even admiration — but subjects.

I bring you the only offering I can, which is thanks.

Ever truly yours
HENRY ADAMS

As the years went by, friends began to wonder more and more if Mrs. Gardner were not lonely in her treasure house. Was she? She would never have admitted it. Certainly in 1903 her life seemed to consist in the preparation of delightful entertainments and the enjoyment of praise.

TRIUMPHS

For her birthday party she gave a concert with the following programme:

FENWAY COURT
APRIL THE THIRTEENTH MDCCCCIII

COMPOSITIONS BY
C. M. LOEFFLER

I. POÈME PAÏEN

II. SONGS
1. DANSONS LA GIGUE!
2. LA CLOCHE FÊLÉE
3. SÉRÉNADE
4. TIMBRES OUBLIÉS
5. ADIEU POUR JAMAIS
6. LES PAONS

III. L'ARCHET

MISS METCALF, MESSRS. LANG, PROCTOR
GEBHARD, KLOEPFEL, BRENTON, MANN
CHORUS FROM THE CECILIA &
MR. LOEFFLER

It was the first performance of the 'Pagan Poem,' which Mr. Loeffler had arranged for two pianos and three trumpets; the trumpeters were placed in an upper gallery across the court, and the effect of the music was very beautiful. Messrs. Proctor and Gebhard were the pianists, Messrs. Kloepfel, Brenton, and Mann, the trumpeters.[1] The songs were sung by Miss Metcalf, accompanied by Mr. Lang; 'L'Archet' was arranged for solo, female chorus, viole d'amour (played by Mr. Loeffler), and piano.

Succeeding seasons saw a great variety of entertainment presented in the Music-Room. On three days in February, 1904, it was the scene of a vaudeville performance in aid of the Massachusetts Society for the Prevention of Cruelty to Children. In December of that year Mrs. Gardner gave a coming-

---

[1] Louis Kloepfel, H. E. Brenton, Joseph F. Mann, *members of Boston Symphony Orchestra.*

out ball for her grand-niece, Catharine Gardner, of which a friend wrote:

> Never before has such a thing been, because it was not possible in Boston. The massing of the candle-light and the bigness and mystery of spaces and objects as they died away into darkness — was what took hold of me. What a good object lesson to our much belighted and benighted friends, who lose all beauty and imagination in a blaze of light from which is no escape.

Another friend spoke of 'the indelible impression of wonder your dance left. Those firelit, candle-lighted rooms were the most perfect of settings, and all others should give up any idea of a ball, after your enchanting demonstration of what it could be.'

On February 21, 1905, at four o'clock, Sir Charles Wyndham and Miss Mary Moore gave a duologue, 'Mrs. Hilary regrets.' In March, 1905, Mrs. Gardner sent out invitations with the innocent, mystifying, terrifying word 'Music'; the artist was Melba, the evening was memorable. After the concert in the Music-Room, while the guests were wandering through the cloister and the galleries, which were illuminated for every party as for that first New Year's Night, Melba stepped out of the Dutch Room where supper was served, and, standing on the landing above the fountain in the court, sang again. Never was music so lovely. The following October, she wrote from England:

> I shall never forget that evening — You, in the centre of your beautiful music-room surrounded by your guests all worshipping at your shrine and saying (*I am sure*) how glad we are to be invited by this wonderful woman who has built this beautiful palace and done *so much* for art in America.

To Melba Mrs. Gardner gave the yellow diamond which had been coveted by the King of Cambodia.

Over the pleasure of these happy days a shadow was cast by the decision of Mr. Leslie M. Shaw, Secretary of the United

Isabella Stewart Gardner, 1888, by John Singer Sargent, oil on canvas, 74¾ by 31½ in.

Fenway Court, the Museum Building in 1904

The Dutch Room, southeast corner

The Titian Room showing Cellini's bronze bust of *Bindo Altoviti* and paintings by Velasquez and Bandinelli on either side

The Spanish Cloister, the setting for Sargent's *El Jaleo*

North Cloister and northeast corner of the Court

The Farnese-Gardner sarcophagus, Roman, II century A.D., West Cloister

States Treasury, that the duties paid on the works of art imported by the Museum would be retained by the Government. During Mr. Gardner's lifetime, before the Museum had been incorporated, duties had been paid without question. Although Mr. Shaw's decision may have pleased those who did not comprehend the value of Mrs. Gardner's undertaking, there were many to lift their voices in protest. Kenyon Cox, the distinguished artist, wrote that she was a 'public benefactor who would be decorated, not taxed, by the Government, if we lived in a truly civilized country.' Another man said: 'Long as I have been venomous against the brutal policy of this country in fining people "ten dollars or ten days" for the offence of artistic taste, you add a new point to my fangs; and I hope some day to be able to express myself adequately as to this iniquity.'

In January, 1904, Mrs. Gardner received the following letter from the Bishop of Fond du Lac:

MY DEAR MRS. GARDNER,

You have erected a Home of the Beautiful to the enrichment of our civilization. The Genius that designed it is not less than the works of genius it enshrines. All lovers of art owe you a debt.

But you have planted your work under a Government that is commercial to baseness, and blind to the culture of the people. All works of high art held for immediate private or public use should come in free of duty. Why should not the Legislature be petitioned to remit the taxes, or would it be hopeless to try and make good Athenians of them?

If I were connected with Harvard, I should advocate its honouring itself by giving you a degree!

And so to all brave efforts good

Follows the snap and snarl of Envy's hateful brood.

With as ever my regards   Yours truly

January 1904.   ✠ C. C. FOND DU LAC[1]

Some time after, her old friend Professor Norton, whose

---

[1] Rt. Rev. Charles Chapman Grafton.

own interests and pursuits made him perhaps appreciate more than any one else the significance of Mrs. Gardner's achievement, wrote:

SHADY HILL, 3 *April*, 1905

MY DEAR MRS. GARDNER:

I thank you for your note and for the cheque . . . enclosed in it in payment for the two paintings by Tintoretto, which I am glad to have pass into your hands. It gives me pleasure to receive the cheque as a sign that you are free from embarrassing conditions into which you were forced by the extortions of our tariff, which is the root of political and social corruption and the evidence of our national semi-civilization.

I wish I could give you pleasure corresponding to my admiration and gratitude for what you have accomplished, and still more for the spirit with which you bear the trials and disappointments which result from the lack of due appreciation of your work and your intentions. I wish that you may live long enough to see the recognition of them from the public as warm and as sympathetic as that which is given to you now by the few who have intelligence enough to recognize the worth of what you have done.

With affection and respect, I am, dear Mrs. Gardner,

Sincerely yours

CHARLES ELIOT NORTON

Two months later, Major Higginson sent her the following note:

BOSTON, *June* 1, 1905

MY DEAR MRS. GARDNER,

If you think that you are to have a peaceful life, die at once! So soon as a person has showed his capacity to help his fellow-creatures and his will to do so, he will be asked again and again.

It is a price and a joy of life. I am glad that you for your own sake and for Jack's — the kindest man on earth — have fallen into that class. You chose the path and are a blessing to many men and women.

Very truly

H. L. HIGGINSON

In 1905, Mrs. Gardner did a thing in which she took great pride and pleasure for the rest of her life: — she offered a series of prizes for tenement-house gardens. It was announced that the judges would consider the difficulties overcome as much as artistic beauty, good taste, and extent of the display; raising

[208]

plants from seed was recommended. Fair consideration would be given not only to window boxes, but also to ornamentation of sides of houses, roofs, sheds, extensions, rear yards, and alleys. Children and adults of all ages and nationalities, were invited to take part. The eighteen successful contestants with their families were invited to 'Green Hill,' on Sunday, August 20th to receive their prizes; five nationalities were represented. No prize-winner was eligible for a prize a second time until three years had elapsed, but might receive honorable mention every year. Mrs. Gardner maintained these competitions through the year 1911; in 1905, there were one hundred competitors; in 1911, three hundred.

Of all the entertainments given in the Music-Room none was more ambitious than the performance on April 23, 1906, of

FIORELLA

COMÉDIE LYRIQUE EN UN ACTE

Poème de
Victorien Sardou
et
P. B. Gheusi

Musique de
Amherst Webber

PERSONNAGES

Cordiani (amant de Fiorella)..............M. M. Kittredge
Gattinara (chef de bandits)...................... Codman
Agostin (Patricien de Venise).................... Carbone
Un Exempt du guet............................ Osborne
Deux Gondoliers...
Un Veilleur de Nuit.....................................
Fiorella...................................Mmes. Child
Zerbine (suivante de Fiorella)......................Seygard

La scène se passe dans le palais de Don Agostin
à Venise au XVIᵉ siècle

Chef d'orchestre................................M. Zach

[209]

ISABELLA STEWART GARDNER

Since the happy season of 1892 in Venice, Mrs. Gardner had seen much of Mr. Webber. His first visit to Boston was made in 1894; in 1896, he returned with the de Reszkes. For the rest of Jean's life, Mr. Webber was his accompanist; in 1902, he began the composition of 'Fiorella,' intending it for Jean de Reszke's theatre. January 23, 1906, he wrote from New York:

DEAR MRS. GARDNER,

You are a magician. How have you managed to make Fiorella seem possible? She seemed quite unpracticable when we talked her over. I am in a great state of excitement about her and shall at once send for copies to Paris — but of course shall not whisper a word to any one. I am longing to know how you think of making up the cast, and all about it.

You are a perfect angel to take so much trouble about it; I know what a lot of thought it requires even to make it *look* feasible.

In tearing haste
Ever yours
AMHERST WEBBER

There were difficulties which would have daunted a less intrepid spirit than Mrs. Gardner. Not more than two or three complete rehearsals were held, but, stimulated by Mrs. Gardner's energy and confidence, and stage-managed by Mr. Joseph Lindon Smith, the performance was a great success. Mrs. Bertha Cushing Child, who sang 'Fiorella,' wrote:

It has all been such a wonderful pleasure — the music itself, the beauty of the palace in the day and its haunting mystery at night — the spell of your personality — it is all so enchanting I can't thank you enough.

Mr. B. J. Lang, who had had a long experience in the preparation of musical entertainments, wrote:

DEAR MRS. GARDNER,

What is a 'Dutch Uncle'? I'd like to talk to you like one! You must *not* do such things as you do. They cannot be done in *your way* excepting by you — therefore even if you were willing to be helped, no one could help you.

TRIUMPHS

It is your pleasure? Granted. You should be denied it when the pleasure coveted entails such an enormous outlay of nervous energy, and when you know the result is open to the possible break-down of singers. Be less generous to the world and more generous to yourself.

I am yours gratefully but dreadfully.

B. J. Lang

It was a wonderful night.

On May 2, 1906, at an entertainment in aid of the Holy Ghost Hospital for Incurables, Cambridge, Massachusetts, Miss Lena Little sang four songs and Miss Ruth St. Denis danced 'The Cobra, or Snake Charmer,' and 'Radha, a Hindoo Temple Dance.' It was one of her earliest appearances in Boston.

November 22, 1907, Mrs. Gardner's guests had the pleasure of hearing again Loeffler's 'Pagan Poem.' He had now arranged it for full orchestra, and dedicated it to Gustave Schirmer, who died July 15, 1907. The music was played by the Boston Symphony Orchestra. This was Mrs. Gardner's last elaborate concert, but it was always a pleasure to her to be able to assist her friends by placing the Music-Room at their disposal. During the winters of 1908–09 and 1909–10, the Kneisel Quartette gave its concerts there, and there for several seasons the concerts arranged by Miss Julia Terry were given. On January 28, 1914, the subscribers to the Flonzaley Quartette Concerts were invited to a private performance of Schoenberg's Quartette in D minor. A performance by Novelli and his company early in January, 1908, was the last brilliant entertainment that Mrs. Gardner gave Boston society. There were many, many other delightful affairs for the smaller circle of her intimate friends, but these did not, as a rule, take place in the Music-Room.

On December 30, 1908, as a New Year's gift to Mrs. Gardner,

some friends performed a little French Christmas play in the Gothic Room. It was so picturesque that Mrs. Gardner asked to have it done again January 9, 1909, for the benefit of the sufferers from the earthquake which on December 28, 1908, devastated Messina. The proceeds of the performance, $1480, were forwarded by Archbishop O'Connell (who was made Cardinal in 1911) as a contribution to the relief fund of His Holiness the Pope. For Cardinal O'Connell she had great admiration; her invitations to the theatre and the opera his position did not permit him to accept, but he did come to see Novelli at Fenway Court, and thanked Mrs. Gardner 'for the exquisite courtesy and honor which the distinguished hostess herself offered to the Archbishop of Boston.' She in turn felt greatly honored by his many courtesies to her.

Great as her collection already was, she wished it to become still greater. No one labored more steadily in her service at this time than Mr. Joseph Lindon Smith. In May, 1903, he wrote that he had bought for her in London an Italian primitive 'large as a grand piano — splendid in color — Madonna and Child with saints around her — full of strong individual character — perfectly sound — absolutely untouched, but showing some marks here and there of cruel treatment in the past — nothing but what can be overcome and put back into shape by a little loving care.' It is signed and dated,

✠ ANNO ·· DNI ·· MLLO ·· C · C · C ·· SETTIMO ·· IULIANUS ·· PICTOR ·· DEARIMINO ·· FECIT .. OCHOPUS ·· TEMPORE ·· DNI ·· CLEMENTIS ·· PP ·· QUINTI · ✠

It has been said that this is the only known work by this master with a signature and date.

Mr. Smith sent word soon after that in Florence the dealer Volpi had shown him a photograph of a 'Hercules' by Piero della Francesca, and he asked if she would like him to get it for her. The trials and tribulations connected with this purchase lasted many years. At the end of May, Mr. Smith returned to Florence to see the fresco, and on June 11th he wrote:

If nothing happens, you will soon be the owner of the

'ERCOLE' by
PIERO DELLA FRANCESCA.

So many things did happen that it was nearly four years before the picture came into Mrs. Gardner's possession and even then an unlucky fate pursued it. On June 28, 1903, the Italian laws relating to the sale and export of works of art were amended, increasing the restrictions. For two years no picture on the Government list could leave the country; for two years Volpi struggled to have the picture removed from the list on the ground that he had begun negotiations for its sale before the law was passed and that Italy was rich in fine examples of Piero. In June, 1905, Volpi was assured that the law would be modified, or at least that certain pictures, including the Piero, would be taken off the list; Mr. Smith was taken by Volpi to see the Florentine official who had authority in the matter, and who assured him the picture would be allowed to leave Italy by the end of June. A copy had been made and put up at Borgo San Sepolcro to replace the original, which Volpi guaranteed to deliver in good condition to Monsieur Robert in Paris. To enable him to be certain that the picture bought by Mr. Smith was the one delivered to him, Mr. Smith took elaborate precautions which he described to Robert as follows:

I have placed across the face of the picture bands of thin tracing paper running from top to bottom and side to side . . . Where these strips of paper intersect I have placed red seals with the letters E V . . . and four times I have written my full name on the tracing paper — one of those times on a separate piece of white paper torn off from a hotel bill, the other end of which I enclose. I then took friends of mine living in Florence to see the picture . . . and they will be in Paris in July, and Volpi knows this, and I told him they stood ready to be called in to see the picture there, if there seemed any reason for it . . . Indeed, I feel quite guilty towards him to *seem* to suspect his honesty, as I have done — but you and I are not doing these things for ourselves, but for a lady who trusts us, and no caution should be spared.

Nevertheless, the picture did not leave Florence in June, 1905; in October, 1906, it was still in Volpi's hands, and on October 6th, Mrs. Gardner received the following letter from Dr. Wilhelm Bode, the famous Director of the Berlin Museums:

FLORENCE, 6th *Oct.*
H. DE ROME

DEAR MRS. GARDNER,

I hear that you arrived here the other day, as you had the intention. I am sorry that I am not able to see you here because I am suffering and must return directly to Berlin, if possible to-morrow, in order to prevent a fresh inflammation of the veins.

Perhaps it may interest you to know that the picture dealer Elia Volpi here (Piazza Goldoni) has the fresco representing Hercules by Piero della Francesca in his house and that he can get now the 'permissione dell' esportazione' from the Government. He believes that you still wish to buy this fresco, but after what you told me in Berlin you have not the intention to make any important acquisition this year and the next. Perhaps you will be kind enough to call upon him and tell him your intention. It will be interesting for you as you will see in his studio some good pictures and sculptures.

Believe me, dear Mrs. Gardner,

Yours very truly
W. BODE

The letter seems to display a certain ignorance of psychology. If Mrs. Gardner's resolve to possess the picture had ever weakened, it would have been fortified by Bode's interest; this was not the first time that they had desired the same master-

[214]

piece, nor was it to be the last, and in no instance did Mrs. Gardner fail to score. Finally, on Christmas Day, 1906, Mr. Smith, who was in Egypt, wrote to Mrs. Gardner that he had just received a letter from Volpi saying 'he was only waiting word from Robert from Paris to start at once himself with the Piero. It seems so good news that it can hardly be true. I hope there may be nothing to block further progress of this famous picture towards Paris. Would that Boston were as free as Paris to welcome it!' This time the picture did actually reach Paris. What further mishaps awaited it will be told later.

In November, 1903, Mrs. Gardner purchased four tapestries from the Charles M. Ffoulke collection; they were known as 'The Château and Garden Series,' and were placed by Mrs. Gardner on the stage of the Music-Room, where they made the setting for whatever performance was given there. In December, Mrs. Gardner contracted with Mrs. Ffoulke for the purchase of eleven more tapestries formerly in the Barberini collection at Rome — a set of five then called 'The Archduke Albert and Archduchess Isabella Series,' [1] another set of five known as 'The Abraham and Rebecca Series,' and a single tapestry known as 'The Museum Piece,' described as 'Boy in Tree and other Springtime Illustrations.' Four of these tapestries were in the United States; the others were in Europe, and eventually joined the Piero. The purchase of these tapestries sealed the doom of the Music-Room, as yet scarcely a year old.

In 1904, Mrs. Gardner purchased from a New York dealer the 'Portrait of Madame Gaujelin' by Degas, formerly in the Manzi collection; at the sale of the Somzée collection in Brus-

---

[1] Now identified as 'Scenes from the Life of Cyrus the Great.'

sels, Monsieur Robert secured for her 'Santa Engracia' by Bermejo, a picture which she and Mr. Ralph W. Curtis had seen and admired as the most interesting thing in the Paris Exposition of 1900, where it was hung in the Belgian Pavilion.

Mrs. Gardner's last trip to Europe was made in 1906. Although the Music-Room was not destroyed and the Tapestry Room constructed until 1914, she had in her imagination a vision of what the new room should be and of what should be done with the space under it, and while in Europe she purchased such architectural fragments and such furniture as the realization of her vision demanded. Perhaps it was because of a premonition that she would never go to Europe again — she had an uncanny faculty for anticipating events — that during this European sojourn she visited all the places which had particularly endeared themselves to her. In Madrid she purchased a tomb-relief of a man in armor and a Gothic silver-gilt cross. When she returned to Paris, she wrote to a friend: 'Prichard arrived in Paris two or three days ago and has started vigorously studying the Louvre. I feel about it and many museums as I did about the Prado — if I could only take hold! Some things are so wonderful — and yet so badly presented — and such a lot of not good. Poor Museums! Strength of mind they do need — and taste.'

The following letters reveal the interest and assistance of Mr. Henry Adams in her purchase of a stained-glass window, probably the finest example in the United States.

[PARIS] 13 June, 1906

MY DEAR MRS. GARDNER,

Your letter has taken a month to reach me, and I answer it at once for fear you may depart and think me faithless. I am lost, but not untrue. Here in my attic I feel like an early Christian or a late primitive — highly decomposed — but sure.

On inquiry I find that the window is still there, boxed up, but withdrawn from sale. I have been promised a photograph of it. If I get it, I will send it to you. I had half a mind to buy the window myself and set it up in my room, but I could not get the measurements and dared not ask the price. If I took it at the owner's price, I should doubtless be cheated and cheat you. You would scorn me justly and I should more than ever throw dust on my head. But then I should have an excuse for keeping the window which I could not buy in cold blood.

Never would I be a party to leading any helpless banker or woman to buy even a bond. Perhaps I would sell them an automobile, but that is honest fraud.

Ever truly yours

HENRY ADAMS

October 23, 1906

WONDERFUL WOMAN,

That any one should exist as energetic as you fills me with marvel but that you should talk of my opinion on a matter of art is altogether contradictory. My opinion remains what it was when I happened to mention the window to you. Obediently, like a swan — no! a lamb! — I went to examine it again on summons, and found nothing to add. Here and there, small pieces of glass have been replaced, but the quality is so inferior as to be evident at once. To me it is a wonderful thing to be six or seven hundred years old, and as fresh as when I was six. Glass and porcelain and some mosaics carry color so, but all else is grass. . . .

Sunday, 24

DEAR MRS. GARDNER,

Our letters run across each other in all directions.

The dealer's name and address is on the letter-heading enclosed.

He tells me that the window is still at his place, but boxed up and withdrawn from sale by order of the owner.

Apparently he has no authority to sell it now, without referring to the owner. This means that one must either ask for a price or make an offer. He has a photograph which he promised to have printed.

I said nothing about your wishes, knowing that any mention of your name would at once raise the price five or ten times.

He has my name and address. If you go there *incognita*, you could safely say that I had *asked* you to inquire about it as a curiosity. He would probably show you some fourteenth-century pieces he has, which are not bad, but

[217]

quite a different thing. *The* window is from Saint Denis, early thirteenth century.

I shall come at once to see you.

Ever yours

HENRY ADAMS

At the end of October, or early in November, Mr. Berenson's zeal obtained for her the portrait of Pope Innocent X by Velazquez,[1] which they both called 'a whacker!' Berenson conducted the negotiations from Paris and Madrid; she herself was in Rome. On October 22d, she spent an hour at the Vatican in the Borgia Rooms, 'more wonderful than ever because lighted up'; she had been taken by a friend prominent in Black circles to call on Cardinal Merry del Val, who 'talked much of O'Connell, our Boston Bishop.'

Her dear friend Mrs. Maud Howe Elliott and her painter husband John Elliott were living in Rome, and did everything for Mrs. Gardner's comfort. Her journey from Rome to Naples she described in the following letter to Mrs. Elliott:

HOTEL ROYAL DES ETRANGERS

NAPLES, *Friday noon.* [*October*,1906]

Well, my dear!

The history of our roves could be long and dismal. I will try to make it short. Owing to the machinations of the Prince of the Camorra (how is it spelled?), J. Elliott, we, Ella and I, went safely alone as far as Monte Cassino, then four Italians swooped down and in — ! And with such a mass of luggage that the compartment was full to the eyes — on we went, when not far from Monte Cassino, slam, bang, all brakes on — and then dead stop, and such screaming, and confusion as Italy alone is capable of. It seemed that my four Italians consisted of an invalid young man, his mother, brother and sister. It also seemed that the invalid was on the point of a nervous breakdown. His trained nurse and the maid were in the next compartment, and the trained nurse threw himself out of the window. Hence the stop and

[1] Most critics now consider this a version by another hand.

the screaming, etc. My Italian family beside themselves with grief over the accident, and principally that the invalid son (aged twenty-five) should not find out what had happened. The train backed to pick up the man, still alive, and the mother, brother and sister had a regular time over it, keeping the invalid in his seat, that he should not know, and themselves rushing over me, backwards and forwards, to and from the window! You can form no idea of the horror of it all. At the next station the would-be suicide was taken out of the train and off to a hospital or something. The maid in hysterics had to be coped with, crowds surrounding our carriage, and through it all, the efforts to keep the invalid son in ignorance. They told me, in English, that they feared the worst from the shock to him. Some people can make a journey in peace and alone in a train without paying for the whole compartment — but no such luck for me. So in future I cannot run risks. You can't think how dreadful it all was. Of course, I am a pig to think of anything but those wretched people — but it was like making a journey with an insane asylum. Of course we were hours late. When I at last got Ella and myself into bed, I thought I should break down. Well, that morning hoping for a haven of rest on board the steamer, a telephone came that she might not sail. I rushed to the office of the ship and find the strike is on terrifically, and they do not yet know when they can go, probably not before Sunday night! I don't know a soul in this place and feel as if the last straw had fallen. However, I pray for the best — Perhaps! To steady my mind I went to Pepe's the antiquario. There I found some *nice* things, *very*, and enough, not so nice, to make me doubly sure that what I said about Miss C.'s furniture was true. . . .

She bought twelve carved chairs, style of Louis XV, two settees of walnut, style of Louis XV, two walnut writing-tables, and a handsome large oval table.

From Paris she wrote on November 11th: 'I have been all day at Giverny with the Tom Perrys and Monet the painter. It was perfect in every way.' Writing again, two days later, she said: 'My days are crammed. I am seeing all the private collections, *now* mostly with Dreyfus [1] — before with Berenson. . . . Lawrence Butler gave me a tea this afternoon and sang — but beautifully. And at 1.30 I went to a rehearsal of a new

[1] Gustave Dreyfus, the collector.

play at the Français. The whole interesting world of Paris there.'

Owing to the tariff, most of her numerous purchases were left in Paris in the care of Monsieur Robert.

The following letters testify that enthusiastic appreciation of her collection was not confined to her friends and neighbors. A Frenchman wrote:

Votre superbe collection ... ferait l'envie de n'importe grand musée d'Europe; vous avez des merveilles et en les apportant en Amérique, vous avez été une plus grande bienfaitrice que cette quantité de gens qui distribuent de l'argent à droite et à gauche. C'est par la beauté pure qu'on arrive à élever les idées, les sentiments. Tous ceux qui sortent de chez vous s'en vont avec plus de noblesse, car ils viennent de se retremper au contact de ce qui est parfaitement beau.

Paul Clemen, Professor of Art History at the University of Bonn, wrote:

Certainly you have now the best private collection in the world — not the largest, but the noblest.... The Wallace Collection suffocates now under the pictures and art objects and in several rooms it looks as by an Art Dealer. In your house one walks quickly through the centuries and through the leading art countries and has always again quite a harmonious and round impression.

And in February 22, 1909, Thorsten Laurin:

I am just now on the point of leaving Boston ... but before I go, I must thank you for the most interesting hours I have spent in this country, I mean the visit in your delightful home, which I consider the most beautiful I have ever seen and I don't ever expect to see its equal anywhere.

The intruder had done for Boston something that no Bostonian had done, something that would permanently enrich the city, something for which Boston was to be forever grateful. Gradually it began to dawn upon the more open-minded Bostonians that, if Mrs. Gardner had been confined within the narrow limits of their conventionalities, if her free spirit had known their inhibitions, her genius might never have flowered. Her daring and self-confidence had made possible Fenway Court, a citadel of peace and dignity and beauty, not the result of a sudden desire for collecting, which has become an American obsession, but the consummation of a long-sustained, slowly developed plan whose joyous execution proclaimed anew the triumph of spirit over matter.

CHAPTER XIII
THE CROWN OF LIFE

MUCH as Mrs. Gardner enjoyed her collection and the constantly expressed amazement at her success, the great pleasure of her later life was the steadily increasing and deepening affection of old friends and the ardent devotion of new friends. She loved love, and every token of affection she cherished; the little gifts of children, made perhaps in their kindergarten classes, she not only preserved, but kept about where she could see them. In her youth she intrigued and amused her intimates; now she inspired their love; indeed, she came to be regarded almost with reverence. Many a woman who has known the pleasure of being considered charming in her youth has found herself neglected and forgotten in old age, but Mrs. Gardner had the happy experience of knowing herself more appreciated, more admired, and more beloved as the years passed. If she were to be described with one word, it would be Mr. Berenson's 'life-enhancing.' The indiscretions and follies of her youth were remembered with smiles; the admiration of her courage, loyalty, determination, generosity, and of her genius became almost universal.

Of all the new friendships that enriched these later years, none made a more profound impression than that of the Japanese artist, connoisseur, philosopher, and poet, Okakura-Kakuzo. Before Mr. Okakura's first visit to Boston, Mr. John La Farge wrote to her: 'I should like to add to any knowledge

The Court, 1956, southwest corner

The Terrace, St. Tropez, 1904, by Henri Matisse, oil on canvas, 28¼ x 22¾ in.

Madame Gaujelin, 1867, by Edgar Degas, oil on canvas, 23½ x 17½ in.

Mrs. Gardner in White, 1922, by Sargent, watercolor on paper, 16¾ x 12½ in.

Mrs. Gardner and A. Piatt Andrew at his house Red Roof, Gloucester, Massachusetts

you may have of him my statement that he is the most intelligent critic of art, and I might also say of everything, that I know of. His very great learning in certain ways is balanced by his perception of the uselessness of much that he knows. I think that he is one of the very few persons whom you should not miss enjoying. . . .' On Sunday, March 27, 1904, Okakura came to Fenway Court. Thereafter, whenever he was in Boston, he and Mrs. Gardner were much together. Each understood the other and stimulated the other. Okakura's most beautiful English poems were addressed to her; to her he dedicated his most ambitious poetical effort, the drama of 'The White Fox.' The moonlight on the walls of the court at Fenway Court inspired the following poem, called

THE STAIRWAY OF JADE

The One
Alone and white.

Shadows but wander
In the lights that were;
Lights but linger
In the shadows to be.

The Moon
White and alone.

The stars have dissolved
To make a crystal night;
Fragrance floats
Unseen by flowers;
Echoes waft,
Half answered by darkness.

[223]

ISABELLA STEWART GARDNER

A shadow glides
On the stairway of jade —
Is it a moonbeam?
Is it the One?
In the Abode of Solitary Shadow?

Mr. Okakura joined the staff of the Boston Museum of Fine Arts, which owes to his knowledge and taste the purification and elevation of its supreme Oriental collections; he taught the community — those who had ears to hear and eyes to see — to comprehend a little the significance and beauty of early Chinese and Japanese art. In his train came Mr. Rokkaku, a worker in lacquer, and Mr. Okabe, a worker in metal, who lived during the summer of 1905 in a little cottage on Mrs. Gardner's Brookline estate; she was one of the three or four Bostonians who seemed to them to feel genuine concern for their welfare and happiness.

As Mrs. Gardner took the deepest interest in the development of the plans for the new building of the Art Museum, she frequently invited the members of the staff, Mr. Prichard, Mr. John Briggs Potter, Mr. Paul Chalfin, and Mr. Bert Hodge Hill, for dinner. Never was she more in her element than when she was discussing with a group of men their specialty; to artists, musicians, politicians, explorers, and scientists she was equally sympathetic. She was the best of companions with whom to share success, the most encouraging in failure; when Mr. Thomas Bailey Aldrich, whom she once called the best host she ever knew because he tried to give his guests every chance to display their abilities, invited her to attend, on October 13, 1904, the first performance of his play, 'Judith of Bethulia,' she regretted that she had 'a previous engagement' — she had already taken tickets for herself and Henry James. Mr. Aldrich then wrote:

DEAR MRS. GARDNER:

It is good of you to have 'a previous engagement' — of that kind! During the evening will you not look in at our box (where I shall be a prisoner) and afterward bring Henry James with you to the Union Club, where we are to have a little supper? We'll celebrate a success, if we catch one, and if we don't, we'll dry our tears with Monopole *extra sec.*

Always yours

T. B. ALDRICH

In 1907, Zorn came again to America and spent the week-end of May 11th–13th at 'Green Hill'; it was due to his intervention that Mrs. Gardner obtained the drawing of 'A Turkish Artist' made by Gentile Bellini when he was in Constantinople. The drawing was found there by the Swedish Consul, Zorn's friend, Dr. F. R. Martin, who was persuaded by Zorn to give Mrs. Gardner the refusal of it. Both British and German museums coveted it. Any one of Mrs. Gardner's friends would have acted as Zorn did; like Mr. Sargent and Mr. Smith, her other friends wished they might make some contribution to her collection. It contains many gifts from artists — the portrait of Henry James by William James, Jr.; paintings by Martin Mower and Arthur Pope; a drawing of Mr. Prichard by Mr. Potter; and several paintings by Denman W. Ross. Mr. Thomas Whittemore gave her a painting by Matisse, a very fine Russian painting of the fifteenth century, and a drawing of himself by Sargent.

It was in the year 1907 that Mrs. Gardner discovered Eastern Point, Gloucester, which immediately became her favorite pleasure resort; of her friends there, the first among equals was perhaps Mr. A. Piatt Andrew, then a member of the faculty of Harvard College, but all the little colony became very dear to her. The last vacation of her life was a month spent at Eastern Point in 1918, when she occupied the house of Miss Caroline Sinkler.

After her first visit to Mr. Andrew in the summer of 1907, she wrote:

Wednesday 2 P.M.
GREEN HILL, BROOKLINE, MASS.

In a few hours, what a change! The land change does not make one into something rich and strange — alas! Your village is Fogland with the sea's white arms about you all. Don't let outsiders crawl in — only me! For *I* care — I love its rich, strange people, so far away. My greetings wall the village — and to you 'I do beseech you (chiefly that I might set it in my prayers), What is your name?' That seems the only way to thank you for my happy visit.

Don't let Miss Davidge forget next Friday P.M. — for 'it is deeply sworn.' I shall expect you and her. Sleeper at midday on Saturday.

Then perhaps I can *say* a bigger thank you, than I can *write.*

Sincerely yours
ISABELLA S. GARDNER

As often as possible on her way to or from Gloucester, she stopped for lunch or dinner with Mr. and Mrs. William Hooper in Manchester. Mrs. Hooper's father, Mr. Charles E. Perkins, of Burlington, Iowa, was for many years president of the Chicago, Burlington & Quincy Railroad, of which Mr. Gardner was a director; whenever the business of the railroad required his presence in the West, he paid a visit to Mr. Perkins, and, as the best Burgundy was reserved for these occasions, Mr. Gardner was known to the children as the 'Duke of Burgundy.' Now Mrs. Gardner had discovered that at Mrs. Hooper's house could be found, besides the best Burgundy in the world, for which she cared nothing whatever, the best corned beef in the world, which was her favorite food. No matter how formal the occasion or how elaborate the menu of Mrs. Hooper's party Mrs. Gardner never failed to request nor to receive cold corned beef.

On August 7, 1908, she wrote the following letter to the author, inviting him to spend the week-end at Eastern Point:

Green Hill, Thursday night

DEAR MR. CARTER,

I am looking forward to seeing you — but not here — I have a little spree up my sleeve for you. Andrew has gone to Europe and has given me the use of his little house if I want to run down for a day or two — So that is where we are to spend Saturday night, and Sunday, coming up as early as you like Monday morning — It will be like a picnic, I take Ella and we all get on as well as possible — No dressing at all — I do hope it won't bore you — Collins will appear at the Art Museum with the carryall for you — at 2.30 on Saturday, and you will take the 3.20 for Gloucester. I will meet you at the station there, and drive you to Red Roof (Andrew's house). I go down ahead of you to get ready —

I have so much to hear, and tell —

I hope you will know me —

A demain —

Sincerely yours
I. S. GARDNER

When I arrived, I found her with bruised and bandaged head — due to the accident she mentions in the following letter to Mr. Andrew — but her spirits were not dampened.

Sunday, August 9
EASTERN POINT, GLOUCESTER, MASS.

MY DEAR A——

So; good morning, from this most wonderful place! When you want 'references' as a friend, send to me. I will give you one, A No. 1 kind. You have always been that to me, and this is the 'comble.' For, I have not been tip-top — and I came a cropper at the Hays Hammonds' last Monday — fell on my head — and so, this is such a wonderful cure. A man from the Art Museum, who is overworked, and tired, is here for Sunday. He thinks it is

Paradise. His name is Carter. Honest, you have no idea how wonderful it is. But there is an A No. 1 blank; that is A.P.A. And no matter where you are, it is not one half as good as this! Such weather, such sunsets, such moon. — The neighbors have been, one and all, devoted to me, as guest of Red Roof. Miss Davidge spent an hour here with M. Le Gendre — and asked me to dinner. I lunched with Cecilia, and that enchanting Miss Sinkler comes and goes. Another hour with her yesterday. And Harry Sleeper, well, there are no words! Ella and Bridget, my two henchmen, are buzzing about like the bees about the bee balm. Ella says, 'Mr. Andrew ought not to lose the pleasure of being here — he is too good.' And, when you hear everything you *will* envy us. I came down on Friday and brought Mr. and Mrs. Sam Abbott, of Rome, and Henry Swift. On the way over (we were in Frick's motor) we went to Bay View by Annisquam where His Grace Archbishop O'Connell has got a place. He is a great friend of the Abbotts from Roman days. I made him come over here too! So, how you would have liked it! Every one of those four guests were as crazy about this place as I. We had picnic supper in the porch. Windows all open and all of us facing the water, with a sunset made on purpose. Then, as they were leaving at 8 P.M., out came the moon! We all thanked *you.* And the Archbishop is coming again, and if he and you are here for Thanksgiving, he has promised to come! But he probably will be in Rome, as he has been bidden. Gibbons is getting well, otherwise O'Connell might be made Cardinal. If you come home before he goes (early November), he promised to come over here to see you. So *there* is an incentive for an early return. But I don't have any illusions about your getting here early. Isn't it splendid, the time you are having? . . . I have been writing this, dressing, and watching the bears. They were so infatuated with everything this morning, that they didn't fight, but made love and were darlings. They stood up, side by side, looking up at me as I talked from the Boudoir window. And the birds! Do come back soon to see it all.

With eternal gratitude

Yours

Y.

Some years later, when she took Henry James to lunch with Miss Cecilia Beaux of Eastern Point, he called the day 'a dense splendid tissue of adventure,' and said he thought Mrs. Gardner had had a 'preposterously pleasant career' because she had everything, she did everything, she enjoyed everything.

THE CROWN OF LIFE

She regularly called Mr. Andrew 'A,' and the little circle at Eastern Point called her 'Y'; many of her personal things were marked with a crowned 'Y.' These initials, 'A' and 'Y,' led to little plays on words that pleased her fancy. Thanking Mr. Andrew for a small bust of Napoleon which he had sent her for Christmas, she wrote:

> The Corsican has weathered the storms, dear A, and arrived two minutes ago. He is a joy, and Y isn't Ys (wise!) * enough to know where anything quite like him could have been found. I *am* so pleased and grateful . . .
>
> * I feel obliged to be explanitive!

The story of another episode is related by Mr. Andrew:

> With another young man I had met her in New York and we had spent together a fabulously crowded day with visits to picture dealers, art exhibitions, a lunch party, a play, a dinner party, the opera, and supper afterwards, which had left my friend and me completely exhausted when we separated about two in the morning. I recall that as we pushed back our chairs from the table, Mrs. Gardner commented on our initials which were 'A' and 'M,' and said, 'That means the morning,' and I had replied 'Y,' which was hers, 'means youth, eternal youth.' I have never forgotten the way she flashed back instantly, 'A, M, and Y, that is the beginning, the middle, and the end'; and so the party ended.

When she got back to Fenway Court she wrote:

> You thought well, dear A.
> Youth is not Youth unless eternal, and Life is not Life without it.
> — Evviva!
>
> Yours
>
> Y.

January 9, 1909, she wrote to him:

> DEAR A
> Thanks, ever so many, for the little note. I am awfully glad to get it, and the messages from M. I wish I could have seen him. I fancy you won't be coming this way again very soon. But if you do, remember your room is ready here — only let me know that I may see you! Sleeper is helping me about my little play that is to be given for the earthquake sufferers. It is the

same play as before — very dear and pretty. Otherwise my life is as usual — Music, people, and constant persecution from our government. Tell me your news and believe me always

Yours

Y.

Thanks for the photos — awfully funny!

The difficulty with the Government was caused by the unceremonious entrance into the United States in 1908 of the ill-fated Piero accompanied by the Ffoulke tapestries and a marble bust of Cardinal Riario. The news that the customs agents had seized these precious masterpieces was as severe a blow as Mrs. Gardner ever received. She wrote me a long letter about this and another difficulty, beginning: 'Please have patience to read this. I want you to know and therefore write,' and ending:

What can I think of this world? Is there justice? And what can I think of the chivalry of people? I am trying to keep up in public, and I don't find it so easy as I did. My only chance seems never to *speak* of any of these things. I simply can't. So I write them to you. I want you to tell Potter and then let me count on your friendship and sympathy to help me through. I try to let my thoughts get all the distraction they can. I am now going into the garden.

After the matter was settled, the following paragraph was published in a Boston paper:

MRS. GARDNER'S MISTAKE

When the duties of $150,000 on the old masters, valued at $80,000, have been paid, it may perhaps dawn on Mrs. J. L. Gardner how grievously she has offended against this great and glorious republic, in trying to import works of art. The law of this republic is very strict with all misguided persons who dare to bring to this land paintings, or statuary, or valuable works of research. What these persons should do, if they wish to be favorably regarded by the law, is import dogs. A snarling, blear-eyed bulldog of uncertain walk and disagreeable temper, valued at $10,000, can be imported free

[230]

of duty. A yelping, howling, snapping poodle, of no earthly good to himself or humanity, but valued at $8000 can be imported duty free. An obese, ungainly and repulsive dachshund of a value of $5000 can be imported duty free. It is expected that all good and wealthy citizens will spend their money in decorating the land of the free with high art of this variety, and if the animals are 'pedigreed,' no duty will be charged. But any millionaire who tries to import works by Titian, Rubens, or Turner, is lucky if he escapes jail. All of which proves us to be a logical, reasonable and highly intelligent nation.

Within a year the tariff on works of art was removed.

On April 9, 1909, Mr. Higginson sent Mrs. Gardner the following innocent note:

DEAR MRS. GARDNER,
May I have the honor of calling on you soon? The doctor will let me do so by the 14th, and if you allow it, I propose to go to your house on that afternoon, say 4.30 to 5 o'clock — and would like to say a word or two about business. You have an investment, which is promising and will be performing by and by — and I can tell you of it.
And I've fixed on the 14th, because we meet that night — and I would anticipate and yet wait in order to be sure.
Yours truly
H. L. HIGGINSON

The investment was Fenway Court; April 14th was Mrs. Gardner's birthday; they were to meet that evening at a festival dinner given by Dr. and Mrs. Arthur T. Cabot; what he wished to say was that her friends desired to give her an abiding testimony of their appreciation. When he called, he presented to her a book, beautifully bound by Miss Mary Crease Sears according to a design suggested by Mr. J. Templeman Coolidge, and containing the following statement signed by as many friends of Mrs. Gardner as could be reached:

We, the signers of this book, desire to give you an earnest expression of our feeling about the noble work done by you for Boston.
You have conceived and built a beautiful house and have filled it with

[231]

treasures of art. To this end you have worked with untiring energy and love of your task, a task involving ungrudging self-denial.

For us and for posterity you have created a museum priceless for refreshment and education, an unique achievement of imagination, skill and ardent purpose.

For this great public benefaction we offer you our deepest gratitude.

This tribute had been proposed by Mrs. Fiske Warren, who wrote: 'We have wanted this book to be something very serious — something civic as in the old days — "to live," as Mr. James said, "in the archives of Fenway Court."'

The day following the presentation Mrs. Gardner received this letter from Mrs. Higginson:

Thursday April 15, '09

DEAR MRS. GARDNER,

Will you be so friendly as to come and lunch with us, next Sunday, at 1.30 to meet my brother, who has just returned from Italy? I hope you will. We want you very much.

I do not believe you know how much we cared for what happened yesterday. Mrs. Warren has been able to give shape to what we all have so long felt — the need of expressing to you our gratitude, our appreciation for what you have done to make this weary world beautiful and interesting. Mr. Higginson and I have often said that it did not seem as if our sympathy and admiration could go on, and on, without some tangible sign of appreciation — some real expression that would tell you how we appreciate the genius, the devotion and the masterly ability which have created the wonderful result which you have established and which have brought happiness and refreshment to us all.

It would be some satisfaction to you to know that you have done this in a way which no one else has ever done, or could ever do. You have made beautiful the life of those about you.

Believe me, with great regard and admiration

Yours very truly

IDA A. HIGGINSON

Mr. Higginson had loved 'Jack' Gardner; in his thoughts he could not separate Mrs. Gardner from him. On December 5, 1908, he wrote to her:

THE CROWN OF LIFE

'Tis our wedding day forty-five years ago — and so a pleasant word to you.

Of your great services and gifts to our city and its people (and to outsiders as well) I am fully aware, i.e., of your great virtues; and of your sins I am ignorant. Possibly these last exist, for we all are 'miserable sinners' — but I can now only regard you as a benefaction and a friend to us and to me by whom you have always stood as staunchly as Jack did — and one can't possibly find a more loyal, courageous, wise friend than he.

And ten years later:

DEAR MRS. GARDNER,

How answer your delightful note? Jack, you and I have held the same views of life and its duties and in doing so may have forgotten *the* painful subject — one's self. It was the natural result. You conceived nobly and have lived beyond your conception — of beauty and duty. Clearly it was your dream, and Jack helped you as he could. To our country full of life and enterprise what dream could have accomplished more? . . .

With my feeling of entire confidence, deep respect and warm affection for Jack I agree heartily about him and am glad to be named with him by you to whom I have felt as I have felt about him. . . .

Yours affectionately

H. L. HIGGINSON

The year 1909 was a fortunate one for Fenway Court. In February, Mrs. Gardner purchased the portrait of 'A Doctor of Law of the University of Salamanca' by Zurbaran; in March, Mr. Berenson proposed Manet's portrait of his mother, Madame Auguste Manet. He reminded her that when she was in Paris in 1907 she had asked him to find for her 'a great Manet, if possible a portrait, and one worthy of hanging beside your Degas.' This portrait he called 'a colossal thing.' As Piero's difficulties had very much embarrassed Mrs. Gardner financially, she was obliged, in making these purchases, to arrange for deferred payments; at first the Manet seemed too difficult, but the reproduction sent by Mr. Berenson convinced

[233]

her that she must have it; he first suggested that she pay a certain amount down and interest on the remainder, but finally arranged that payment be deferred for a year. In October she paid for 'A Woman in Green and Crimson' by Pollaiuolo, which she had purchased in 1907.

In Mrs. Gardner the love of fun and of unconventional entertainment never died; such hearty, robust humor as May Irwin's gave her great pleasure. During the winter of 1909–10 she had the good fortune to be taken to a show called 'The Red Moon,' given at a theatre not attended by society; the players were octoroons, and Mrs. Gardner admired not only their sincerity, but particularly the way they put their feet down. She went many times to see them and recommended 'The Red Moon' to all of her friends whom she considered up to it. The following spring Mr. Andrew wrote from Washington, D.C.:

Only a line to tell you that remembering a chance remark of yours made months ago, I went to an unmentionable theatre here in Washington the other night to see Cole and Johnson in the 'Red Moon' — and came back so flurried with the merits of the show that I have been sending all of male Washington over which I have any influence. The theatre is one to which female Washington could not go without being utterly emancipated and disguised — or I should have sent them thither also.

So the bread you cast upon the waters is helping Cole and Johnson to keep alive.

What a splendid counsellor you are, whether with regard to gardens, the medals of Pisanello, the achievements of Cole and Johnson, or n'importe quoi!

Mrs. Gardner was too thoroughly vital to exhibit any æsthetic affectations; hating prudery, she could tolerate honest, red-blooded vulgarity more easily than the cynical, sophisticated licentiousness which rewards so richly our theatrical producers.

THE CROWN OF LIFE

To gratify a longing of Mr. Okakura, she gave him in 1910 a snow-white Angora kitten; the following letter is from him:

DEAR MRS. GARDNER:

Our name is KOWUN, which means the 'Lonesome Cloud.' It also signifies 'The Gift by Favor,' and again the 'Messenger of Bliss' — all these we hope are appropriate titles symbolic of our quality and high descent. We have discarded names like 'Haima' which suggests the snowy realm of India, 'Mishio,' the crested foam, 'Sogettse,' the frosty morn, because our coat at present is far from being immaculate white.

Kowun (they may call us Kōtan in moments of tenderness or even Kō-chan if they are silly) may have reference to the Ode by Tao-Ying-Ming which begins:

> 'All Things
> on Things are supported;
> I, the lone-some Cloud,
> Resteth on none but myself.'

We delight in the name, for we are not lonesome. We, like a cloudlet in the sky, curl, unfurl, and swirl on in immense glee. We sleep beautifully. Our only lament was over some hairs singed in snuffing a candle with our tail.

With homage and humble greetings to the seat of the Honored One

We remain Your most obedient

KOWUN

and

OKAKURA-KAKUZO

November 22, 1910.

In 1911, Mr. Okakura went back to Japan, and the cat was given to the artist, Dodge Macknight; October 4th, Mr. Okakura sent the following letter from Tokyo:

DEAR KOTCHAN

Ages have passed — are you changed any? Swans sailing acrossed the ocean have brought tidings of your wherabouts and I am glad that fate has dealt kindly with you.

When you left I have felt the loss deeply — My breast has missed your nightly tread, the table was suddenly large without your prowling presence. Even now I write with your picture before me. You have killed all the cats in the world for you are alone, — the only one dear to me.

[235]

Have you caught your first mice yet? Did he taste nice? Perhaps you enjoy chasing squirrels, there is great pleasure in the quest of the unattainable. You and I know that wonder is the secret of bliss and that with reason comes the death of the beautiful.

I hope you that have not made the acquaintance of the feline feminine — treacherous things who pretend to understand you and has only claws to match their eyes. Be cautious of forming friendship with tomcats — even of the best sort. They can teach only what they acquired through pain; you must learn all through the gate of gladness. Be courageous, for bravery is the key into life. Never be ashamed of yourself — Think of your high lineage and under whose protection you were brought to me —

Kochan! are you lonesome? Loneliness is the lot of many worthier than you or me —

With the best greetings
Your friend
KAKUZO

I am sending you a small parcel of Japanese Catnip — and hope that it may agree with you.

Although Mrs. Gardner appeared to the world effervescent and gay, although her conversation is remembered as a steady flow of wit and of surprisingly varied information, perhaps there was an undercurrent of loneliness, perhaps Mr. Okakura saw deeper than others, and there was even an occasional moment of sadness. To a friend she wrote:

GREEN HILL, Thursday

DEAR ——

You are always so kind and thoughtful to me that it touches me very much — I am peculiarly sensitive to that sort of thing and one's own efforts in that direction seem so often to miscarry, that perhaps, although you may think it is silly, you may like to know that I feel all you do and thank you.

I *really* do feel sure that always, my 1st thought (and an abiding one) is 'others,' but I don't seem to have the knowledge which makes my thought of service — So I notice more than usual, perhaps, all the things you do and say and I thank you for my part — I go to Commencement to-day, and hope and expect to be with you to-morrow at supper — Do manage the Races —

[236]

and Deane I count on — No word yet from the Loefflers, so surely my letter miscarried —

Yours

Isabella S. Gardner

The number of people, plain everyday people as well as artists and musicians to whom her thought was of service in ways that showed a vividly comprehending sympathy, can only be guessed — they remain anonymous.

A friend seeking her backing wrote: 'You are the recognized leader in so many useful ways that whatever receives your endorsement carries a certificate of worth.' In November, 1910, she was asked semi-officially by a director of the Boston Opera Company to use her influence to secure more general public support; the opera was Mr. Eben D. Jordan's child, but Mrs. Gardner might have been called one of its godmothers. The rôle of godmother particularly suited her; it did not entail the expense of maintaining the child nor the responsibility for its behavior, but entitled her to take a lively interest in its training. Not a performance of the opera was missed by Mrs. Gardner unless she was ill in bed; to some of the singers, notably Alice Nielsen, Maria Gay, Zenatello, and Vanni Marcoux, she was devoted. Both Pavlowa and Maurice knew the practical benefit of her friendship. When Lady Gregory brought the Irish Players to Boston, Mrs. Gardner was one of their most enthusiastic adherents; in her Music-Room, Lady Gregory gave a lecture on her method of play-writing. When the world was thrilled by the heroism of the musicians on the S.S. Titanic, who remained at their post playing hymns while the ship sank, she obtained permission to place in the corridor of Symphony Hall a tablet:

ISABELLA STEWART GARDNER

In Memory of
the devoted musicians

Wallace Henry Hartley
Bandmaster
John Frederick Preston Clark
Percy Cornelius Taylor
John Wesley Woodword
W Theodore Brailey
John Law Hume
Georges Krins
Roger Bricoux
who were drowned
still playing
as the Titanic went down
April 15 1912

Nearly every year Mrs. Gardner gave a party to celebrate her birthday. For one of them Mr. Joseph Lindon Smith arranged a little play of Venetian intrigue; for another, in the year 1911, he prepared a charming presentation of the story of Pan and Syrinx. It was a happy moment in her life; she had just been elected a member of the Hispanic Society of America, and of its Advisory Board, and Mr. Archer M. Huntington, the President, had written: 'It would be childish to praise alone what you have built when it is within my power to frankly admire the author of the greatest work done by an American woman.' At the party a Japanese dancer, in whom Mr. Okakura was interested, mimed Japanese legends, and Dr. Denman Waldo Ross read the following letter:

BOSTON, *April 19th*, 1911

DEAR MRS. GARDNER:

I want to express for myself and for this company of friends which has come together to celebrate your Birthday, the affection with which we regard you and our admiration for what you have done for us and for everybody.

There is no one of the Fine Arts in which you have not taken serious interest; no one of them to which you have not given a generous patronage.

THE CROWN OF LIFE

We have seen your devotion to the arts of Dancing and Music, to the Drama and to Literature. As for the arts of Sculpture and Painting you have illustrated them in a Collection of Masterpieces which is known all over the world. You have built this beautiful house, yourself the Architect, and you have filled it full of Treasures. You are, not only the lover of Art and the Collector, but the Artist, having built the house and having arranged all the objects which it contains in the order and unity of a single idea, — an idea in which you have expressed your whole life with all its many and varied interests; this to our infinite satisfaction and delight.

We want to say this and much more than this, and we want to wish you many happy returns of your Birthday, — still many years of happy days and after that a blessed immortality.

DENMAN W. Ross
for one and for all

When the party was over, Mr. Okakura gave her this poem:

THE TAOIST

She stood alone on earth — an exile from heaven. Of all the immortals she was the flower.

Time receded in reverence at her approach, Space bowed the way to her triumph. The wind brought to her its untrammelled grace, the air lent to her voice the balm of its own summer. Blue lightning swept in her glances, clouds draped the flow of her queenly train.

Infinity asked of Wonder:
'Below and above, in thy wanderings amongst the stars, hast thou heard the name of this fearless Spirit, who laughs with the thunder and plays with the storm, whom fire burneth not because she is fire itself, whom water quelleth not for she herself is the ocean?'
Quoth Wonder: 'I know not.'

Life asked of Change:
'In form and out of forms where the Transient dwells, hast thou heard the name of this peerless Spirit who mocks at thy moods and scorns thy bond, whose sadness is a joy, whose shadow a sunshine, whose very loneliness a world of gladness?'
Quoth Change: 'I know not.'

Glory to the Nameless! sang the swaying pines of the forest.
Glory to the Nameless! echoed the billows of the sea.

On the birthday
of the Presence
1911

CHAPTER XIV
OMEGA

FOR the evening of February 5, 1914, Mrs. Gardner invited a few friends, not more than six or eight, to come to the Music-Room at Fenway Court at eight o'clock. Miss Alice Nielsen sang, Mr. George Proctor played — it was intimate and delightful; as the mirror was rolled back and Mrs. Gardner led the way into the court, she said: 'This is the last time that any one will go through the mirror.' In an adjoining room there was a supper prepared by Mr. Martin Mower — a gay little supper, and yet somewhat sad, for it was a milestone. Time was demanding recognition; the next day the mirror was to be taken down, the doorway was to be sealed up, the demolition of the Music-Room was to be begun. Mrs. Gardner, more vivacious, more energetic, more lively than any of the younger company about her, had decided that she must no longer delay the alterations which were to give Fenway Court its final form. Most of the materials had been in her possession since 1906; in 1908, she began to show friends the plans for the new rooms, so that in case of her death they might be carried out. Now, though the significance of the enterprise was a little melancholy, every one was grateful that the result was to be the work of her hands.

Throughout the spring and summer she labored; when she had a moment of leisure she sorted and arranged the tiles which in 1909 her friend Dodge Macknight had bought for her in Mexico; there were nearly two thousand of different patterns, which had formed the pavement of an old church; these she herself arranged to decorate the walls of the Spanish Cloister that was to replace the central part of the lower half of the Music-Room. This Cloister had one purpose — the suitable exhibition of 'El Jaleo,' Sargent's painting of a Spanish dancing girl. The picture did not belong to Mrs. Gardner; it was owned by Mr. T. Jefferson Coolidge, but he had said that some day it should be hers. It had been lent by him occasionally for public exhibition, and each time, according to Mrs. Gardner, it had been ineffective because it had been lighted from above; the picture represents a stage lighted with footlights, and all the shadows are thrown up. To express not only her conviction in regard to the proper installation of the picture, but also her high estimate of its worth, she prepared for it a more elaborate setting than for any other work of art in her collection; she built an alcove, marked off by a Moorish arch, giving the effect of a little stage, and placed a row of electric lights along the floor. When Mr. Coolidge saw these arrangements, he decided to give Mrs. Gardner the picture at once. People who had known it for years said they had never really seen it before, and that Mrs. Gardner had done as much for it as Sargent himself. The figures stand out in such bold relief that one lady, seeing it from a distance, asked whether it was sculpture or painting. No other work of art at Fenway Court interests artists so much.

By building a new floor at the level of the Music-Room balcony, the upper half of the old room was made into a large hall suitable for the exhibition of the Ffoulke-Barberini tapestries. Mrs. Gardner liked big rooms, and she liked to use every part of her house; in the Spanish Cloister, with its floor of blue tiles and its easy access to the garden, she gave a series of little suppers during the summer of 1915; after the Tapestry Room was finished, she regularly received her Sunday afternoon visitors there, and served them tea at the refectory table.

As soon as the transformation of the Music-Room was accomplished, she started to make over the little apartment in the opposite corner of the ground floor; by removing a partition she obtained a pleasant, well-lighted room, which she called the 'Macknight Room.' She had been an active friend of Mr. Macknight for many years and owned many of his pictures. The Macknight Room is the most intimate in Fenway Court; after Mrs. Gardner became an invalid, it was her downstairs sitting-room. In a narrow passage beside it, she placed association books and other souvenirs; as the space was so limited and so crowded, she called it the 'Vatichino.'

Notable works of art were still being added year by year to her collection; although many of them are paintings, it was her desire now that the collection should indicate the catholicity of her taste. In 1912, she bought a Persian lustre plate, called the finest that had been found; in 1913, Mr. Smith got for her an alabaster canopic jar; in 1914, she bought two Chinese bronze bears dating from the Han Dynasty, and a Chinese stele, one of the best pieces of Chinese sculpture that had come to the United States up to that time. In that year she also bought three old masters, a portrait by Lorenzo di Credi, a Madonna by Bernardo Daddi, and the lovely portrait of a girl by Paolo Uccello.[1] In 1915 she bought a portrait bust by Anna Coleman Ladd, and in 1916 a landscape, 'Yoho Falls,' by Sargent.

Meanwhile, the war in Europe had broken out and with

[1] Formerly attributed to Domenico Veneziano.

startling rapidity had developed to terrible proportions; no one felt its horror more deeply than Mrs. Gardner, no one foresaw more clearly nor dreaded more intensely its frightful possibilities. She was too intelligent to be deceived by propaganda and too old to shout for sham ideals, but she could extend a generous helping hand. Her young friends were going to France to drive ambulances, and when Mr. Henry D. Sleeper undertook to organize and finance this splendid service she was among the first to contribute. She was told by Cardinal O'Connell that her gift to the Knights of Columbus for their war work was one of the largest they had received. She hoped desperately that President Wilson might keep us out of war; the prevalent hysteria exasperated her, nor did any warnings to the effect that her conduct was unwise, if not even dangerous, affect her. She would not be false to her convictions, and she could not believe that the war, terrible object lesson that it was, would end war, or make the world safe for democracy, or secure the rights of subject races. When the war had been so gloriously won, newspaper editors began to deplore the fact that patriotism and the maintenance of an effective attitude of belligerency required the dissemination and acceptance of so much that was false; Mrs. Gardner deplored this fact during the war.

While she was dining one evening in the public dining-room of one of Boston's leading hotels, the orchestra played 'The Star-Spangled Banner'; Mrs. Gardner rose, but almost immediately sat down, in a furious temper. Did she sense that some one had requested it in order to see what she would do? A resident of the hotel said it was the only time he heard it played in the dining-room. More attention was paid to her than to the national anthem, and every one was relieved when the music ended. It was said that any one but Mrs. Gardner would have been mobbed. As soon as dinner was over, she sought the manager of the hotel and told him she thought it was an insult to the national anthem to play it under such conditions; at a banquet, where it might have a definite, honorable place in the evening's proceedings, well and good, but not in a restaurant where it bore no relation to the emotions or activities of the hearers. The manager said that it was never played except by request, but that a request could not be refused. If we ever learn to observe the etiquette of the flag, we may then develop an etiquette of the national anthem. At least let it be forbidden in restaurants.

A public hostility toward Mrs. Gardner had been aroused by her devotion to the leader of the Boston Symphony Orchestra, Dr. Karl Muck. There was no doubt of his genius, which Mrs. Gardner greatly admired, and for years she had been a friend. Now that he was in difficulties, she would not be unfaithful to her ideal of friendship. This was not the maudlin sentimentality of the woman who pours out her sympathy on a man in prison of whom she never heard before his arrest; it was the fidelity of a great soul who must be true to herself and could not be false to her friend. More than one person who would not have acted as she did said to her: 'I'm glad to think you are my friend; I know that if I get into trouble, at least you will stand by me.'

Early in the spring of 1919, Mrs. Gardner asked me if I would like to give up my position of Assistant Director of the Museum of Fine Arts and come to work at Fenway Court; she said she did not feel very well nor very strong, and that even a grass-hopper seemed a burden. There were a few definite things she wanted done, but chiefly she wanted me to become acquainted with her collection because, as she told me, she had designated me in her will to be the first Director of the Isabella Stewart Gardner Museum. She had already disposed of her Brookline place, 'Green Hill,' and planned to spend the rest of her days at Fenway Court. There was no sadness about it — there was only the practical common sense of a courageous spirit looking the future squarely in the face. Although she made no secret of her plans, only the Gardner family and her business man fully understood them, and from the family she received the same affection and coöperation that her husband had given her.

The summer and the autumn passed as usual; Mrs. Gardner made little visits, never being away more than a night; she attended the lectures given at the Harvard Summer School by Professor Charles T. Copeland, over whom she was as enthu-siastic as any Harvard alumnus; she went to the football games; for Christmas she gave her friends photographs of pictures at Fenway Court, sending them a week or two early as usual; on Christmas Eve mass was said at midnight in her chapel; and Christmas Day was spent receiving and acknowledg-ing the usual large number of gifts. The next morning she said she had a little headache and felt rather dizzy, but in the eve-ning she went out to dine at the house of Mr. and Mrs. Arthur F. Johnson; it was a merry evening — Mr. Sargent was of the com-pany and she was very happy. After she got home and had gone to bed, she was taken ill, and from that illness she never re-covered. Her right side was paralyzed, but as long as there was any hope of recovering her strength and regaining her activity she invented explanations of what might prove a temporary disability — it was the grippe, it was a heart attack, it was — something that made idleness a pleasure. With a stiff upper lip and a straight eye she set herself to the solution of her problem, to the mastery of this unexpected fate.

More than the admiration for her genius was the admiration of her friends for the courage, the patience, the cheerfulness with which she met enforced inactivity. For weeks she was not well enough to sit up, but during those weeks she did not fail in her habitual graciousness to her friends. Barely a month after her illness began, she learned that Professor Barrett Wendell was to be the new president of the Tavern Club and she sent a note of congratulation, to which this was his reply:

358 MARLBOROUGH STREET, 1 *February*, 1920

DEAR MRS. GARDNER:

No one but you would ever have taken the pains, in illness, to send just such a message as comes from you. Only that word *pains* — unless it be true of the illness — is all wrong; for through all the years I have known you there has never been a time when you have not gladly and helpfully spoken just the word one needs to persevere. You can hardly help feeling.

The rest of the letter is a tribute to preceding presidents of the club and an expression of his sense of the honor done him.

February 4, 1920, George Arliss wrote:

I can't tell you how sorry I am to hear that you are not well. I missed you dreadfully on my opening night here. I remember with a good deal of pride that on a previous visit you got up from a sick bed in order to come to my first night, and so I know you must be pretty bad this time.

Before she was able to sit up, she insisted on being carried into the beautiful big room which she called the boudoir, and there decoratively arrayed she spent her days reading and destroying old correspondence. At first she was unwilling to see visitors, but, as strength slowly returned and she became aware that months and perhaps years of inactivity were before her, her love of companionship and of participation in life asserted itself and friends were welcomed. Now, more than ever before, she found happiness in the friendship of women, and her women friends found her increasingly gentle and touchingly affectionate. No word of complaint was uttered, no trace of bitterness appeared; she wanted her friends to think nothing was the matter, and it was her effort to be as gay and engaging as ever.

Although she never regained the ability to walk, or to write except with difficulty, she did recover an extraordinary degree of strength, and made the most of every bit she could muster. She still wanted to use all her house and was carried about in a gondola chair she had brought from Venice. When summer came she went out in the automobile every morning, and spent the afternoon in the garden with her decrepit old dog Roly at her feet. During the night of July 16 word was brought to her that Roly was dying; in a fever of haste she was carried down to the garden and sat by him till the end.

Her house and her walled garden were filled with the fragrance of flowers; as she sat under a little arbor, she looked down a brick walk bordered by petunias and overhung by a great willow. Every morning a pupil of Mr. Proctor played on the piano in the Tapestry Room, and other musical friends, especially Mr. Loeffler, came constantly to give her pleasure, by their music and their companionship. When she sat alone, which was not often, she read; the Brookline Public Library, whose management she much admired, sent her the best detective stories as well as more serious books. Although a friend gave her the privilege of borrowing books from the Boston Athenæum, the privilege was of little worth to her, because the library's regulations required that such a borrower appear in person or send a signed order.

Her last old master was purchased in May, 1921, a Madonna and Child by Giovanni Bellini. Between June 1, 1919, and November 1, 1923, she bought six water-colors by Sargent and an oil sketch by him of Madame Gautreau (of peculiar interest to Mrs. Gardner), a water-color by Charles H. Woodbury, 'La Gitana' by Louis Kronberg, whose work was already liberally represented in her collection, a portrait head by Arnold Slade, a sketch by Manet, a small sarcophagus called to her attention by Mrs. Henry L. Higginson while she was in Rome, and a bronze 'Diana' by Manship, who wrote to her in 1918, 'There is no inspiration in the world to me like that of being with you.'

In June, 1921, Professor Frank Jewett Mather invited her to be a member of his 'Special Committee on Old Painting' of the National Gallery of Art, Washington, D.C. He wrote that he knew her health would make it impossible for her to take an active part in the work, but her name and good-will would be most helpful as indicating that the finest old paintings were desired for the nation.

An Austrian art expert who came to see her on a Sunday in January, 1922, wrote: 'The scent of your flowers, the impression of the genius in your art collection and *your own youthfulness* are vibrating through my soul. I shall write to my children in Vienna that I found here that which I have missed for years, a true Sunday.' Her mental alertness, her graciousness and charm, the pervading power of her personality did not wane. About this time a young clergyman, who had recently come to Boston, was taken to see her, and then to see her collection; when he came to the door of the Tapestry Room, which seemed in the dim light of the late winter afternoon to be of immeasurable size, he gasped and said: 'What a big room! — but if Mrs. Gardner should come into it, she would fill the whole place.'

Several times she went on Sunday mornings to see the decorations by Mr. Sargent that were being put in place in the Museum of Fine Arts; on March 9, 1922, she went to a rehearsal of the Symphony Orchestra to hear John McCormack sing three Irish songs with music by Loeffler. But her most strenuous undertaking was a trip to Gloucester to hear the first afternoon ringing of the carillon in the Portuguese church which had been dear to her since the beginning of her acquaintance with Eastern Point. The following letters, before and after, were written to Mr. Andrew:

FENWAY COURT *July* 17, 1922

DEAR A—

It is getting nearer next Sunday, and I am more and more anxious to be able to be there; but the nearer I get, the more frightened I am. However, this is what I plan unless all gives out: — It is suggested by the Lorings that I spend Saturday night with them, going to bed on arrival. With a late and lazy morning Sunday I think I can motor to the bells for the afternoon ringing, perhaps see you all, and hurry back to bed, and home Monday morning. Then, if all goes well, I should love to come down later, before you go off to Washington, and sleep in Miss Sinkler's bachelor apartment and see you all. But I always go to bed so early that my hours have to be considered. Of all this later. Looking ahead, I'm terribly pleased and thrilled, but *may* have to telegraph at the last moment I can't come.

My love to all —

Y.

ISABELLA STEWART GARDNER

FENWAY COURT, *July* 24, 1922

DEAR A —

Here's the promised note. It was all perfect from beginning to end, and I got home and was in bed at half past seven. I hope your dinner was as great a success. When I see you next here, I shall be as full of the perfections of the afternoon as ever. It *was perfect.*

Love from

Y.

Friends tried to persuade her to let Manship make a bust of her, but she knew that either bronze or marble would express too completely her physical aspect and might fail — although she admired Manship's work — to express her. When, however, Mr. Sargent was induced to ask if he might make a watercolor portrait of her, she accepted with alacrity. The result is one of his masterpieces. It was done September 14, 1922, in the Macknight Room. Swathed in white, an ageless spirit, sphinx-like, looks out of eyes that have plumbed human experience, a spirit that comprehends human nobilities and human frailties, and comprehending all pardons all, a spirit that loves and has never known fear.

On the morning of October 20, 1922, Mrs. Gardner took her usual morning drive; Centre College was to play Harvard in the afternoon, and Mrs. Gardner, sharing the general enthusiasm for the team from the little Kentucky college which had defeated Harvard the previous year, turned instinctively toward the Stadium. The streets near by were filled with people who could not hope to see the game, but did hope to see the team, possibly even to get inside the enclosure and see a little practice. Not a crack anywhere. A football official, however, a friend of Mrs. Gardner, invited her to drive onto the field, and then, practice over, the Centre College team ran the length of the gridiron and one by one they were presented to her. The following April she received an appeal for funds:

> Centre College of Danville, Kentucky, is trying to build a concrete stadium to take care of her growing needs.... We would like very much to dedicate a section of our Stadium to you and Mr. Gardner. We feel that the high ideals for which Mr. Gardner stood are daily exemplified by our athletes on the gridiron, and it would be an honor to dedicate a section to Mr. and Mrs. Jack Gardner — the name to be permanently inscribed in the concrete structure the entire length of the section.... Say it with cement.

It was the only appeal Mrs. Gardner ever called 'delightful'; it was so much more entertaining than the flood of requests from colleges and universities to contribute toward endowments which would enable them to increase professors' salaries, or build laboratories, or do other commonplace and obvious things.

In a letter written November 15, 1922, to Count Hans Coudenhove, who had asked if she had any animals and where her house was, Mrs. Gardner, over eighty-two years old, sitting helpless in her chair, gave this account of herself:

> ... I haven't a horse or anything now, but I am trying to keep up my courage. I'm quite an invalid, but cheerful to the last degree. I think my mind is all right and I live on it. I keep up a lot of thinking, and am really very much alive. I live in one house, everything else having been sold. This house is very nice, very comfortable, and rather jolly. It is on the outskirts of Boston, not in the country. I have filled it with pictures and works of art, really good things I think, and if there *are* any clever people I see them. I really lead an interesting life. I have music, and both young and old friends. The appropriately old are too old — they seem to have given up the world. Not so I, and I even shove some of the young ones rather close. I really have energy.

Toward the middle of May, 1923, Mrs. Gardner had an ill-turn which she thought meant that the end of her earthly life was near. She prepared for it in accordance with her religious faith, and then waited patiently. Never had she been more disappointed than when she realized that she was still to live. Her work was accomplished; reading was becoming an effort; even the visits of friends, much as she enjoyed them tired her; interviews with distinguished foreigners, however highly recommended, were more a burden than a pleasure.

During the summer, an English lady, reputed to be a great beauty, whose portrait had been painted by Sargent and by Charles Sims, came to Boston with a letter of introduction from Sargent to Mrs. Gardner. She asked if Mrs. Gardner could receive her on a certain day at eleven o'clock, and if she might see Mrs. Gardner's Sargents. Mrs. Gardner replied that she might see the pictures, but that she herself would be taking her morning drive at that hour. When we started out in the motor, I expressed my surprise that she had not arranged to see Lady ——. 'Why should I want to see her?' 'Because she is considered quite a beauty, and because Sargent would not have given her a letter to you if he had not believed that meeting her would give you pleasure.' 'What makes you think she is a beauty? What does she look like?' Having only seen reproductions of two portraits of the lady, I made the best answer that I could, and the subject was dropped. After doing our first morning errand, Mrs. Gardner asked if we needed to go downtown; if we did, she thought perhaps she had better go home first. As she had had more than one ill-turn in the motor, and I was always anxious about her, I nervously told the chauffeur to go at once to Fenway Court. When we had started in that direction, Mrs. Gardner remarked placidly: 'You said so much about Lady ——, that I thought we might as well see what she looks like, so we will sit in the motor across the street from my door and watch her arrive.' As we approached, Bolgi, who was on the lookout for Lady ——, came running to see what accident had brought us back so soon. Mrs. Gardner's scheme had to be hurriedly explained and Bolgi urged back to the house, instructed to make no sign. We took our position opposite the door, and after a few minutes of placid waiting, Lady ——'s motor drove up. Her chauffeur rang the bell and found she was to be admitted. We heard her voice as she gave him a few brief orders; when she stepped out of her car, we saw her close-fitting hat and her coat; to our delight, she decided to leave this in the motor, and we saw her dress; of her face, except for one fleeting glimpse, we saw only the tip of her nose. Entirely satisfied, we went to finish the day's errands.

The autumn dragged slowly along; when Christmas Eve came Mrs. Gardner was unable to attend the midnight mass, but her discouragements and her weariness were kept secret as far as possible. She would not be beaten by her fate; replying to a Christmas letter she said: 'Be as happy as you can, and appear even more so.'

In the spring of 1924, it was evident that her strength was failing, but she persisted in her daily routine; although she knew that over-exertion would cause an agonizing heart attack, she would not shut herself away from life. On her morning drive, she did not want to go out into the country, but down through the business streets where there was something to see. In July a fraternal organization held a convention in Boston;

the decorations of the streets, the men in regalia and the bands of music were so entertaining that on July 8th she was not content with her morning expedition, but, although the day was excessively hot, insisted on driving downtown again in the afternoon. Soon after she got home, she suffered a heart attack so severe that the doctors knew it foretold the end. Although she was not expected to live through the night, her vitality was still so great that she rallied and for a few days was comfortable and able to see her dearest friends. The end came quietly and peacefully in the evening of July 17th.

All the details of the preparations for the funeral she had arranged. On the morning of the 18th, her body was taken downstairs and placed beside the Spanish Chapel, with its inscription 'In Memoriam'; she was covered with the purple pall that she had bought to cover her husband's coffin; on the wall at her feet a long black crucifix was hung; on either side of the coffin stood two tall, massive bronze candlesticks with candles burning day and night; between them were two prie-dieux where nuns remained in constant supplication. Prayers for the dead were read that morning by Father Spence Burton of the Society of Saint John the Evangelist, and each succeeding morning mass was said. Friends came day and night and the effect of this brief period of waiting was solemnly beautiful. On Monday morning, July 21st, a requiem was sung by Father F. C. Powell, S.S.J.E., who had brought Mrs. Gardner Holy Communion once a fortnight during the last year of her life, and at noon the funeral service was held at the Church of the Advent. The hymns were those she chose for her husband's funeral. She was buried in the Gardner tomb at Mount Auburn, where she rests in peace between her husband and her son.

By her will she established Fenway Court 'as a Museum for the education and enjoyment of the public forever.' The dream of her youth had been carried out.

THE END

INDEX

[257]

INDEX

Burmah, 81
Burton, Rev. Spence, S.S.J.E., 254
Busoni, Ferruccio, 140–141
Butler, Lawrence Smith, 186, 219
Byard, Theodore, 167, 172, 178

Ca' d' Oro balconies, 201
Cabot, Dr. and Mrs. Arthur T., 231
Cambodia, 68–75
Campbell, Mrs. Patrick, 187
Canopic jar, 242
Canterbury, Archbishop of, 192
Cardinals
  de Lorraine, 4
  Agostini, 102, 109
  Rampolla, 149
  Schönberg, 149
  O'Connell, 212, 218, 228, 243
  Merry del Val, 218
  Riario, 230
Carlos, Don, Duke of Madrid, 130
Carmencita, 117
Carter, Morris, 227, 230, 244–245
Cass, Lewis, U.S. Minister to Italy, 14
Catalogues
  Choice of Books (1906), 100
  Choice of Manuscripts and Bookbindings (1923), 100
Catena: Delivery of the Keys to S. Peter, 149
'Cathedral Pilgrimage,' England and France, 49–51
Cavenaghi, 159
Cecilia Society, 200, 205
Ceiling, painted (Dutch Room), 168
Cellini, Benvenuto: Bust of Bindo Altoviti, 169
Cenci, Francesco (red velvet baldacchino), 152
Centre College, Danville, Ky., 250–251
Chairs
  From the Borghese collection (Titian Room), 125
  Style of Louis XV (Tapestry Room), 219
Chalfin, Paul, 224
Chalice, 180
Charitable Eye and Ear Infirmary, Boston, 33
Charles I of England, 3–4, 157
Cheney, Edward
  Dante, 98
  Venetian manuscripts, 100
Chest, French, carved (Gavet collection), 163
Chicago, Illinois, 187
  World's Columbian Exposition, 137, 139

Chicago, Burlington & Quincy Railroad, 140, 226
Chigi, Prince
  'Chigi' Botticelli, 177
  Tintoretto portrait of a lady, 202
Child, Mrs. Bertha Cushing ('Fiorella'), 210
China, 63–68
Chinese stele, 242
Choate, Joseph H., 192
Choate, Mabel, 192
Choir stalls, 180
Christmas play, 212
Church, Frederick Edwin: Heart of the Andes, 20
Church of the Advent, Boston, 49, 120, 192, 254
Cima da Conegliano: Madonna, 162
Civitali, Matteo: Madonna and Child, 197–198
Clemen, Prof. Paul, 220
'Cleopatra's Barge' (sleigh), 16
Cleveland, Pres. Grover, 92
Cochran, Hon. W. Bourke, 187
Coello: Juana of Austria and her niece, 162–163
Collins, Alfred Q., 128
Constantinople, 45–46
Coolidge, Archibald C., 192
Coolidge, Harold Jefferson, 187
Coolidge, Joseph Randolph, 18, 24, 86
Coolidge, Mrs. Joseph Randolph, 85
  née Julia Gardner. See also Gardner, Julia
Coolidge, J. Templeman, 231
Coolidge, T. Jefferson, 129, 192–193, 241
Copeland, Prof. Charles T., 245
Copes, two XV century green velvet, 152
Cornaro, Caterina, Birth of (painting), 152
Corner-stone, 185
Corot: Landscape, 54
Coudenhove, Count Hans, 109–110, 251
Cox, Kenyon, 207
Cram, Ralph von, Prior of the Order of the White Rose in North America, 4
Cranach: Adam and Eve, 131
Crawford, Earl of, Library, 100
Crawford, F. Marion, 56, 143
Credence, French Gothic (Gavet collection), 163
Credi, Lorenzo di: Portrait, 242
Crivelli: S. George and the Dragon, 169
Curtis, Daniel, 109
Curtis, Ralph W., 125, 133–135, 152, 176, 216
Daddi, Bernardo: Madonna and Child, 242

INDEX

[259]

INDEX

INDEX

INDEX

Masaccio: Portrait, 170
Massachusetts Charitable Eye and Ear Infirmary, Boston, 33
Massachusetts Society for the Prevention of Cruelty to Children, 205
Massenet, 148
Materna, 101
Mather, Prof. Frank Jewett, 248
Matisse, 225
McCormack, John, 249
McCurdy family, 5, 7
Médicis, Catherine de, 4
Melba, Mme. Nellie, 142, 206
Melozzo da Forlì, 181
Memmi, Lippo; Madonna, 168
Mendelssohn Hall, New York, 190
Merry del Val, Cardinal, 218
Meryon: Etchings, 100
Messina earthquake sufferers, Benefit at Fenway Court for, 212, 229
Midnight Mass, Christmas Eve, 192
Milan, Poldi Pezzoli Museum, 15
Millet, Jean François, 54
Mino da Fiesole: Relief, 197
Monet, 219
Monks, Dr. George H., 171
Mont-St. Michel, 119
Moore, Miss Mary, 206
Moro, Antonio: Portrait of Mary Tudor, 197
Moroni: Portrait, 154
Morse, Prof. Edward Sylvester, 59
Mosaic pavement, from Villa Livia, 168, 192
Motto: 'C'est mon plaisir,' 188, 203
Mountenay-Jephson, 153
Mount Gardner, peak in Okanogan County, Washington, 121
Mower, Martin, 225, 240
Muck, Dr. Karl, 115, 244
Munich, 166
Museum of Fine Arts, Boston, 54, 138, 158–159, 195–196, 224, 249

Naples, 168, 218
Napoleon, chiffoniers, 54; flag, 55
'Neptune' knocker, 55
Nevin, Ethelbert, 145
New England Conservatory of Music, 123
New England Women's Club, 160
New York Agricultural Society, 8
New York (City), amusements, 19–22; (firemen's procession), 20–21; Central Park, 21–22
Nichols, Edward, 162, 183, 190–191
See also Sears, Willard T.
Nielsen, Alice, 237, 240

Norton, Prof. Charles Eliot, 54, 93–95, 97–98, 100, 170, 181, 194, 201, 207–208
Norton, Richard, 168, 177, 179–180
Novelli and his company, 211–212
Nuremberg, 46

Oakley, Kruger, 19
Oakley, Wilmot (uncle of Adelia Smith), 10
Oberammergau (1890), 119
O'Connell, Archbishop (later, Cardinal), 212, 218, 228, 243
Oddie, Lillie (Lily), 12, 19–20, 22
Okabe, 224
Okakura-Kakuzo, 222–224, 235–236, 238–239
Okill, Miss Mary, 11
Olmstead [Frederic Law], 174
Orchids, 96
Order of the White Rose, 4
O'Reilly, John Boyle, 83

Paderewski, 122–123
Palazzo Barbaro, Venice, 109, 120, 128, 146, 178
Papanti's Dancing School (Boston), 26, 29, 30
Paris, 13–14, 125, 127, 134–136, 145, 153, 164, 169, 179, 216, 219
Parker, George F., 113–114
Parker, H. W., 114
Passini, Ludwig, 130, 133, 178
Paton, Thomas, 8
Paul V, Pope, chairs, 125; halberd, 150
Pavlowa, 237
Peabody, Frank, 31
Peabody, Joseph, 19–20
Peacock Room, 103
Pearls, 35, 128, 149, 167
Peirson, Charles L., 188
Penang, 80–81
Penicaud enamel, 153
Perkins, Charles E., 226
Perkins Institution for the Blind, 56, 197
Perry, Mr. and Mrs. Thomas, 219
Persian lustre plate, 242
Persian rug, 145
Pesellino: Madonna and Child, 126; cassone panels, 169
Peyre, Emile, collection, 169
Phippen, J., 114
Piero della Francesca: Hercules, 213–215, 230
Pintoricchio: Madonna, 197
Pnompenh, 69–70, 72–75
Poldi Pezzoli Museum, 15
Pollaiuolo: A Woman in Green and Crimson, 234

INDEX

[263]

INDEX

[264]

INDEX